The Rubber Tree

—THE—
Rubber Tree

MEMOIR OF A VIETNAMESE WOMAN WHO WAS AN ANTI-FRENCH GUERRILLA, A PUBLISHER AND A PEACE ACTIVIST

by Nguyen Thi Tuyet Mai

edited by MONIQUE SENDEROWICZ

McFarland & Company, Inc., Publishers
Jefferson, North Carolina, and London

British Library Cataloguing-in-Publication data are available

Library of Congress Cataloguing-in-Publication Data

Nguyen Thi Tuyet Mai, 1931–
    The rubber tree : memoir of a Vietnamese woman who was an anti-
French guerrilla, a publisher and a peace activist / by Nguyen Thi Tuyet Mai;
edited by Monique Senderowicz.
    p. cm.
    Includes bibliographical references and index.
    ISBN 0-89950-954-1 (lib. bdg. : 50# and 70# alk. paper) ∞
    1. Nguyen Thi Tuyet Mai, 1931– . 2. Vietnam—Politics and
government—1945-1975. 3. Nationalists—Vietnam—Biography.
4. Publishers—Vietnam—Biography. I. Senderowicz, Monique.
II. Title.
DS556.93.N5262A3   1994
959.704—dc20   94-2055
                                                                      CIP

Manufactured in the United States of America

McFarland & Company, Inc., Publishers
    Box 611, Jefferson, North Carolina 28640

To all those for whom the subject of Vietnam has been like a thorn in the side, may this help to remove that thorn.

To my daughter, Khôi, thank you for your patience, your perseverance, your organizational skill, and above all, your understanding. I also thank my husband for verifying the accuracy of the historical facts that I refer to in my personal account of events. Finally, I would like to mention the wonderful contribution of my loving, playful dog, Buffo, who was a great writing aid and foot cushion...

Nguyen Thi Tuyet Mai

To Boobi, many thanks for your stamina in the endless tedious tasks, and most of all, your quasi-constant support during the entire project. And to our wonderful little treasures, Binah, Benji, Tati, and Batata, may this serve as an umbilical cord to connect you to your past and nourish you for your future. With love,

M.S.

Contents

Preface

MANY PEOPLE have asked me why
South Vietnam fell to the North in 1975. To this question I had no specific
or simple answer. A lifetime can pass by before one realizes what it was
all about. It has taken me sixty-two years to gain the proper perspective.

As one of the Vietnamese students educated in the United States to
return to Vietnam in the early fifties, I lived through the Vietnam War
as a witness and a participant. During the Vietnam War, I felt divided between Vietnam and America. As did many soldiers, I felt a terrible uncertainty about my duty, and indignation at the purposeless destruction.
Moreover, it was a nearly unbearable frustration for me as a Vietnamese
to see the imminent loss of my country written on the wall while Americans were being misled by predictions of victory such as "we can see the
light at the end of the tunnel."

The story I have written here about myself is not meant to excuse
or explain the misjudgment, corruption, greed and apathy in South Vietnam, but perhaps a glimpse into that society would give some insight into
the complexity of the war.

It is strange how America came into my life. I was brought up in an
upper middle class Hanoi family and was part of the Saigon elite during
the Vietnam War. The first time I ever heard of America was in 1945 in
the midst of songs and lectures praising "Uncle" Ho Chi Minh and "My
Quoc" or Beautiful Country, a name the leaders of the Vietnamese
Revolution used for America. Three years later I had been a guerrilla
fighting the French and "My Quoc" had become an enemy of the
Revolution.

Then in late 1953, I found myself being quoted in the *Congressional
Record* as one of the first supporters of Ngo Dinh Diem when he was
discussed on the Senate floor by Senators Mike Mansfield and John Kennedy. A year later, at my wedding, I was being escorted to the altar by
our friend, the late Dr. Wesley Fishel of Michigan State University in
East Lansing, who would go on to become one of the closest advisors

to President Ngo Dinh Diem. The other professors of the Michigan State University Advisory Group would eventually become key figures in the nation-building process to create the government of South Vietnam. But of course, none of these connections made any impression on me at the time.

Returning to Saigon in 1954, I carried on with living my life as I was brought up to live it. I had high hopes for the future of Vietnam, but things deteriorated and eventually I saw the opportunity for a great democratic Vietnam in Southeast Asia wasted. In 1961, my husband resigned from the government and wrote his book *Is South Vietnam Viable?* In it he exposed for the first time the hidden truth about the Diem family corruption. Diem was overthrown in November 1963, but the legacy of his family's corruption had taken roots in South Vietnamese society.

Through the course of the following years and a most unpredictable series of events, America gradually became an integral, direct part of my life, until finally it even came to be my adopted home. In the winter of 1970, while my family was trying to settle down in California, I awoke one day after traumatic orthopedic surgery, my leg in a cast, to the news of my mother's death. The agony was overwhelming. I wondered if this was called destiny. I had somehow survived three decades of relatively risky living without bodily harm within a dangerous society—but there I was, immobilized for months as a result of a tobogganing accident... In my state of depression and feelings of helplessness over the sudden loss of my mother, I came to realize that Death could come and claim me anytime, anywhere, taking with it my secret feelings, wiping out my footprints and rendering meaningless my life on this earth. With this sudden realization, I thought it was important for me to reflect on my life and to write down my thoughts.

For the first time in my adult life, I was finally given time for myself—eight months for the compound butterfly fracture to heal; eight months' time for me to sink into the depths of my being and recover my past, jotting it down as my mind freely travelled. Then my leg was healed and I had to carry on with the chores of my daily life, postponing my writing for another fifteen years, until 1985, when a car accident shattered my knee and nearly immobilized me again for about two years.

This time as I reopened the chapters of my past that I had written before, I felt somewhat less "pressured." South Vietnam's agony was no longer in my daily thoughts. It had finally collapsed in 1975. Regrettable as it was, it was an acceptable ending for me. As a Saigon insider witnessing the corruption of the anti–Communist side, I had known for a long time this would surely come. At least the destruction and killing of the meaningless war ended and relative peace returned to the people. With my children grown up and gone, and with less bad news from Vietnam (because of the United States embargo, which made communication with Vietnam more difficult), I was psychologically liberated to resume my writing.

Before I knew it, the story of my carefree childhood covered the first chapters of my writing. The puzzle about life and its complications slowly faded away. I was now impressed with the simplicity of an old society where people were living in harmony with the peaceful flow of the river, rising and going to bed with the sun. Children had fun playing with their neighborhood friends and enjoyed such simple things as a swim in the river or climbing a tree.

This journey to my past turned out to be a reality when I got a chance to revisit Vietnam in 1990, when it began to open up as a burgeoning free market economy. I returned to my rubber tree and I reconnected myself with my relatives and the surviving members of my 1945 guerrilla group. With the latter, I marvelled at the fact that after so many years of separation and "hostility" between us, we could easily pick up where we had left off, way back then. In their company, I rejoiced at the thought that we could forget the opposing ideological camps we had belonged to during the war, and reunite as simple Vietnamese, "born from the same womb" as our Vietnamese ancestors had impressed upon us.

With my cousins and my former guerrilla friends, I had no problem communicating, as we appeared to be sharing the same traditional Vietnamese values. I admired the spartan lifestyle and the spirit of sacrifice that they seemed to have inherited from their fighting days. But these elderly revolutionaries, who made up half of the older generation, were about to be replaced by the younger generation. These younger people seem to be motivated only by money. They consider the older generation somewhat obsolete and they think that they are more up-to-date with the modern gadgets—often black market products—they proudly exhibit as signs of superior intelligence and modernity. They seem to form a new class of well connected opportunists, bent on making money fast, even illegally, without any concern for their social responsibilities. Meanwhile their less fortunate compatriots, the majority, are having a hard time earning an honest living in a country which is badly lacking in job opportunities because of poor organization.

With each of my subsequent returns after the first in 1990, the peaceful scenery I had seen in Vietnam had changed quickly for the worse: more noise, more pollution, more crime, more disease, more people, more waste... Even the historic gravesite of Dinh Tien Hoang, the founder of the first dynasty of independent Vietnamese kings, was carved up for sale! It was an impressive array of natural granite formations, strategically aligned in such a way as to facilitate defense against enemy intruders, a scenic place of unique historical significance being destroyed by the very people who should have known better. Things deteriorated so fast. One got the frightening impression of riding a roller coaster down a steep hill at a deadly speed.

*   *   *

I begin my story at a carefree and innocent juncture in my life. I love Vietnam as I love my mother. Talking about it makes me feel good and writing about it helps me keep my memories alive. I feel like the flower in that Vietnamese poem:

> Flower, what do you live for?
> Poet, why do you ask such a strange question?
> I live because I love to live,
> I never think about what I live for!

In Vietnamese:

> Hoa oi hoa song de ma chi?
> Thi si nguoi sao hoi la ky?
> Em song chi vi em thich song,
> Em chua he nghi de ma chi!

Oakland, Thanksgiving 1993

A note about names used in this book: Whenever necessary, names have been changed, though the historical facts are respected. Most Vietnamese names frequently referred to in this memoir are translated into English for easier reading. Vietnamese names of historical significance are left intact.

xii

1

IT WAS 1943 in Bien Hoa, a small town northeast of Saigon. It was one of those wonderfully hot, sluggish afternoons so common to the memory of my childhood. The heat and stillness were such that time itself seemed stagnant, and to the energetic child of twelve that I was, oblivious to care and constraints, this meant but one simple thing: play.

Of particular attraction this afternoon, while returning to school from break with my good friend An, were the lotus flowers perched on the branches overhanging the river along our path. Like outstretched arms, the long branches seemed to beckon to us. Lotus seeds tasted good, and lotus flowers were pretty. We ran to the tree.

We searched for some branches to enable us to hook some lotus stems to shore, but the branches were too short. We stepped down into the water—first to our knees, then to our waists. Soon we were shoulder-deep in water. We were able to pick one or two seed cups. We tried the big seeds, but they were too old, and the green stem in the middle of the seeds tasted bitter. We waded farther out to reach the more tender seeds and select other flowers. The small seeds tasted sweeter, and the budding flowers were prettier than those in full bloom whose petals fell too easily. We were having fun splashing, making silly comments on the seeds and flowers, and spitting out the remains.

Suddenly, there came shouts from the middle of the river. "Catch them! Beat them up! Kill them! Thieves . . . Thieves!"

Through the clearing between the branches we saw a woman and a boy on a small round rattan boat coming towards us, their arms gesticulating in rhythm with their barking threats.

"Chet cha [Dead father]! They saw us!" we exchanged in whisper and

1

quickly spun around, trying to run to shore with the lotus flowers and seeds.

At this point, we were up to our chins in water. The mud bottom was slippery and uneven. It had potholes. We found ourselves sinking into its bottomlessness. We extended our arms to grab onto and support one another, kicking and struggling to get our footing. But the mud had another trap. It sucked our feet deep into the soggy earth when we stepped too hard on it. We screamed, pulled, pushed, and gulped large mouthfuls of muddy water. Finally we reached firm ground.

We looked at one another, smiling. Each of us was still holding onto a big bouquet of lotus flowers and seeds. Behind us, the woman and boy were still shouting their curses. When the beautiful flowers had first appeared, they had looked as boundless and uncontrolled as the river itself. It had never occurred to me that they might have an owner.

We ran back to school at full speed, giggling all the while, making it just in time to place the flowers in our teacher's pot. The flowers were much too beautiful to be thrown away.

We had barely finished arranging them when the school drum struck three times, which was the signal for us to line up for our teacher's inspection before entering the classroom.

"Stop! Mai. An. Why are your clothes all wet?" asked Miss Ngoc.

"We... uh... we were in the water," I answered.

"What water, and why were you in the water?"

"We... uh..." I glanced at the lotus on her desk.

"We fell into the water," An interceded.

"Go kneel down. One on each side of the blackboard," instructed Miss Ngoc.

After the other students sat down and pulled out from their desks the assignment of the hour, Miss Ngoc walked behind each long bench, her hands behind her back, leaning forward over the students' heads to check their work. Meanwhile, at the side of the blackboard, I knelt erect, my arms crossed in front of my chest. I wished that she would come to thrash us quickly, so we could be released. Now and then my eyes wandered over to my friend and to the chalk tray where the rattan rod, the thickness of my finger, lay. Out of boredom I tried to guess how many beatings I was going to get.

Miss Ngoc, our seventh grade teacher at the Primary School for Girls, was a good-looking young lady of about twenty-five. Her complexion was creamy white with a touch of pink. She had large cheekbones and a Saigon accent and wore her hair in a chignon behind her large head.

She stood about five-feet-five, used little make-up, walked very fast, and had a very bad temper.

A twenty-minute break had come and gone. My friend and I were bored to the point of dozing off. Now and then we were jerked upright by the piercing snap of the teacher's ruler against a desk.

Napping soundly while kneeling, I was suddenly awakened by an urgent cry, "Teacher... teacher... my eyes!"

Miss Ngoc stepped quickly over to the end of the classroom where Tu was holding her face with both hands. She pried Tu's hands open to look into one of her eyes. Then, with her index finger pushed into Tu's eye, she explained to Tu that a white veil had partly covered Tu's eye, and that she was trying to pull it back. The whole class, including An and me, surrounded her. A moment later, Miss Ngoc succeeded in pulling the veil back to the corner of the eye. She was now holding it there to make certain that it did not creep back out again; her face was as green as a banana leaf.

We students all began talking at once in the forbidden Annamite language. The classroom was a place where all students had to speak in French, write in French, and learn only French history and geography.

"Little sisters, go back to your seats," Miss Ngoc said, as if she did not know that she, too, was speaking in Annamite. "I'll try to get Tu some help."

We obediently returned to our seats, and Miss Ngoc left with Tu. As soon as they were out of sight, commotion erupted. We all began redescribing the incident among ourselves in Annamite, agreeing and disagreeing on the details. We had never heard of such a thing as that veil. Later, the aunt of one of the students said it could happen from exposure to too much sun or from internal heat caused by consuming too much of the "hot" fruits—green bananas, tamarinds or goyaves. She knew someone who knew of a boy who had gone blind because the veil could not be removed after it had covered the whole eye. The veils were probably cataracts.

After that day, we had more admiration for Miss Ngoc and accepted her wild outbursts of temper with less reluctance. When Miss Ngoc got angry, especially at students who did not understand math, she would use the rattan rod to beat them—on their hands, arms, behinds—wherever, and whenever, even in the middle of their writing! I had shown respect to my teacher because my mother told me to do so. But I had had no reason to admire her until that day. She had been very brave. What if her own sharp fingernails had caused Tu to go blind? Instead, she had saved Tu.

3

There were only two students in class that Miss Ngoc did not scream at or beat up—the two best dressed ones. They both always wore white pyjamas style shirts and trousers neatly pressed while the rest of us were always in our exercise uniforms: blue shorts and white short-sleeved shirts. Lai always ranked first in class. The daughter of the man who collected honey buckets, she came from the poorest class because her father, dealing with septic containers, owned the "dirtiest" business. Lai was the most serious and looked the sweetest of us all. She talked only when asked and always kept her clothes clean, with the iron creases always neatly intact. Phan, the other well-dressed girl, was the daughter of a rich contractor. She was also quiet, but not as intelligent as Lai. In the past, the teacher had occasionally beaten her for mediocre work.

Tu, the one suffering from the eye affliction, was of a poor, common family. Her attitude was very mild and submissive. Even if Miss Ngoc's fingernails had caused her to go blind, there would have been no lawsuit. I never heard of a lawsuit coming from poor people. There would have been mean gossip though, which was much worse than the law.

I had heard gossip about the three girls who lived in the pension house behind the candy shop in the woody area near the end of our street. My older sister, Bright Moon, and I met these girls every Thursday in our home economics class.

The three girls were sent by their parents from across the river to study at the home economics school created by the director of public elementary schools. The director was a friend of my parents—a nice, soft-spoken gentleman, casual and good-natured in comparison with my parents and their other friends who were very formal and spoke very deliberately. The three girls looked a little older and more mature than Bright Moon and me. They talked sweetly, wore pressed white blouses and black flowery satin trousers which were made specially in the rich province of Vinh Long, famous for its fabrics and shrimp puffs. Mother had forbidden us, particularly my older sister, from seeing them. But, in her absence, we always did anyway. I didn't think Mother knew who they were and how very attractive, polite and well-mannered they were in class.

There was a boy who happened to live near where the girls stayed. One Sunday, our Catholic priest had given me a good scare with his hellfire and damnation "sermon" on this boy. He made it clear that whoever came near the boy would also be condemned for breaking God's Ten Commandments. He denounced him with such downright condemnation that I thought God was present in the priest's body to condemn us all. I somehow connected that religious power with the French and believed that the priest represented them in governing our public lives the way our parents ruled over our private lives.

The priest lived like a Frenchman, in a large house behind the church. He ate French food every day and passed down harsh judgments. His power was as absolute and fearful to us as that of the French chief of police who was known to have imprisoned and tortured many "misbehaved" natives in his own huge living quarters. He was our neighbor, separated from our house by a "haunted" vacant lot. It was said that the vacant lot was haunted by angry ghosts from the souls of those beaten to death by him.

The priest had not said what sin the boy had committed. I wondered if his sin had something to do with the girls, like what had happened to me once after a choir meeting. The priest had called me into his office and applied a furtive kiss on my cheek. I had a feeling instantly that it was wrong. First, because he had looked around prior to doing so to see if there was anybody within sight. Second, because no one but my mother had ever kissed me and that only on my forehead as a blessing. The priest had then said that he liked my voice, but I was sure that that did not entitle him to kiss me as he had.

I dropped choir and brushed aside the complicated incident. I told myself that I would understand better when I grew up. Until then, I had better stay away from trouble, I vowed to myself. My mother never discussed her problems with us nor with my father nor her friends, as far as I knew. So I felt that my problem was nobody else's business and that this was a chance for me to apply my father's favorite saying—"Regardez en haut, cherchez a s'élever toujours" (Look up, seek always to elevate yourself)—by looking ahead, moving forward, and not belittling myself with inferior thoughts. In spite of myself though, gossip did come now and then to trouble my mind.

One afternoon, while visiting my friend Phan instead of going to the teacher's apartment to earn extra credit as my mother expected, the question of lawsuits came up. Phan's house was a grand villa; it occupied almost half a block in the commercial center of town. Comparing it to our house, a rented brick building only one-fifth the size of Phan's house, I knew that her father must be a very wealthy man. Yet the status of her father as a contractor gave me a sense that the family belonged to the class of "commoners."

The "merchant" class was held a notch below the farmers and two notches below the doctors, administrators, and engineers like my father, who were considered to be "intellectuals." To be rich meant to be a merchant, and to be a merchant meant to be servile and dishonest. Nobody

5

had told me these things in so many words, but I must have picked it up from being raised in my social class which was ranked first on the scale of societal respect according to our popular saying: "Si, Nong, Cong, Thuong" (Intellectuals first, then Farmers, next Artisans, last Merchants).

Several maids were standing on the veranda watching over Phan's baby sisters and brothers. I was playing with a toy car. They had many toys. We had none at home, not even a doll. Mother did not like us to play with things that she thought would make us turn into "sissies."

One of the maids pointed her chin at my fingers. "Why are your hands all swollen?"

"I was beaten," I responded.

"By whom?"

"My teacher," I answered matter-of-factly.

"Yes," Phan said, "Mai receives the most thrashings in class!"

Then Phan turned to me, "I really can't figure you out, Mai. Some weeks you rank number two or three, but then other times you slide all the way down to twenty or even twenty-five in class ranking. You must not be dumb, because Miss Ngoc always calls you to the blackboard when Lai gets stuck with her math. Why is that?"

"To beat me up," I answered straight away, as I had contemplated the matter myself and come to that conclusion a long time ago.

"But you always solve the math problems when we get stuck!"

"Maybe because I get so scared," I said, shrugging my shoulders.

The maid then said, "You should go tell your mother. Phan here does not get thrashed any more because her mother threatened to sue her teacher if she ever touched or screamed at her again."

I was shocked. Reporting on my teacher? Never, I resolved to myself in silence.

My mother never noticed my bruises, and even if she did, she would consider them part of my "education." She would never talk about the goings-on in the adult world in front of us, let alone tell the maids. Neither would she ever allow it to enter our heads to question our superiors, not to mention sue them! I decided not to go to Phan's house again.

Most of my afternoons were spent trying to find ways to avoid siesta at home and to go to school early. On one of these successful afternoons, I was rewarded with a rare treat. I had finished a math lesson for a friend. In return, she gave me a boiled sweet potato topped with ice cream flavored with coconut juice costing half a penny. I could never have afforded it because I never received any allowance. Besides, Mother believed that street food was dirty and that it was ill-mannered to eat in the street.

A long time passed after the last cool bite of the treat had melted slowly in my thirsty throat, but still the school drum did not sound. I looked around for something to do.

All at once I saw the yellow flowers in the front yard of the French directrice's house which stood next to the school. I moved closer just to take a better peek at their leaves. This type of flower has leaves that can be rubbed thin until their veins are smashed, I thought to myself. I put one leg across the fence and broke off a leaf. Gently I rolled the leaf in the palms of my hands to lightly smash the fibers. Then, with careful fingers, I tore the leaf bottom laterally, leaving one side of the skin a millimeter or two shorter than the other. Next, I peeled off the long side skin further down, making a space for me to blow my breath in, until the whole leaf totally swelled up and looked like a long thin balloon. Magic! A long flat leaf had suddenly turned into a balloon the length of my arm! Proud of my masterpiece, I stored what I could of it in my pocket and walked farther inside the garden to look for fatter, longer leaves.

There were yellow and red irises lined up in three rows of perfect symmetry. They looked beautiful. I picked one stem, then another, then yet another. I counted half a dozen good ones all together.

Just then, a Chihuahua ran out from behind the house, jingling its bell collar to announce its presence. I jumped out of the flower bed and ran toward the low fence. The tiny dog had a loud mouth; it barked like crazy after me. I heard the door behind me open, but I was already safe in the schoolyard, behind its surrounding walls. When my classroom doors opened, I took out the teacher's flower pot and arranged the fresh-picked bouquet in it.

We students had just settled down in our seats, and the teacher was just coming round her desk when she noticed the flowers.

"Beautiful flowers! Who..." She had not finished her sentence when in marched the French directrice, a strikingly handsome lady in her thirties. She pointed at the pot and said in a loud, angry voice, "Those flowers are mine. One of your students stole them from my flower bed. Who was that insolent thief? I demand that she get up here!"

I froze behind my desk in the first row. I stared at my teacher, who now had turned pale with shock.

"Miss Blanche," my teacher addressed the directrice, "could it be possible that you are mistaken? It's hard to think that the students would dare do such a thing—especially to you," she said in a controlled tone.

"Mistaken?" Miss Blanche shrieked, "I saw the girl with my own eyes! I saw her back! She ran away with these flowers!"

7

I could feel a ray of electricity shooting sideways from Miss Ngoc's eyes in my direction.

"I am sorry that your flowers were taken. You can rest assured that I will take care of the matter. I appreciate your telling me."

"I demand that the thief be called out!" exclaimed Miss Blanche.

"Sorry. This is my class, and I will handle it my way." Miss Ngoc looked firmly into the French directrice's eyes and walked toward the door. "Please leave us," she said.

The French directrice stared at Miss Ngoc for a long moment. Her mouth opened as if to say something. Then abruptly she spun around and left, her heels knocking hard on the brick floor.

Miss Ngoc took the rattan rod out and hit it several times on her desk while yelling a long moral lesson. My ears perked up waiting for my name to be called. Big terms like *obedience, discipline, rules, directrice,* and *people's property* drifted in and out of my ears making it difficult to concentrate on my name. After a few minutes, the whacking sound ceased. I saw my teacher open her notebook and heard the students arranging their school tools on their desks. I hurriedly followed suit.

When the drum signaled the afternoon fifteen-minute break, I walked past my teacher to line up before dismissal. While I lowered my head, as one must dutifully do to show respect, I caught my teacher's look, followed by her terse command: "Go to the blackboard and stand there until the end of the break."

I meekly walked to the blackboard. There I crossed my arms and turned my head to face the huge blackboard one foot away. I was surprised that she did not make me kneel down. Maybe the punishment was being delayed to give me time to meditate over my crime—the way Mother always did. This was unusual for my teacher, who taught us math and dictation with her rattan rod, striking us all over our bodies without warning and upon the slightest of our mistakes.

I really didn't know why I managed to get into trouble all the time, especially with adults. To me, the beauty of flowers was like the beauty of the river, the sunset, the big branch of my favorite "rubber tree," or a sad song. When my senses came in touch with them, my body just felt like melting away to be a part of them. I lost all awareness until something like a barking dog would bring me back to reality. Three times I almost drowned in the swift river thinking that I would be able to swim naturally like dogs did without having to learn how!

My teacher had been afraid for me. That was why she didn't identify me. That was very brave of her, even braver than when she had put her finger into Tu's eye to save her sight. She could have been accused of

helping a thief, which is what I had been called by the French directrice, and a thief could be imprisoned and receive brutal punishment —
especially one who stole from the French. I thought of the song about
a thief who stole mangoes from Ong Lon's (Mr. Big's) garden. He was
caught by the police and sent off to a prison in the Con Son Island, which
was reserved for those committing crimes against the French. I felt much
admiration for my teacher who had dared to stand up to them for my
sake.

In my daydreaming I heard Sau say, "Did you hear how beautifully
our teacher spoke to the French directrice?"

"Of course. What did you expect? I never doubted that her French
was perfect," responded Tien.

"That's not what I mean. I mean the way she was able to make the
French directrice back down, using her own language. *And* made her
leave the classroom."

"Yes. And very mad, too."

"Good for her. Our teacher wasn't afraid to show who was boss in
her classroom."

I followed the conversation with keen interest. French people didn't
walk in our quarters, go to our markets, or come to our houses. They lived
in a world apart. I hardly ever saw the French directrice. She taught in
the French classroom that was only for French children and some highly
well-to-do Annamites. My little brother went there, fifty feet away from
our classroom, in the same lot but separated by a grassy courtyard. Ours
was only dirt packed. I never talked with my brother in school.

Now an incident that had happened to our family a while back began
to make better sense to me.

We were riding in our black Citroën on one of our family outings.
Father sat in the front with our chauffeur. I saw a broken tree trunk lying
across the road, and our chauffeur swerved around it to avoid hitting it.
Then a Frenchman appeared in another Citroën from the opposite direction. Our chauffeur backed the car up in panic. The heavy Frenchman
jumped out of his car and stamped his way over to us, his face red with
anger. Our chauffeur hurriedly got out of the car and stood on guard at
its side. The Frenchman confronted him menacingly, his large body taking on even greater proportions next to that of our chauffeur, who
although the same height, was much thinner. Without a word, he violently struck a powerful slap on our chauffeur's cheek. As soon as I heard
the slap, the car door slammed on my father's side. I saw my father move
quickly around to the front of the car, like a tiger on the attack. The next
thing I heard was another slap. The Frenchman's cheek, marked by my

9

father's fingers, looked drained of blood. He and my father stared defiantly at each other. Not a word was spoken. A long moment passed, and then finally each returned to his own car and drove away in silence. For a long time, no one said a word in our car. Even Spring Field, my little eight-year-old brother, who went to the exclusive French school adjacent to my public one and who was usually very talkative, kept to his own thoughts that day.

A week later, at my mother's card-playing gathering, I heard my mother's friends laughing and joking excitedly about the slapping incident. They requested that my mother confirm what they had read about in the *Ngay Nay (The Times)*—the country's most prestigious newspaper. Then they exclaimed about the way the report was written up: full of nuances, mocking humor and pride, especially in the closing, when it said that the case was brought to court but dismissed.

That was when I realized I had been under a cloud of fear that something was going to happen to my father. My mother and her friends seemed to be happy and proud of him though. I was, too.

A new thought occurred to me then. I began to distinguish the French from the Annamites. I used to accept without question that all adults were my superiors and should be treated with respect, whether Annamite or French. Now, if the French were not fair to us Annamites, I would no longer have to think of them in that way.

As I stood now at the blackboard, I wondered whether and when I would get punished. Like our chauffeur, who had stood at attention awaiting punishment from both the Frenchman and my father, I had expected a serious spanking for my wrongdoing. I was surprised to be only mildly scolded. I guess I was lucky. Had it been one of our people in the place of the French directrice, she would have discreetly discussed my problem with my teacher adult to adult. This would have put my teacher on the spot. Then, in turn, I would have been beaten to near death by her. She would have thought I deliberately disobeyed her and had given cause to others to question the effectiveness of her teaching.

The ways of adults were complicated. One never knew when they would strike. My duty to myself was to try to remember the different circumstances in which they applied their rules and try not to antagonize them.

2

Our colonial brick house looked
out over an empty lot to the Mekong River. Our view of the immense
rice paddies and the railroad station was blocked by a garden of lemon
and areca nut trees belonging to our landlord.

I was sitting with Bright Moon and Spring Field, my sister and little
brother, around the copper tray waiting for lunch to be served. Gold
Cloud, my frail little sister playing nearby, had asthma and was constantly
watched over by her nurse. My other two smaller sisters and baby brother
were also somewhere in the background, their nurses hovering over
them. Since they were too young for me to play with, I hardly ever noticed them.

The cook came to move my mother's rattan chair to the shiny, satin
brown, solid wood bed, which also served as the table around which we
now sat. First the cook's aide used two long bamboo paddles, twice as
wide at the bottom as at the top, to fluff up the rice in the large earthen
container placed in the specially woven basket lined with red quilted cotton to keep in the warmth. The steamy hot vapor of the Eight Fragrance
rice emitted an enticing aroma. Sau, the cook's aide, was careful not to
scoop less than three times, nor to fill more than two-thirds of the tiny
antique bowl for my mother. This skill had taken a long time for Sau to
acquire. She had had to repeat the procedure several times and be cor-
rected all too often in front of our hungry eyes. Mother was meticulous
about that.

We waited for Mother to serve herself first before beginning to dip
our chopsticks into the communal dishes. Only after seeing our mother
set down her bowl and chopsticks, which were made of carved ivory with
copper tips, could we be allowed to leave the "table." With great care, so

as not to be caught being ill-mannered, we swallowed the last of our portions. Each of us wanted to be the first to leave, but nearly always, we ended up by folding our arms in front of our chests and reciting almost simultaneously: "Reverend Mother, I have finished eating. May I be excused?"

Once satisfied that we had behaved well at the table and all finished our food, Mother would stand up, give each of us a final look of warning and admonish, "Take your siesta." Then she would saunter off to her bedroom. As soon as the bedroom door was shut, each of us would disappear to our favorite corner, not to see one another again until suppertime at eight that night.

As usual, this afternoon I went first to the veranda overlooking the street and the field on the river shore. Mother had forbidden us to play in that field which seemed to belong to nobody. I stood tippy-toe on the balcony and looked over the hibiscus fence to the river beyond. Not a soul was in the street. The bushes and grass on the forbidden field appeared as though they themselves were taking a siesta in the scorching sun. Beyond the field was what I liked to call my "rubber tree." The green mass of its leaves gave protection over its huge trunk which extended over the swift cool waters of the Mekong River. The tree beckoned me. I slid down to the other side of the balcony and walked to the hole under our fence dug out by our neighbors' dogs, who used it to visit our house. Spotting no one, I crawled over to the other side and into the haunted field. There I straightened up, ran over the thorny grass and across the street to the far side of the forbidden field, and followed the path to my rubber tree.

Normally, I would go directly to my tree, climb my favorite branch, and balance myself on the farthest limb which was a ten- to twelve-foot overhang above the water. Then I would wrap myself around the branch and look down at the fish swimming briskly in the water. Some days I could spot a fish as big as the forearm of a man. Now and then, a small boat would pass by carrying a boy with his fish and shrimp traps. Live shrimp would be jumping around in the bottom of the boat, and some would be grilling on a little earthenware stove. I would often wonder enviously if these boys didn't have to go to school. Whenever I tired of looking over the river, I would usually amuse myself by scraping the bark of the tree, rubbing the white sap onto my hands and arms and waiting for it to dry before rolling it into a bouncing sphere as big as a ping-pong ball. However, because of a discovery I had made two days before, today I changed the course of my actions.

Two days before, while crossing the forbidden field, I had spotted a rabbit. Feeling an urge for a good chase, I had run after it. I had forgotten that the field was haunted by a vicious, ghastly ghost, said to be the rightful owner of the lot, who had passed away a long time ago. People have seen it appear with its head severed. It is rumored that it has even killed a few curious people who have been foolish enough to venture into its territory. In any case, during my chase, I had stumbled across a shrine about the size of my mother's chair. It sat squarely on a brick foundation, two steps above the ground. Upon spotting it, I decided to drop the rabbit chase and instead tiptoed toward the shrine to have a peek inside. On a square tile of about a foot, I saw a small bowl of rice holding sticks of burning incense. In front of the incense, there were two saucers decorated with colorful cakes. I stared at them for some time, then went back to my rubber tree. Yesterday, I returned to the shrine and saw that the cakes were still there, fresh and colorful as ever. I ventured to poke my finger lightly on one of the pretty buns and was surprised to find that it felt warm. With that discovery, I once again returned to my tree.

Today, I decided to visit the shrine again and found that the cakes were still there. I was very puzzled. Since the cakes were not yet eaten, it must have been either because there was no ghost in the forbidden field or because the ghost did not like those cakes. I pondered a minute. Then, by habit, I started the prayer I said before meals; only this time I asked the ghost's blessing instead of God's.

"Please bless my food, ghost. You understand. If I don't eat them, they'll get spoiled." I watched for a sign of approval. A long time passed before a breeze swooped down and shook the grass where I had concentrated my attention. "Ah, he approves." I tiptoed up the steps of the tomb and raised both of my hands to touch the cakes. As I did so, I thought I heard my name called. Quickly, I grabbed the delicate cakes that were lying in the saucer and ran over the thorny weeds, across the street, and back through the dog hole. With one swift jump, I cleared the balcony. Safe at last, I squatted down in my hiding corner and pulled out a cake. To my surprise, all of the cakes had found their way securely into the pockets of my shorts. Biting into the first cake with an unsure expectancy, I could still hear my heart pounding and my name resounding: the ghost had been calling me. All of a sudden, the living room door swung open. Out came Tam, my adopted sister. Tam shot a horrified look at my secret corner where I was about to pop a cake into my open mouth.

"Hey, what are you eating?" Petrified by the surprise encounter, I stared at Tam without answering. "You won't tell me, ha? I'll tell Mother," and with that she spun around and disappeared behind the door. I made an attempt to stand up and run after her, but it was too late. The door had already closed on me. "Tattletale. I hate people who report on others," I thought, putting the rest of the cake in my mouth while preparing to be called in. Tam's threat was not idle. She always reported immediately to Mother about our clandestine outings, unless of course Mother was asleep, in which case she would only postpone her tattling until later. Reporting on us was her way of being loyal to Mother, who had adopted her and saved her from hunger five years ago. On a visit to our grandparents in North Vietnam, Mother was convinced to adopt Tam and my bigger brother Middle, whose parents had been killed in a flood that had ruined the harvest of that year. Maybe Tam was just doing her duty; all the same I hated her tattling.

Two more cakes were eaten by the time I heard the long sounding drum from the boys' school two miles away. I ran to the locked gate and climbed over it. My speed did not slacken until I reached my school. "Tam Ta Ta," sounded three beats from my school's drum. The girls were just then lining up in front of the classroom. I joined in.

Class finished at five. By then, having forgotten that morning's incident, I calmly walked home, looking forward to receiving two of my mother's homemade biscuits for an afternoon snack. On reaching home though, I was met by my mother's stern command, "Go inside. Lie down."

The designated torture bed for thrashing, my father's napping spot, was in the same room with my parents' modern springy bed which was padded with a thick hot cotton mattress. In my blue shorts and white shirt, I crawled to the middle of the wooden bed, flattened myself out on my stomach and straightened my arms alongside my body.

I lay still for a minute, my head to one side, facing the window. All at once I felt like crying. I let my teardrops fall from one eye across my nose to join with the tears from the other eye, together drifting down to my temple and onto the bed. On contact with the wood of the bed, my tears spread out and formed a little pool of water between my cheek and the wood that it was pressed against, giving a nice cool feeling. Enjoying that feeling, I pulled my hand up and pushed my index finger under my cheek to spread the water down and inward. Soon both my arms were raised and my hands were trying to reach out to the sides of the wooden bed. My fingers barely touched the edges of the bed, which was made of one single piece of solid wood. I wiggled my body right and left trying to reach down the sides to measure the thickness of the wood. "A good six inches," I thought. I slid back to the middle of the bed. The salty tears had become sticky. I turned my face to the other side facing the wall. The dull wall stared back at me. My eyelids grew heavy. In my dream, I heard myself wishing that my mother would not choose Tam to pick out the spanking rod. Anybody else but my newly acquired enemy.

Rods were selected from hibiscus stems. The length had to be uniform, but the width depended on the picker. A thin rod gave a burning sensation, but its end got smashed after four or five whacks. As a result, its terrible beat-up appearance would make Mother feel that she had inflicted enough pain. A thicker rod bit deeper into the skin. Its pain stung a lot longer, and it remained sturdy for a lot longer. Some old rods had knots that would leave very painful welts and bruises.

A sharp whacking sound on the wood startled me awake. I turned my head and saw my mother already sitting in her blue rattan chair in front of me. "Move down," she ordered. I slid my body down, adjusting it level to the rod she held in her hand. The trick was to present the most meaty part so that the pain would go away quickly after the thrashing, yet there would be terrible looking superficial red marks left on the skin.

"You know what you did wrong?"

"Yes, Mother. I am sorry. I will not do it again."

"What did you do wrong?"

"Honorable Mother, I ate the cakes."

"Where did you get them?"

We children were forbidden to eat foods that were not prepared at home, that is, unless we got permission from our mother. I described where I had found the cakes.

"Those cakes are freshly made and brought there by some worshipers. They are taken home afterwards, to be replaced by new ones the next day."

"I'm sorry, Mother. I didn't know that. I will not do it again. I promise."

My mother gave me three whacks for stealing the cakes and another one for going in the forbidden field.

"Think about it."

When Mother left the room, the rod was left balancing on my bottom. I knew that if I kept the rod well balanced, Mother would come back some time later and let me go. I lay there and thought of my little brother. If it had been him, he would have received at least ten or fifteen blows. He never cried and never showed pain. The harder the stroke, the tighter his jaws. He said Napoleon never cried. He had played Napoleon in a play at his school. I had learned from him to yell very loudly at each whip. As a result, I received fewer whacks. When my mother returned later and dismissed me, I pulled myself up and walked to the bathroom where my adopted brother was already waiting.

"It wasn't too bad, was it? You must thank me for the small rod. I was the one who picked it."

"Thank you," I said, wiping my nose with my hand. I kept my promise to my mother, since I had been taught that it was a sin and the mark of a base person to break a promise. Never a spanking came twice from the same situation, only from others. Ah, so many forbidden things! They were overwhelming. They crowded your little head to the point where they burst from their compartments, mixed with one another until you vaguely remembered that everything was forbidden to you when adults caught you doing it. Even eating, sleeping and doing your homework were sometimes wrong when adults thought it was the wrong time. I ended up doing what my senses dictated to me, simply to avoid being confused.

When Middle organized an excursion into the yard of the neighbor who was also our landlord, we immediately thought it was a great idea. Even Bright Moon and Tam jumped at the opportunity. Three times we had tried. Three times we had not been able to get past the owner's dog who was always napping beneath the overhang of the house.

But we were a brave lot, especially Middle. We were not afraid of the dog nor of its owner. It was our mother's finding out about the excursion that really worried us.

Today, on our fourth attempt, Middle again cautioned us not to touch the areca nut tree or the leaves of the betels that crept onto it. "The owner will kill us if we damage it."

"Why are they so precious?" Spring Mountain asked.

"Ask Bright Moon. Soon her future husband will need those inseparable leaves and nuts to ask for her hand and to give them to the relatives and friends as an announcement of his engagement, unless she wants to stay an old maid for the rest of her life. Hee, hee, hee," Middle giggled. We remained silent. It was a serious matter.

We managed to reach the dog's sleeping corner, but the dog was nowhere in sight. Middle turned around and winked at us. His big smile showed his long white horse teeth. Our spirits rose. We passed over to the the rear of the house in bigger strides after him. We would do whatever Middle told us.

A faint voice was heard coming from the direction of our house. Middle spun around. He put his right index finger to his lips, but we were already silent as clams. He cupped his other hand behind his ear, and we all heard his name called out sharply. Then we saw Middle run past us. We followed suit. From outside the fence enclosing our property, we saw, in between the thick leaves, our mother standing next to the dog hole. Above the ground where the hibiscus trunks were thinly spread out, I saw the embroidered hems of her satin pants, and I shivered with fear. We had trespassed on the owner's property, another forbidden field. We turned to Middle who stood like a martyr. Our eyes were transfixed on his. We expected our heroic leader to crawl through the hole first. Middle knew it. He hesitated a second, and then his face firmed up. He scratched his left earlobe, then with a smile he went down on his knees and crawled through the hole. Thwack, thwack. "Ouch. Sorry Mother."

When the last of us had gotten through the hole and received our thrashings, we were ordered to go in and wash up. We went to the bathroom, a room the size of a large kitchen. Middle scooped the water with a smooth coconut shell the size of a rice bowl. It had one hole on each side for the handle to pass through. The container, as large as a wine barrel, was made of ceramic, colored in earth brown. Middle poured the water on our feet for us to rinse them, then poured some water in the brass portable sink for us to wash our hands and faces.

While waiting for my turn, I thought of the bathroom in the home of my parents' friends, the director of public schools and his family. They lived in a villa given to them by the French. It was behind the boy's school and had a yard spreading out to the Mekong River. There was one bathroom downstairs and one upstairs. Both used running water from the pipes. The toilet upstairs looked out on the river. That was my favorite spot, second only to my rubber tree. I hated our bathroom at home, which was hidden beyond the three "maids" rooms and the garage. It was dark, small, and smelly. Whenever possible, I managed to be present at the director's house, allowing a decent amount of time to pass before excusing myself to use the flushing toilet with a view of the river. It was a good thing that his wife's two younger sisters were friends of Bright Moon. Bright Moon's friends were hand-picked by Mother, and it was Mother's order that I accompany my older sister at all times (like those escorts of the princesses in the *Livres Roses* I guess). In this case, I didn't mind because I could roam anywhere in the house or garden until I was called to go home. I felt pretty comfortable with Mrs. "Directrice" since she was my spiritual mother at my Catholic confirmation when I was eight and I got to call her Ma Doc (Mother Directrice).

I hated myself whenever I quarreled with their son, André — his baptismal and French citizen's name — who was my age. In these situations I had to resort to the French house next door. They also had a son my age whom I had met one day while he was roaming alone in the Annamite school yard. There were no other French families nearby, and the

Annamite boys did not want to play with him. He had looked lonely, so I offered my friendship. We exchanged greetings, and he invited me to his house. I was introduced to his mother, a sweet French lady about my mother's age, thirty-five or so. He then asked his mother's permission to show me his airplane in his bedroom. His plane hung from the middle of the ceiling and took one-third of the space. It was a beautiful plane in metallic blue. Before leaving his house that first time, I had asked him to show me his bathroom. Satisfied that it also had a flush toilet, I had said goodbye and promised to visit him again. Since the boy did not dare to venture away from his house, I only visited him when I was on enemy terms with my sissy friend, André.

André always wore his silk pyjamas buttoned on the side, the latest style. Even so, I liked him when he sang. In his gutsy moods, he would jump up on the breakfast table when his parents were not around and perform before us girls. One of his favorite songs was:

> Mine. If you love me please swear.
> Swear? I don't care. I will swear.
> Mine. You will buy me a house, a house of my own.
> Of your own. Okay, of your own.
> Mine. You must buy me gold bracelets and necklaces.
> Yes, yes, yes.

The older girls would laugh and applaud vigorously. I, too, enjoyed his performances. Yet, I was puzzled by certain songs he knew. My mother would certainly not like to hear those songs coming from her friend's young son. There was a record my sister used to play at home. On it was a song about a fifteen-year-old girl whose blossoming beauty made men's heads turn. My mother did not speak French, but she had determined that the song was "immoral" based on some "Sh, sh" sounds emitted by the male singer. For that reason, she had taken the record away from my sister.

3

IT WAS ONE OF those carefree after-
noons without class. My mother and her friends had just returned from
a bicycle ride. From the center room, I could hear Mrs. Chief of District
laugh in the antique living room. (Wives were called by their husbands'
title.) She was always cheerful, and her laughing sounded like fire
crackers. The high school directress talked about the snack they were
having with their tea. The beautiful Mrs. Administrator was also there.
I played my mandolin softly; their merry conversation drifted by my ears.

Suddenly, my mother, red from the sun and exercise, entered the
room and told me to accompany my big sister, Bright Moon, to church.
I walked to the backyard and found her already settled in the fluffy white
cushion of our rickshaw. I climbed up the wooden landing and told her
to scoot over.

"You're rude," she said.

"Why do I have to always follow you?" I snapped. I was furious.
Because of her, I always had to drop whatever I was doing to accompany
her.

"Go ask Mother," she replied, looking away. The rickshawman picked
up the wooden bars and leisurely pulled the cart toward the gate. He was
someone from the neighborhood who came to pull our rickshaw whenever Mother needed to go on short errands.

Halfway to church, Bright Moon turned to me and looked critically
at my shorts and shirt. "You go to church like that?"

"Oh, I forgot." I looked down and saw my bare legs. No words were
exchanged after that. Arriving at church, Bright Moon walked straight to
the seat reserved for my mother. I was not properly dressed, so I walked
around the grounds of the church in search of something to do while

waiting for her. At the front of the church I saw Brother Anh, the son of a wealthy doctor in town. He stood in the middle of the main entrance, legs slightly apart, arms crossed. He seemed to be lost in thought, staring straight ahead toward the altar. I followed his gaze and saw my sister kneeling piously, like one of the holy statues surrounding her.

"Hi, Brother Anh." Startled, he looked toward me in shock. A second later, "Oh, hi, Little Sister."

"Why don't you go inside? Because you're not Catholic?"

"No, no. I mean, yes. I'm not a Catholic, but I still can go in. In fact I might go in now, and I might also even become a Catholic."

I was now standing side by side with Brother Anh. He put his big hand on my shoulder. I looked up and saw his big smile and was surprised to notice the distance from my face to his. Brother Anh went to school in France. He drank a lot of milk and ate lots of butter so that he looked much bigger than the majority of us natives here. His eyes returned to my kneeling sister. I saw my sister kneeling erect and attentive. She must have been aware of Brother Anh's presence. Brother Anh seemed to forget that I was there. Gently, I tapped the hand on my shoulder to say goodbye. After waiting around a bit, I got bored and decided to walk home.

In half an hour, I was in my little sister's room plucking away at my mandolin. My mother walked in, a paper fan in her hand. She gave me an approving smile which froze abruptly midway. "Where is your sister?" she demanded.

"Reverend Mother, she is at church."

"At church—and why are you here?"

"I ... uh ... I forgot to wear my dress, so I couldn't get in."

"Who is with her?"

"Reverend Mother, there was nobody with her."

"Did you meet anybody?"

"Yes, Mother, I met Brother Anh in front of the church."

She frowned slightly. Then, suddenly, I found myself assaulted with the round handle of the fan. Mother hit me again and again. I covered my head with my hands while repeatedly murmuring: "I am sorry Mother, I am sorry ... sorry ... sorry."

My mother's anger subsided after half a dozen hits that left my hand covered with bleeding lines from the sharp metal hook of the fan.

"Get out of here. And tell Tam to go fetch your sister," she ordered as she turned to rejoin her guests. "Thank you, Mother," I said and scuttled out to go find Tam, then to go to the corner of the house.

I sat on the foundation sill, fuming. I did not know why my mother had gotten so angry. As far as I could recall, this had been the first time that my mother had beaten me that way, for no fault of mine. And she had even had such a good time riding her bike with her friends. By and by, I heard the whistling of the train in the distance. I climbed up the foundation, hooked one of my arms around the gutter pipe to steady myself and tried to look over the fence through the rows of areca trees. There I could see the faded redwood-colored train crawling out from the brick station beyond the rice fields. It came and went twice a day.

"Toot, toot." The black head sent up a long black column of smoke that drifted back along the nine cars that I counted. The faint whistle in the distance always stirred a sad appeal in my heart. I wished I were on that train going to see my "real" mother, the mother who presumably lived in Hue. Sometimes, when my mother became angry with me she would say that I could not be her child, that she was not my real mother. At times, I wished that that were true. Especially today. My real mother must be dark skinned like me. Mother here had told me many times that I was "black like charcoal" and that my hair was "messy like a crow's nest" and infested with fleas. My clothes, that began clean in the morning, would always be stained with dirt and mud by evening.

"You are not my child. You are the daughter of Miss Hong in Hue," my mother would sigh, shaking her head sadly as if I were a hopeless criminal.

"Sorry Mamma," I had once replied, feeling deeply sorry for my mother that I looked the way I did. Remembering a story that I had read in one of the *Livres Roses* about an ugly girl who had become pretty and got married to a prince after a hot bath, I helpfully added, "All that you need to do is to scrub me good in a bath of boiling hot water. I'll turn white again."

I saw my mother's face light up with a smile, her head tilted back on her long white neck, her eyes closed. I was pleased to see that my mother was pleased.

No problem there, I had thought — baths I could handle. But, to keep my head far apart from those of my friends so that lice wouldn't jump from their hair to mine, as Mother had told me, was asking for the impossible.

One of my favorite games was to go with my friends to the graves that were abandoned, or to the rice paddies late in the evening to detect the singing of the loudest cricket. We would join our heads close together in front of the designated hole. Once done, we would take turns putting our hands in the long dark hole to find the cricket and pull it out. A prized cricket had shiny black jaws equipped with a set of strong black clamps and a firm thick line of gold color across the top of its head, right where the skull met with the bright black wings. When a good cricket was found, we would put it in a matchbox carefully lined with fresh green grass for food and aired with a few holes punched through the sliding lid. The prized cricket would then be shown around to friends, who would then call up a fighting match among the neighbors. Even Bright Moon, who considered our games childish, would stand by to watch whenever the cricket fighting party was held on the veranda of our house. It was very exciting to hear the crickets singing loud and clear already in competition the night before the fight.

Middle played the role of leader in all our games. At Middle's signal, the boxes were opened and the crickets pulled out by their beards (two antennae) at the sides of their jaws. We would again gather round, our heads touching, to admire the crickets and comment on how beautiful and strong they looked. The owners would then hold the crickets' beards up and whirl them round and round on them. When the wings of the crickets spread out in the act, we would then lower them to the ground to face one another. A dead silence would fall. All eyes would concentrate on the crickets that now moved steadily, wings half out and curved up, tails raised, heads lowered, and jaws wide open. They would move slowly towards each other at first, until their jaws hit — at which time *wham*, the fight would begin. Their jaws would lock, their bodies sway from side to side, and their wings flip in and out. In our excitement, we would jump up and down, swing to and fro, and roar cheers of disappointment or approval.

When the crickets slowed down, those that looked beaten would be withdrawn from the match. Their owners would caress their broken wings and jaws, murmuring, "You are brave, you are strong," over the arrogant shouts of the others.

After the cricket fights, we would sit and chat with excitement until the sun set and our hungry stomachs told us it was time to scuttle home for dinner.

"See you tomorrow," we would say. "Tomorrow" or "ngay mai" is a wonderful word in our language. It could mean the next day or any indefinite time in the future. "Ngay" means day, "mai" the morning star. Every day has the morning star, so one didn't feel the need to commit to a specific time. Time was God given and taken. It could be long or short. Tomorrow or forever after.

As I stood dangling from the gutter pipe to look across the fields, the thought of cricket and crab hunts chased away my desire to go searching for my real mother. Instead, my eyes drifted over the field towards the graves in search of a potential hole for a prized cricket. I smiled at the promising outlook.

The gate was my favorite playground when I did not feel safe to wander far from home, that is, when I knew my mother was awake in the house. It was there, at the gate of the house, that once a day, after siesta, the maids would gather with the cook's aide, who had the key to the gate. The whole household assembled there, except for my mother, Bright Moon, and Spring Field, my brother next to me in age. Whenever Mother was not around to observe, one of the nurses could be seen carrying my baby sister at her side—Mother had ordered that all the nurses carry the children in front of them with their legs together so that the children would not grow up to be bowlegged. The cook seldom spoke on these occasions because she had a northern accent and had to repeat herself several times before the others understood her. She looked sad all the time. It had been over five years now since she had left her home town near the Red River in the north. The old, mean nurse, no longer good for anything, was also always at these gatherings. She oversaw the household in my mother's absence and the maids' conversations in general. People from three or four other families in the neighborhood joined the daily gatherings to exchange news from their households and the market.

Every day, a Chinese man would come and park his cart on the sidewalk. For half a penny, he would sell a glass of sweetened gelatin made out of seaweed, or crushed ice molded into the shape of a glass, flavored with one of six different tastes, each one identified by a distinctive rainbow color from the jars lined up on the front of his dessert cart. In the afternoon, the "star trees," tall as pine trees, forming two rows alongside the street, would cast their shade on the group and fan them with their leaves waving in the river breeze. Around this time, the fat snack vendor would also appear. It took him about two hours to waddle over, stopping all along the way from his house, three miles across the first bridge to the island. He carried a bamboo yoke with a basket on each end. The basket he carried in front was lined with dried squid and fish tendons. Two small jars of sauces were placed in the middle—one containing a sweet and sour bean sauce, the other, pickled red peppers. For half a penny, he would select two dried squid or two cut-up dried fish tendons and broil them on the burning charcoal covered with ashes contained in the rear basket. People loved to eat these dried seafoods. They were chewy, strong smelling like Camembert Cheese, and easy to share with others by shredding them alongside their fibers.

Everybody also loved the fat vendor. He was so fat that his chest spilled out like a woman's breast. They called him "lai cai" or "homo." They said that because he was half woman and half man, he could not have a wife. I heard their comments and was very much puzzled by them. One day, I left the crowd to follow him, pretending that I had something to do in the direction he was heading. When I reached him, I spoke my mind: "Mister, they said you are 'lai cai.' Are you?"

He giggled and walked on.

"Are you?" I insisted.

"Hee, hee, hee . . . Noooo," he chuckled in reply.

"They said you don't have a wife."

"I have a wife." He raised his voice at the word *wife* in protest. "She prepared all of this for me to bring to the market . . . hee, hee, hee," he giggled again.

Satisfied, I left him. The next time I heard them announcing the coming of the "lai cai," I protested excitedly, telling them that he was not and that he had a wife. "It's true. He told me so," I added, defensively.

Everybody broke out into robust laughter, telling me how dumb I was. "Next time look at his tits," they said mockingly, and I thought that *they* were dumb not to believe him. Who else would know better than himself?

On one of those hot, lazy summer afternoons, I was loitering at the gate, enjoying the maids' jokes, when two Annamite men in European suits arrived. They said they had an appointment with my mother and asked if someone would be kind enough to announce their arrival. I volunteered and led the way. The door to the living room was already wide open, and a colorful "tea" was set on a side table. They stood at the door while I walked into my mother's bedroom to look for her. My mother was in her long, light-jade-colored dress, sitting on a low chair in front of her dresser. "Reverend Mother, there are two men who wish to see you."

My mother nodded and walked out to the study room, then through its door to the main living room. The men introduced themselves as representatives from the École des Beaux Arts (School of Fine Arts). She asked them to have a seat and took a seat herself near the tea tray. She asked me to serve the tea from the teapot that sat inside a bamboo basket the shape of a jar. The basket was lined with a thick red cushion. The teapot, powder pink in color, was decorated with white Mai flowers— plums that bloomed in early spring. The antique teapot looked fragile next to the large cups and saucers that were sky blue with patterns of white flowers intertwined with delicate green branches.

"Ah, I am delighted to see that you use our tea cups," the director said. He looked up to see his school's bright-colored jars, three feet high, standing behind the sofa, surrounded by antique bowls and plates. "And the jars too. They look so elegant among the antiques."

"Your artwork is beautiful. The French touch gives it an exquisite shape and color. The modern and the old blend together very well," my mother said. I was very surprised to hear my mother express herself with such ease, and in public, too.

"We are proud to be near the École des Beaux-Arts," she added.

"Thank you. You give us too many compliments," the director said, embarrassed, but looking very pleased.

I wondered when my mother had acquired the tea set. I had never seen it before. But then, my mother always locked everything away, even magazines that were brought from my father's trips. I also did not know why my mother received her visitors here in the main living room, instead of in the antique room where she always entertained her friends at card games.

The director picked up his cup and saucer and asked for permission to drink. "If I may invite you to drink?"

"Please. Before it turns cold," Mother replied timidly. He had one sip of tea, then continued, "Madam, as you said, our work is unique, and we try to keep it original by combining the French art and techniques with our traditional ones to produce a modern Vietnamese creation, which is very much in demand in France. Unfortunately, because our school is so small, we have only thirty students and few facilities, and our production is very limited. One consolation is that there is quality work being done by chosen students who come with the best recommendations from their apprenticeships all over the country. Our sculptures — the black bronze busts of the Tonkinese woman [North Vietnamese], the Cochinchinese woman [South Vietnamese] and the Thai woman — are very famous. Next year we plan to have a full standing statue of a woman that represents the beauty of the Annamite people. That statue will be the soul of our school and will stay on the pedestal right at the entrance to the school in front of the 'Sens Unique.' We are very excited about it." He stopped and took another sip of tea.

"That is a beautiful idea. I share your joy," Mother said, sparkling with excitement.

"We ... Uh ... we ... in order to make the statue we must find the lady who represents that beauty. We ... cannot invent one. The lady has to be a real woman with the features, height, measurements, and expression of a beautiful Annamite woman. Uh ... we heard rumors from our students and checked around with respectable friends. I mention 'respectable' because we also want the chosen lady to be of good family. Otherwise she could not symbolize the beauty that we admire and of which are are proud." He raised his cup and saucer again and seemed to wait for my mother to ask the question.

My mother raised her cup for a small sip while looking down at her dress. A moment passed.

"Uh . . . as we said, we checked around and were told that you have a very beautiful daughter, Miss Bright Moon. In fact, I saw her going to church last week: slim, pretty, and gracious. She looked tall, must be five feet four, five, six? Her long shiny black hair reflects hope and purity. I knew right away she was our dream statue."

I saw my mother looking attentively at the man. Her face looked puzzled, as if she were disturbed at the terms he used to describe her oldest daughter.

"It would be very nice if she could be our model," the director added.

My mother suddenly turned her poised face away and firmly placed her saucer and cup on the corner table beside her.

"I wish you could tell me what exactly a model does," she said in an even tone.

"A model just sits on the platform. The students will study her manners, expressions, and proportions. Some will sketch her on paper, others will work directly with the clay." He looked at her and noticed the change on her face. "Of course we will be there all the time to supervise them."

"Hm . . . just sit and let the boys study and take her proportions? I am sorry, Mr. Director. As much as I wish to be of help to you, I do not think that my daughter will be available to model." She paused, "She has to go to school in Saigon and . . . But you might like to check about Mr. Vinh's daughter. He is a known respectable teacher. I heard that he has a pretty daughter."

Her polite refusal greatly vexed the director, whose eyebrows drew together into a frown.

"Please understand that we did not make a light decision. It took us a great deal of time to gather the right recommendation. We think the choice will bring honor to all of us in the city and abroad."

"I understand," Mother said with a warm smile.

"We are very sorry." The men gathered the art busts that they had brought to show as samples of their work and stood up slowly. They looked puzzled. "Good-bye, my Lady." They backed out a few steps toward the door before turning away.

"Good-bye, respectable gentlemen." She followed them with her eyes until they had crossed the veranda steps. Then she turned to me and indicated with a nod for me to close the door.

That night, I decided to sleep with my brother in the study room. I had no fixed bed assigned to me. Being a girl of no importance, I could go from my big sister's bed to my brother's, or to one of my little sisters' in the room for babies and nurses, or to my parents' room and sleep on the bed of torture.

There was no outdoor play that night. Mother had the study room door wide open to the small court that led to the kitchen. She had her small earthen stove right on the first step, and Middle was helping her with the cooking. The dish that they were cooking took three or four days to prepare. Everybody had helped in their free time to pick out the tiny hairs or black spots that stuck to the white membranes of the swallows' nests. These membranes — saliva of the swallows — had been soaked for days before the sorting and cleaning. My mother had supervised the entire preparation very closely and told us not to waste any membrane as they were very expensive and the best quality was difficult to find.

As my mother and Middle took turns constantly stirring the pot and watching the mild fire, I lay near my brother's wooden bed, watching and thinking. I thought about my mother's conversation with the men from the Beaux Arts school.

"So they think my sister is pretty. Hm. What's pretty? I think the two misses in the brick house by sister Phung's house are pretty. One has a round face, the other a long face. They fit the description of the two beautiful sisters in the poems mother sings when she thinks she's alone. They ride in a horse carriage brought in from France — so romantic. Why weren't they approached by those men? Maybe they're not respectable. Some folks wonder why they aren't married at their ages — twenty-two and twenty-five. And they're so rich! They look so lovely in their shiny polished horse carriage painted in black and trimmed with fine gold lines. Both have curly hair. That's it! Respectable girls don't have curly hair. The younger one with a round face has her curly hair hanging loosely about her shoulders, while her long-faced sister puts her hair up in a loose, sweeping chignon. Oh no, to think of it, they don't look like Thuy Kieu and Thuy Van because they have curly hair."

I recited to myself the verses written by Nguyen Du describing the beauty of the sisters Thuy Kieu and Thuy Van. Everybody knew some verses of Nguyen Du's novel. I remembered: "Mai cot cach, tuyet tinh than . . . ." (Gracious and strong like Mai flower branches, pure like snow. Limpid like autumn water, eyebrows curved and young like the edge of a spring hill.)

"Maybe, maybe Bright Moon has that."

"One of her smiles will overturn a nation. Two of her smiles will overturn the defending walls!"

"Ay, ya, ya, nothing as such in her," my head protested in mockery.

Thuy Kieu knew musical instruments, played chess, painted, read and wrote poems, and sang.

"Ah, that's why Mother is working hard at making Sister learn music. Bright Moon doesn't want to learn the piano though. She only likes to sing and listen to music. Mother doesn't know that. She spends much money to hire a female piano teacher to come all the way from Saigon every Thursday afternoon."

I was asleep when my mother came to me with a bowl. She lifted my head up and said softly, "Drink this. Be careful not to spill it."

In my dreamy, sleepy state of mind, I allowed the cool, tiny, jell-like membranes to swim with their pleasant, sweetened juice slowly past my tongue and palate into my thirsty throat. It was delightful. When I finished, I gave the bowl back to my mother who, in the dim light, used a small spoon to clean around the small bowl and passed it back to me to lick clean. Then my mother made the sign of the cross on my forehead, pressed her lips on her thumb, then transferred the kiss onto my forehead. "Go back to sleep daughter."

A surge of love seized me. I felt like throwing my arms around my mother and saying, "I love you, Mother." But I didn't. Nobody ever did. So I lay back down and watched her wake up my brother and hand him another bowl just brought over by Middle. After him would be Bright Moon, who slept in the outer room, and so forth. By that time though, I would already be sound asleep with the jelly bits still savored in my mouth and the cool sweet taste in my memory.

4

THE SHORT SUMMER had gone. The big day for my mother was here. The Citroën was out of the garage, parked now on the driveway near our main entrance and ready to take us to our schools in Saigon, eighteen miles from our town. The chauffeur in his white pants and shirt was dusting and polishing the hood of the black car already sparkling dustless in the shining sun. The maid brought out my sister's luggage, two large brown leather cases strapped tight by a buckled leather sash on each side. They contained mostly the clothing enumerated by the nuns of St. Theresa's College (high school), commonly known as the white dress school because the students there wore white dresses and white pants and the nuns white habits. Half of one suitcase was packed with homemade Petit Beurre biscuits and ruoc — shredded pork to be eaten with rice soup, French bread or by itself like beef jerky, letting the shreds dissolve the slightly burnt grilled flavor between one's palate and tongue until most of the flavor disappeared and the remaining shreds became like chewing gum.

"How I wish to have some now," I thought, sliding myself into the front seat to the right of the chauffeur. I knew my mother must have packed some of the delicious food for me, too, not enough though — not like for my sister, because my sister was going to a rich school, where everything was expected to be impeccable and abundant. She had been there for three years.

The idea of richness had come to me the first time I went there with my mother to see my sister entering the school. The nuns had looked like angels, with the brims of their starchy white hats spread out wider than their shoulders and curled up at the tips as if ready to fly on contact with a strong wind. Their dresses were full and spotless white, long black

29

rosaries clinked at their sides. Only the sound of the rosaries could be heard in the huge yard full of nuns and students. I was glad my mother did not send me there. Anyway, if my sister had passed the public college exam she would have been sent to the same school I was attending now.

This would be my first year in the public "Collège des Jeunes Filles," otherwise known as the purple dress school. I almost had not made it. Every year, over a thousand girls from all over the country came to take the exam, but only a hundred passed and were chosen. I was somewhere in the eighties. My teacher had been very disappointed with my results. She had called me to her apartment in order to redo what I could remember of the eight-hour test, and I had received my last beating for faults in spelling and grammar that I had overlooked in the dictée—the dictation. I didn't mind that. I knew that if it hadn't been the dictée, it would've been the math or composition. Anything could happen when my mind drifted.

Luckily, somehow I had passed the sewing test this time. Last year I had had to stay back in the seventh grade because I had not known how to sew a buttonhole. When the French inspector had left the room for a few minutes, Lai, the daughter of the septic tank collector, who was sitting in the same row on my left (we sat in alphabetical order), had drawn my attention with a little scratching noise she made. I had looked up from my drawing of the buttonhole to her. She had raised her sewing and had tried to show me something, but I was scared and ashamed to look. Lai frowned, made a scornful sound in her throat, and pushed the piece of fabric nearer for me to see. "No cheating," I had said to myself and covered the left side of my face with my hand, pretending to busy myself with the drawing. My school sewing had been done by a few friends who had exchanged their sewing for my math problems. I had gotten a zero for my sewing in the exam. I had seen it in the indignant look of the French supervisor who collected my work after the two-hour test—a mere colorful picture of a button. To have a zero in any test meant to have flunked the whole exam. I had walked out of the classroom, head down, not daring to meet Lai's eyes.

After staying back one year, I now moved on to the first year of high school at the age of thirteen.

We arrived at my sister's school. The students in white were walking noiselessly to and fro on the wide dirt-packed lanes swept clean of dust. I felt very intimidated seeing their serene look among the huge tamarind trees.

Again all seemed holy and impeccable. After several hours of following my mother back and forth in the long courtyard, waiting in offices, and watching her whispering with the nuns, my sister was finally taken away. Her eyes were a little red when my mother brushed off the strand of hair from her forehead.

My mother and I went back to the Citroën that was waiting for us near the gate. There were not many cars in those days. Besides the few cars owned by the French, there were only two or three cars owned by Annamites in our city of Bien Hoa. The French had given my father one for his inspection trips. On the days or months that he worked in his Saigon office, he did not need the car, so it was left at home for the family to use. Our Citroën rode silently through the quiet black tar streets among rows of large, tall tamarinds, star trees, and wide cement curbs. Charming brick villas were hidden behind long brick walls surmounted by vase-shaped colonnades spaced to give a view at eye level of the inside.

Finally, the car stopped at a brick house in a busy street. I was surprised that it was not at the school where I had taken the exam. My mother gestured me to follow her into the house. The main entrance doors were wide open, perhaps in waiting for her. A lady walked out, greeted my mother, and led her to the living room. She said that my father would be back at five and that the room was ready for me. They chatted awhile. Then the lady went out and waved at the chauffeur, who stood ready to be given instructions. He walked in with my luggage: one leather suitcase and two large rattan bags full of fruits and wrappings.

He left the rattan bags in the living room then followed the lady to the room designated for me — just a large room with a small wooden bed and a dresser. My window looked out on the cement yard where rain water and city water were kept in huge cement containers. It was there that all washing was done.

My mother left that evening after taking a ride in the Citroën with my father. The next day, my father and I rode our bikes to my school where he registered me at a small open window in the building to the left of a huge iron gate. He left me there and went on to his office.

I was alone in front of the giant gate. Two panels of intricately decorated artwork spread out over the entranceway some sixteen feet in width. I looked around and saw only strangers gathered in groups, mostly dressed in purple tunics over white or black pantaloons. They all wore different shades and styles of purple ribbon in their hair, some simply forming a band, others tied in a bow in front or on the side. The long-haired students tied their bows in the back of their hair at shoulder length. A few wore white "ao ba-ba" — long-sleeve shirts — like me. They all looked serious and sophisticated.

I felt out of place, frightened. Everything seemed so awesome: the long rows of two-storied buildings, the neat bright green grass, the wide paved lanes, the guardian behind the iron gates, the girls with their fancy women's bikes and their bulky briefcases tied on their seat racks. There were hundreds of students on the court, yet neither the air nor the bodies seemed to stir. The silence made me feel timid; the bulky briefcases made me feel inferior. Every time I glanced from the luggage up to the faces of their owners, they seemed to know it in advance. Their eyes had already shifted elsewhere. In this school, girls came from different backgrounds, different social classes. Maybe they were all just as insecure as me but didn't want to show it. The older girls, who I guess had been there before, whispered among themselves. Then the bell rang long and menacingly. The giant gates swung open, and the girls rushed in and parked their bikes on the wooden racks at the end of the building near their classes.

The new girls, about one hundred in number, were directed to their rooms where all the teachers were French except for the math teacher, a fat Annamite with eyes bright like those of a tiger and a gait heavy as an elephant yet speedy as a rhinoceros. I did not know what to make of her at first. To see a fat Annamite was as rare as to see a French teacher. At the end of the day, I decided that the math teacher was a very likeable person. Her sincere smile and her eagerness to make the students learn distinguished her from the French teachers, who seemed very haughty with their upturned noses and swift Parisian accent, apparently intended to make things harder for us to understand. Their cold, proud look didn't seem to take us into their view.

That afternoon, following the landlord's direction, I took the trolley to Chinatown to buy ribbons and a few school kits as instructed by my teachers. I had fun taking my first rides on the two-carred trolleys and even more fun seeing so many little shops, selling almost the same things, all owned by Chinese who spoke broken Annamite.

On that first Saturday morning, we students had to parade in pairs in our purple dresses along the shady blocks that went past the Cercle Sportif, the Riding Club, and beautiful villas and lawns owned by the French people. The parade looked like two long lines of purple fabric pulled by stiff purple bows on top. It moved quietly, indifferently under the direction of our supervisors—one French and one Annamite. Suddenly I noticed the frontline bodies moving this way and that, their heads bowed or turned, and their giggling clearly perceptible all around.

"What? What?" I asked myself in surprise. I turned my head to look at the student beside me. I didn't have to wait long before the answer came in a high cat-like, soprano mixed with a male, duck-like alto. Both voices reverberated from the windows a few dozen yards behind the brick wall of the boy's high school — Petrus Ky High — where quite a few heads appeared.

"If you love me, please swear," sang in unison the cat-like soprano voices.

"Yes. Yes. I'll swear," answered in unison the male duck-like altos.

"Ah ha!" My mind jumped as if I had just caught a prized cricket. "Now I know where André got his song." The pleasurable discovery stayed with me during the rest of the school parade.

The parade of the purple dress college ended at noon. I rode my bicycle back to my rented room. My father was already waiting for me in his white shirt, shorts, and tennis shoes. He asked me to change into my uniform of old days, the blue shorts and white shirt. He gave me a colonial oval-shaped hat like his, a hard casquette that looked like an upside down boat. We were going to ride our bicycles all the way home, twenty miles from Saigon. The first time I got to bike with Father, and for such a long trip! Together we rode our bikes across town, passing the Thi Nghe Bridge where long logs belonging to the lumber yard on shore floated side by side and covered almost an entire portion of the river under the bridge. Small sampans weaved around the logs. A lullaby echoed from underneath the bamboo roof of a sampan where a mother was putting her child to bed. She was singing: "Mother don't beat me all the time. Let me go to the market to buy you a fish and boil it with mangoes for you to sample." Her long sad voice trailed mockingly among the huge logs of wood stripped bare of bark.

At Thu Duc, ten miles from Saigon, we stopped at the market for a snack. Each café owner had five or six tables and a few chairs in front of his small kitchen. There was a choice of a dozen different plates of sweet desserts, salty soups, grilled pork, chicken, and fish to delight me. I loved my father for this. I had always loved him, no doubt about that, but today's love came in a form and shape I thought I could touch, feel, and adore. Not only was I allowed to eat those goodies, but I was also encouraged to be picky about my choice.

My father advised me as to what was good, and wasn't, and why.

Markets had their own schedules. A market would be cleared of produce and meat vendors at around noon. One end of the market remained open all day for booths carrying fabrics, baby clothes, cooking earthenware, and serving utensils. Vendors of coffee and snacks would come and replace vendors of fresh food when these left for the other end of the market. Businessmen, travellers and drivers of buses, limousines, horse

33

drawn carriages and cyclos (rickshaws), all stopped at this central location between Saigon and Bien Hoa for lunch, dinner or breaks.

After having rested, my father bought two dozen of Thu Duc's famous ham sausages, the size of two fingers, made of pork and pork skin, wrapped in banana leaves. "A good processed ham tastes chewy, lightly sour," my father said. He hung them on his steering bar and proceeded onward. "Your mamma loves these." He made another stop at the rubber plantation and bought two pounds of Camembert cheese, made by the French couple who owned the plantation. My father and the Frenchman stood and chatted in French at the front steps of the villa. I walked to the rubber trees to check if there was any milky sap left in the bowls hung by wire around the tree trunks. Each tree had a portion of its bark cut diagonally at eye level so that its sap could drip into a bowl. The bowls were dried of sap.

My father called, and I returned to see him already on his bike. We rode on to Bien Hoa. Father stopped once again to buy the most famous grapefruits at one of the two bridges linking the island to the peninsulas. He told me that the real sweet kind would have wrinkled skin and not be much bigger than a large goyave. Their pulps would be long and more juicy than other kinds, and their inside pockets easier to break apart. In one day, I learned more about food from Father than I had ever learned from Mother through the years. Mother never talked to me this way. She only gave orders.

We arrived home at about five o'clock in the afternoon. My mother met us in the study room. She looked happy and pretty. Father went in and took a bath. For the first time, I was anxious for a nice cool shower. I felt like a grown-up. I came to the dining table wearing my long white trousers, white shirt, and a purple ribbon in my hair.

When everybody had sat at their places after prayer, my mother gave me a look of approval and spoke to the space in front of her: "College has changed your sister's hygiene standard." Then she smiled to the air. I was happy that she approved of my new outfit.

That evening like every other weekend evening, dinner took place when the sun had completely set. The electric light in the garden was lit and a long table placed on the cement court that connected the main house to the kitchen and maids' quarters. Ever since I could remember, I had had the notion that Saturdays and Sundays were my mother's celebration days. We would start with a long dinner on Saturday night. The tablecloth and napkins would be starchy white, the plates, forks, and knives sparkling. The French cuisine cook, who had nothing to do but get drunk during weekdays, would stay sober all day Saturday to cook his specialities and serve us with pride and arrogance in front of the other maids. Though a native, he had learned his cooking when he was a "garçon" on a French plantation.

We children, seven of us by 1945, would sit on both sides of the table, the three older ones to one side and the other four in their rattan high chairs with their own nannies standing behind them. My mother would ceremoniously start the dinner with the Lord's Prayer. A complete silence would reign over the table when she said her prayer; then my baby brothers and sisters would start babbling. The maids would say soothing words to try to get them to open their mouths. Then they would quickly shove in the food before the babies could turn their heads or close their mouths. My father would talk to the cook and the maids who took care of the younger ones inquiring about their work and the children. The cook made his own French desserts, a variety of delicious creamy cakes that changed depending on the meal he served at the time. Sometimes, my mother would add her own vanilla ice cream which took her and Middle one long day of constantly turning the ingredients round and round inside a container held in a wooden bucket of ice and salt.

On Sundays we went to nine o'clock mass. My mother had bought two seats in the middle aisle of the second row (instead of the first row to show her modesty). The seats and kneelers were covered with red velvet cushions. Whenever she came home from her boarding school, my sister and I would sit with our female peers in the left row. The poor people also filed up according to gender behind the children on the side rows.

Normally, if Father was not away, after mass we would go home, have a copious Annamite lunch, and then have a siesta. The maids also took siestas until the sun cooled down. After siesta, my parents and the three eldest of us children would take a ride through the plantation road with the driver and our father in the front seat. I felt very happy whenever I got to ride with my parents.

Today on our outing we passed the asylum for insane people — a city in itself, lined with many, many flat buildings and separated from the world by huge iron gates. The tallest building, where seriously insane people were kept, had small windows enforced with iron bars — windows so small they looked like pigeonholes in the large building. I saw a madman, half naked, wrap himself around the iron bars and wave to us like a monkey.

After the asylum we passed countless rows of rubber trees, then a long stretch of brick wall lined with large white vases three feet tall (these vases were made in our special École des Beaux Arts). At every third vase stood a cactus plant with its thick leaves pointing to the sky. At the same height as the vases, there bloomed the yellow, pink, and white flowers of the cacti. The wall served as the front boundary of the French plantation owner's villa, which could not be seen from the road because it was hidden behind trees and climbing flowers.

At the end of the brick wall, the rubber plantation reappeared. Here, people could be seen working silently, each man or woman bent over a tree collecting rubber sap. Their faces were dark. Their eyes when they looked at you showed only the whites which were all yellow; many had huge sties.

"Daddy, who are they?" I asked my father almost in a whisper. The women and men looked to me like frightening ghosts who could cast bad spells if they became angry.

"They? Oh," he said after a moment, "they are northerners like us. Except they were bought by French plantation owners to work on their plantations. You see, in North Vietnam we often have floods from the Red River coming from China. The floods killed thousands of people at one time and left many families with no food. These northerners volunteered to sell themselves to save their families from starvation. They left the money paid behind, so that their parents could feed themselves and care for their children."

"If they gave all their money to their parents, how do they live here?" I asked timidly.

"Look behind the hibiscus bushes yonder. See the long straw roof? That's where they live — community life — sort of. Their food and clothing are given by their owners. They do the cooking inside their huts or outside behind the bushes."

"They look so dirty. Are the skirts also given to them by French women and dyed black to keep them from looking soiled?" Secretly I thought they looked shameful, worse than ugly animals. Their expressionless eyes frightened me.

"No, no," my father laughed. "Tell her, Mother, how these women would look at their best."

Shiny black silk skirts and reddish brown dresses slit down the middle in front and tied in loose knots below the waistline; wide triangular kerchiefs covering their chests; two or three silk tube-like belts of pink, pinkish purple, sky blue, and water blue, tied around their waists, draped along their ankle-length skirts and knotted in parts to keep their money and precious belongings.

"Oh, how beautiful!" I exclaimed while imagining the women in sight with such colors and richness to their outfits.

36

My father continued, "And a black scarf over their hair wrapped in a black velvet tube showing a few inches of shiny hair at the end. That, against their fair skin, rosy cheeks, shiny dyed black teeth, and black eyes — only in your mother's case they were brown." He recounted all this with delight, then suddenly, "Ah, she was beautiful. Sweet, modest, mysterious, in that scarf tied in the form of a crow's beak."

A soft "ahhm" escaped from my left. I turned and saw my mother's blushing cheeks, her lips slightly parted in a shy smile, her eyes closed and her head slightly tilted backward.

I looked the other way and smiled. My father also turned back toward the "ahhm," then returned his gaze to the front of the car. After a pause he added, "It's true Mai. They looked beautiful in their clean clothes and with their healthy complexions."

Sitting behind my father in the back seat, I imagined he wore a big smile and his eyes were sparkling.

We rode a long time and came to a clear field of grass and wild bushes. Now and then a rabbit jumped out of the grass to cross the street.

The sun set, and the sky was turning pinkish grey. Father was probably in a good mood after his reminiscence of his courting. He told the chauffeur to stop at a spot where no trees or houses were seen for miles. Then he asked my mother to step out of the car with him. Taking his double barreled shotgun from the Citroën trunk, he showed her how to hold it up to her shoulder and look through the sight. It was delightful to see them this way. My mother was very privileged to be taught how to shoot. I had never seen any Annamite with a gun. I guess the French gave my father a car and a gun because he had to travel so far into dark jungles inhabited by tigers, wild boars, and bears in order to explore the possibility of building his highway — Road Number One — the only road to connect North and South Annam with Cambodia and Laos. It was to link remote plantations of rubber, tea, and coffee with sea and mountain resorts throughout Indochina.

He told mother to stand with her legs apart, left leg forward facing, right leg perpendicular, etc. I listened attentively. When he was satisfied with her position, he told her to cock the hammer with the barrels empty of bullets. My mother learned fast. When she got used to it, he loaded the gun and aimed towards a rabbit about to cross the street. He said, "I'm not going to kill him. I just want to show you how the gun sounds." One blasting shot. The rabbit jumped up and disappeared into the grass across the street.

"Very loud," my mother said calmly.

"I'll let you do it this time," Father said.

37

"Thank you. No. I don't think I want to." Mother smiled shyly but determinedly.

They went back to the car. My brother asked excitedly, "Why didn't you shoot it, Daddy?"

"Well," my father said, "we have plenty of food at home, don't we? We don't kill unless we need to, do we?"

"Besides," I excitedly interjected, "rabbits are like people. They suffer too. The cook said that when you clean a rabbit and pull his skin off, he puts his forepaws together to beg you to stop hurting him. Isn't it so, Daddy?"

Father smiled, "Y — es. Well, it looks like it, because of its reflexes. I don't think it feels anything after it's dead. But we feel for it."

"Yes," I thought, and I sadly remembered our pet tiger cub.

The tiger cub was whining two rooms away. I got out of bed and went to him. I sat on the floor, holding him on my lap. He stopped crying. I sat there a long time with him until both of us fell asleep. When I awoke in the night, I decided Cubby needed to sleep in a cave, where he would normally sleep with his mother. Above my head there was a hole in the wall, made to hold a telephone, but my family didn't have one. I put Cubby up in the hole pretending it was his cave and left the chain attached to the hook where my mother had tied him. I petted Cubby back to sleep, then went back to bed myself.

The next morning I ran to Cubby and found him hanging from the chain, feet off the floor and head limp to one side.

"Oh, God, I killed my Cubby. I killed him. I strangled him," I whimpered. I hugged him, tried to untie him, to open his eyes. But Cubby made no sound. His warm limp body flopped helplessly onto my lap.

"Cubby, I love you. You know I love you." I clenched my teeth, closed my eyes. "I promise never to be so thoughtless, so stupid again. Cubby, I promise."

His death and my guilt overwhelmed me.

The morning after I had to get up early to take the train with my father back to school in Saigon. I only remember my little brother, Spring Field, the brave little "Napoleon" who wouldn't cry when he got beaten screaming and crying loudly when he saw dead Cubby. I felt sorry for him and very guilty. I was surprised, though. He had never played with Cubby.

Then I remembered something like that happening before. It was one day in summer. We were walking together to the backyard to check out where Mother was before setting out on our game in the street. We saw her sitting on a wooden stool, busying herself with scratching the tummy of her pink pig. She looked up and saw us. She turned to the bucket at her side and scooped out an aluminum bowl of water and poured it on the pig's tummy.

She said, "The pig is getting too big. I'm going to have to sell it. The Chinese man is coming this afternoon to pick it up."

I heard a loud shriek. "No. No. You won't sell him," my brother yelled and tore away from where we stood. He ran to the pig, grasped its hind legs, pulled them back and forth. "You won't sell him. Promise you won't sell him," he screamed, his big eyes and face all red with tears.

My mother and I looked at him in surprise. I had never seen my brother play with the pig or the bear cub that my mother tied to the clothesline pole or our dog that everybody said was cute and smart because the dog came from Phu Quoc, the island famous for fish sauce and smart dogs.

Mother ignored his tears. She told him firmly that he should play with the pig while it was still there and that she would not be keeping it any longer. "We must do what we must do," she concluded, her usual quotation.

Once he calmed down and knew that she was determined, he insisted no more and walked away alone to the side of the house where the passage was covered with high bushes and a thick hibiscus fence. I thought he wanted to cry quietly by himself.

Mother's other pet, a baby bear, she kept tied to the clothesline post and nursed with a milk bottle. My little sisters had their own nurses, so I hardly ever saw her nurse them. One day, while she was feeding the little bear a French policeman came into our backyard. My father was away on an inspection trip.

The French policeman very politely explained to my mother that he and his "friend" (a young Annamite girl, daughter of a prominent doctor in town, generally known as a bad girl because she was seen with a Frenchman) had watched mother's little bear from over the fence for some time. They loved it so much that they wanted to know if mother would be kind enough to let them buy it from her. He would be willing to pay a high price for it. She would do him such a favor!

Mother did not understand French but she saw the way he caressed the bear and knew what he wanted. She smiled and kept shaking her head while he kept cuddling the bear and trying to explain to Mother how fond he was of the little cub.

He finally had to leave without the bear.

39

The little bear was given by a Moi (Mountaineer) who visited my father often at his post in the forest. My father called him Rhade, a name given by the French to the mountaineers in that region.

The Moi were a race apart. They lived in the mountains, grew their own patches of rice and corn, and burnt them after a few harvests to keep the soil fertilized. They wove beautiful baskets and small pieces of pretty colored cloth to cover their loins. Sometimes, a few would come to the nearest market to exchange their products for salt and medicines. They ate wild deer and boar which they killed with their own bows and arrows.

Rhade had brought the bear cub when he came home with father one weekend in the Citroën. He was tall for an Annamite. He had black curly hair, large black eyes, a big nose, a masculine face, nice long legs, a muscular body, and shiny brown skin. Father said Rhade loved to bathe in the spring and use lots of soap, his new discovery during one of his visits to my father at his post.

That weekend, my father asked Rhade to show us how he used his bow and arrow. The bow was made of bamboo about two feet long, its end pulled by a string taken from animal skin, cured, and twisted together. The arrows were a foot long and were kept in a bamboo holder about one foot high, which he tied around his waist. Rhade went with us to the yard and pointed at a branch of a star tree about twenty yards away. We all looked up, doubtful that such a small bow could do the work. Rhade set out to show us. He took his bow and arrow out and aimed directly toward the sky above him, his head tilted to one side. With one quick jerk of his right arm the bow and arrow released a snapping sound of something sharp whistling through the silent air. The small branch, some twenty feet above the ground and twenty yards away, fell from the star tree, taking with it a dozen leaves.

"Incredible!" Middle yelled. "I didn't see him aim at the branch. He pointed his arrow to the sky. Didn't you see?"

All of us children began talking at the same time. The maids standing in a group some yards away joined in the admiration.

Rhade smiled a big smile, revealing his strong white teeth. He looked tall and brave and spoke very little and only in French, for his tribe had more contact with the French than with Annamites.

That night I went to sleep on my sister's bed. My sister had not come home from St. Theresa High School in Saigon this weekend.

The mosquito net was already spread out. It hung loosely from a square piece of wood about two feet wide, nailed to the twelve-foot-tall railing. Its full drape-like shape curved like a waterfall from a cliff to settle under the French mattress. I pulled out a portion of the net and chose one of the *Livres Roses* stacked on the shelf at the head of the bed. Late in the night I heard my mother ask from her room behind the door, "Mai, are you sleeping?"

"Yes Mother," I said, quickly switching off the light and about to drop my book under my pillow. Suddenly I remembered Bright Moon was not home. I flung the book across the bed, moved to the middle and spread my arms wide open. Tonight I didn't have to be sure that my legs were crossed when I lay on my back or that I pulled one leg up when I lay on my side. My sister did observe these positions, which Mother taught as part of being a good, well-mannered lady. When Bright Moon was around I wanted to show her that I too knew what were good manners. For now though, I felt free as a princess in her big bed surrounded by a cloudy cascade.

In this state of mind, I fell asleep and continued my dream of the "Flying Rug" from the *Livres Roses*, thinking of Rhade. Rhade helped me to visualize a prince in person, and a blurry Bright Moon with a veil played the part of the princess, when she was not acting like a sissy, meek and obedient even in her own bed.

5

IT WAS MY third month in the "purple school." I was in my French composition class when the surveillante came in and whispered something to my French teacher, who nodded. Then the surveillante walked stealthily toward me and whispered for me to gather up my belongings and follow her. I shovelled my things into my briefcase, and as I did so I pictured myself being thrashed and thrown out of school. "Oh God!" My head screamed. "I shamed my mother. I must have done something wrong. What was it? Please would someone tell me?"

Walking in front of me, the surveillante did her best not to attract attention. Her heels touched the floor without noise. Yet I saw heads turn from silent classes and French teachers throw us disapproving glances.

We were now crossing the large lawn heading towards a separate building, and I recognized my father standing with his bicycle; his sturdy body dark against his glaring white shorts and pullover. He wore these to work, play tennis, and take his nap. My father was my symbol of freedom. "He will free me," I thought as Father pushed his cycle towards us. The stiffness of the surveillante seemed to mellow. She spoke sweetly with her casual southern accent: "Mr. Engineer. Here is your daughter." Then she turned to me with a big smile and told me to fetch my bicycle and go home with my father.

"That's it? All that trouble for nothing?" I wondered suspiciously. "Wait a minute. Adults often exchanged big smiles to hide what bothered them inside."

Sure enough as we left the iron gate, my father said, "War has broken out. I am taking you back to Bien Hoa." I turned to him, surprised. He looked serious, and his eyes were concentrated on the distance. We rode

42

on in silence, but I knew Father would explain when he thought the time was right.

I wished adults didn't think it impolite to ask questions. Sometime in the past I had heard of World War II, but its meaning and effect on me were as remote and unclear as when I recited: "Our country, France and our ancestors, the Gaules" in my geography and history classes.

So war had now arrived here. I wondered what war was like. As we rode along, the Saigon streets spread wide and grand in front of us. Tall shadowy tamarinds and flowery flame trees lined the walkways. Behind the curbs and whitewashed walls were pretty French villas. "Such a quiet, solemn atmosphere," I thought, when suddenly the twelve o'clock siren startled me with its alarming shriek. The few cars that were present and the bicycles and pedestrians all came to a halt. Above us something sounding like thunder came tearing through the sky. People scurried to hide against the edges of curbs and walls. I followed my father. We dropped our bicycles and flattened ourselves against the street curbs. Looking upward, I saw nine planes pass in V formation, drawing white lines of smoke across the blue sky. Then the planes were gone.

I looked around and saw people pressing themselves in the niches of walls and curbs, as though they wished to become invisible. I thought we children did a better job in our hide-and-seek games. Some people started getting up from their hiding places. It was quite a scene to see the young, the old, the rich, the poor, even a French lady, all hastening to lie flat on the ground.

Presently, the siren blew again, and we hid ourselves again. Someone in the crowd was shouting: "These are Allied planes. They are looking for the Japanese."

I wondered what the Allied planes would do if they found the Japanese. And whose side they were with. Were we on their side? Some weeks ago, I had seen a truckload of Frenchmen, guarded by an armed Japanese. The natives who stood watching threw them packs of Bastos cigarettes, behind the Japanese guard. The French caught them and waved back with a smile. In school, two years ago, we used to sing to Maréchal Pétain as our hero. It seemed that then he told us to be on the side of Hitler and the Japanese. How come now the Japanese imprisoned the French? It was a big mystery to me.

Anyway, here we were, in the middle of war, whatever that meant. Suddenly I was stopped in my thoughts by swinging baskets that were colliding with the front wheel of my bicycle. We were crossing the Gia Dinh Bridge two miles away from Saigon. Vendors of hot snacks were chanting the names of their goodies, their chanting blending with the lullaby from

43

a sampan below. I wondered if they, too, had seen war. They appeared to be very cool and indifferent in the aftermath. Adults had a way of covering up their feelings. Just half an hour before I had seen them running like mice to take cover.

In Bien Hoa that night at dinner, I saw Bright Moon. So she had also been sent home from school. Mother probably went to pick her up. I guess Mother knew everything, though I did not see any change in our daily habits.

After siesta the next day, I went to my usual place at the gate to join the maids. In the last three months I had been so busy with homework that I had not joined them. I was surprised to see them ignore me completely now. I wanted to ask if they knew about the war, but they tried to avoid my eyes each time I looked at them. They went on joking and sharing among themselves the dried squid they bought for half a sou from the "gay" vendor. I wondered if they considered me a city girl now because I had lived in Saigon for a bit. Perhaps they didn't like my white pants and long sleeves which made me look more upper class than the shorts and short sleeve shirts I used to wear. My sandals also made me stand out among the barefoot maids. They insisted on making me a stranger to them. Nevertheless, the next day after siesta, I again went to the maids' meeting at the gate. They still ignored me.

I stood alone in my white long pants and blouse—a sophisticated city girl with whom nobody wanted to be friends. I had just gone to school away from home for a short time, yet the past seemed to have slipped away forever into obscurity. Even the neighborhood kids did not come by any more—the boys with whom I had played hide-and-seek at night for many years: the one who thought he was my boyfriend and had struck me once on my face because he thought it was his privilege not to be discovered by me in one of our hide-and-seek games; the one who chose to visit my brother and me at the exact time when we were being punished and had to kneel down in the middle room where traffic was the heaviest; those with whom I met for the cricket fights—all had vanished like a dream. The classmates with whom I had gone through the six years of elementary school were also gone—too old to play any more. It was time for them to be little mothers and attend to their families' business.

Now and then I saw Bright Moon at her usual place, perched on the wide windowsill abandoning herself to the lyrics of French music playing on the gramophone, the "Dog and His Master," with the picture of a cute dog and the arm the shape of a small saxophone.

And where did my little brother disappear to? He didn't come to chitchat anymore. The only time I saw him was one night when I was sitting on the balcony and heard a scream in front of the gate. I looked out and saw Spring Field holding a long bamboo pole tied to a big paper star lit by a candle inside. He was halfway up the locked gate, kicking and waving the half-torn star. At the top of the gate he jumped still screaming into our yard, and I ran out to catch him. On seeing me, he pretended, of course, to be cool and shot up from his fall as if nothing had happened.

"What's the matter?" I asked.

"Ghost . . . a ghost was chasing me," he said, and a chill ran down my back.

"Where did you go?"

"To the Japanese class."

"Japanese class?"

"Yes. Japanese class to learn Japanese. Our interpreter said the Japanese are here to help us defeat the French. Then we will all become one big, strong country, the 'Sun' country like their flags, under the same emperor. No longer will we be slaves of the whites. Hey, I thought you were so smart. Don't you know all the men have to go to the Japanese night classes?" Then he walked off to the house. Brother was only eleven, and he obviously wanted to act like a man. He was not scared of anything except of ghosts, which frightened even adults, who talked of them with respect.

Later, I was pondering my little brother's incident when from the river I saw him approaching accompanied by a young man twice his size. My brother was round, not fat, but round and brown-black in his blue shorts. Water was dripping from his swim trunks. His bright eyes seemed to be blinking at me with excitement. The man wore white shorts and a T-shirt. They both smiled at me. The young man had very large black eyes, sad looking but warm. I smiled back at them, happy that I apparently was accepted again. During the entire afternoon, the young man's face kept reappearing in my mind. Every time his image crept in, I felt warm all over and strangely happy. That night and many nights afterwards, I heard flute sounds floating from the apartment Spring Field's friend had entered. It sounded so melancholy that I felt sad and yearnful.

In the days to come, I would see him come from time to time to our house, dressed in starchy white pants, a shirt, and canvas shoes. The young man, Khoi (Handsome), would walk his brand new blue racing bike, shiny with chrome, with my little brother always tagging alongside. Then one day Khoi's eyes met mine. I saw sparks of affection for me in the deep wells of his black pupils. I dwelled on that look for days.

Khoi came to ask my mother's permission to take Spring Field on little outings: to the rocky mountains five miles away from home where they made marble tables, flower pots, and memorials for graves; to the spring ten miles away and across two bridges; to a village known for this or that in some remote place I had never visited.

I waited for my brother to tell me about his outings. Sometimes I wondered, sulking, "What's wrong with me? Have I changed so much now that I'm thirteen?" I would talk to my brother silently, "You've grown to be eleven, too! Why don't you come and share things with me anymore? Why doesn't anybody come and share things with me anymore?" This exclusion, I thought, must be the cost of growing up.

Weeks passed. Late one morning, Mother left for Saigon. I was still in bed reading one of my *Livres Roses* stories when I vaguely heard my sister reciting something from her window bench two rooms away. Strange, I thought. Normally, she was softspoken and spoke only when addressed. This was the way we were taught to behave. The recitation became louder and louder. She apparently meant for me to hear. I put down the book and listened:

> Little one, give me a little love.
> So that my heart'd not feel so lonely.
> Knowing the two soft breezes are intertwining.
> And I so alone, so alone it leaves me chilled.

A love poem! Immediately I pictured the crumpled papers wrapped around rocks that Chi Nam, the assistant cook, now and then picked up from the front yard and shared with the other maids. They would giggle and pass the paper around, then rewrap it for Chi Nam to bring to Mother. Subsequently, Bright Moon would be called to Mother's bedroom and given a moral lecture. On leaving the bedroom she would be weeping.

Bright Moon continued to read very loudly for me to hear. Finally I threw down my book, ran to my sister's room, and tried to snatch the piece of paper that she was holding. But she quickly squashed it into her pocket.

"Who wrote it?"

"Your friend next door. Who else?"

"Give it to me then," I said.

"No. I'll give it to Mother when she comes home."

The earth seemed to split open under my feet. I stared at her, stupefied. Then anger seized me. I cried, "Stupid you. You think you are one of the maids?"

She lifted up her face proudly, frowned, then said, "I'll give it back to Tam."

Oh, but this was worse than death! My adopted sister always reported on me.

I tried to go back to my book, but what I read made no sense. That night when my mother came home, we ate dinner as usual. After dinner, feeling exhausted, I went immediately to sleep in Spring Field's bed. I felt a weariness, as though my mind was too heavy for my head to carry. I knew that the next morning Tam would find the right time to talk to Mother.

I was ready to be summoned. Mother was not at breakfast. Afterwards I went to the balcony, yearning for some familiar sights. I hitched myself up the veranda to look over the fence at the big tree by the river — something I had not done since my return from college. The sight of the big tree stirred me. I sank into a dreamy state of mind.

"Sister Ba. So there you are. We've been looking all over for you!" Tam snorted. Slowly I opened my eyes and gazed at Tam as if she were a character from some book written long ago.

"I'm here," I said calmly a moment later. But actually I was burning with anger.

"Mother wants you."

I slipped down from the veranda and walked through the doorway, oblivious of Tam standing in the middle of it.

"Yes, Mother. You called me?" I crossed my arms in front of my chest to show respect. My mother sat in her blue rattan chair placed between her huge desk and the wide door to the cement yard and the kitchen.

"Sit down." My mother's eyes indicated the end of the wooden sofa. I carefully sat on the edge, still keeping my arms crossed on my chest. When in front of adults, we — the children and the maids — were to sit only when told, and only on the edges of chairs — a mark of respect to higher-ups. Children and maids were to understand that they were not equal to their elders, the wise, educated parents and masters.

I sat there, waiting, unaware that I was about to witness a trial by my mother.

Then I saw Chi Sau walk up the concrete steps to my mother and say, "Madame, the lady is here."

My mother looked up from her magazine and said, "Ask her to come in."

A small lady whom I had never seen before walked up the steps and stood on one side of the door, the side nearer to me. She wore the black trousers and black shirt of people of the labor class.

47

"Greetings to Madame," she said in a central Annam accent. Her skin was very fair. "You sent for me?" Her soft voice vibrated a little.

"Yes. Sit down, please," my mother said.

There was no chair anywhere around. The wooden sofa was large but not near her. Its corner was too close to my mother and too far from the lady. The further corner would be blocked by the sight of my body. I looked at my mother, who looked at the ground where the lady stood.

"Excuse me." The lady dropped to the floor, her legs posed on the lower concrete step.

"I understand the boy who used to come here and play with my son is your younger brother," my mother said.

"Yes, Madam." The woman seemed unsure of how to respond.

"From your accent, you both come from Central Annam?"

"Yes, Madam."

"Have you been here a long time?"

"I came here with my husband five years ago. We have a business here and have been living in the apartment since."

And your little brother? Has he been here long?"

"No, Madam. He has just graduated from high school in Hue this year. So my parents sent him here to spend the summer with us. He postponed his return because the situation is so unsettled and the trip home at this time may not be safe for him."

"You know what has happened?" My mother sternly looked down at her. From my place, I also looked down at the lady. She had very round black eyes, not large as her brother's but round and small like pigeon's eyes. It was hard to see the expression in them. After a pause, my mother continued, "I want him to get out of here, get out of this town. If he does not, I shall report to the police. The inspector lives next door."

Suddenly tears poured from the lady's eyes. She lifted the shawl which she used to cover her hair and with it wiped her tears. There was silence in the room. I did not dare to look at either my mother or the lady. A sense of injustice invaded my heart. Out of the corner of my eye, I saw the lady's skinny shoulders draw together, her tiny white hand firmly wipe and rewipe her reddened cheeks. She must have felt extremely humiliated and indignant to wipe her cheeks so intensely. Then the lady said in a surprisingly dry and clear voice, "I'll try. I don't know how but I'll try. May I be excused?" The lady stood up and walked backward down the two steps that led to the concrete court. She walked backward to show reverence, but her hands clutched tightly her shawl as if in repressed anger. Normally one would salute with one's hands on one's chest to show respect, or hold them in front at the waistline to return a salute to an equal. I shared with her her anger. I thought it was very unjust of Mother.

I glanced at Mother who appeared not to notice. My mother turned to me, and I was surprised to see that there was a touch of sympathy in her eyes. Suddenly, I had the impression that she was only carrying out the duty of a high-class mother, as was taught to her. Years of training under Mother made me realize that she did a lot of things because of the pressure of her class. But, still, it wasn't fair. "You may go now, but stay in the house."

During the next two days, I went from my bed to the balcony, keeping clear of the rest of the household. My mind felt like the inner tube of a bicycle, ready to explode in the hot air. People were cruel and mean, I thought. It was the first time the meaning of "cruel" had full impact on me. I knew that Mother was able to put up such a court scene because the lady was a poor merchant who was from the central part of Annam. The merchant class meant the bottom class, especially to the mandarins of the imperial city of Hue. Hue dwellers were much more class conscious than even northerners. Mother's cook, who was brought from the north, was extremely polite and obedient. She called us children "mistress" or "master." The southern maids called us by our names, gave us nicknames, and sometimes even slapped us in front of Mother when we poked into their things.

It normally took a few hours of waiting before Mother gave a thrashing for a small mischief. The love letter was an enormous crime. It would require more time before Mother took action.

One day, from the balcony, I saw the chauffeur busy cleaning the Citroën, which was now parked near the front gate. A suitcase was brought out. My sister got in the car, and then Mother. I heard Mother tell Chi Sau to lock the gate immediately after the car exited. I knew the precaution was for me.

My father came home that night with Mother and without my sister.

In the late afternoon of the following day, Tam called me into my mother's bedroom and asked me to lie down on the wooden sofa where we children waited for our thrashings. I saw the hibiscus branch already lain there, stipped clean of its green bark. The rod was as large as my finger. I knew Tam was observing me, so I pushed the hibiscus aside to show my defiance and lay down on the cool wood.

Tam went out and shut the door. "Well," I said to myself then caught myself at this unprecedented feeling of revolt. I had thought thrashings were a punishment Mother carried out as a duty to teach us to be good people. It was a normal thing to do, and I almost always knew when a beating was to come. It was also normal for me to try to avoid being caught at a wrong time. All things considered, one was lucky if no spanking was received in a week's time. Today, however, I was obsesssed by a feeling of oppression.

Resentment loomed in my thoughts. I kept wondering what I had done that was wrong. Then it came to mind that maybe the man and I had loved each other and that maybe the wrong thing we did was to *love*. My conclusion brought on another puzzle. All through the stories in the *Livres Roses* Mother bought for us to read, love was the main subject, love and the suffering following it. Even princes and princesses loved and got punished. True, they always reunited and lived happily at the end, but the end was described only in a paragraph or a short half page! Maybe Mother was right; maybe I was in love and had to be punished and go through pain. Still, I resented the fact that I should be humiliated by the same punishment she had given me as a child.

The door opened. Father came in instead of Mother. Another surprise! Father had never beaten me. Once, on his way home in the Citroën, he had caught me riding on the steering bar of a man's bike with three girlfriends, one on the seat, another on the cross bar, and another behind, on the luggage rack. We were struggling to push ourselves through the pedestrians on the narrow walkway of the Binh Loi Bridge. He had simply told us to get off the bike and off the bridge. I had thought then that Father had caught us doing something very seriously wrong and was surprised that he did not tell Mother about the incident.

Father was now sitting in Mother's blue rattan chair. He picked up the rod, not looking at me, and just said quietly, "Your mother asked me to give you five spankings." He touched the different parts of the rod and applied it five times on my buttocks — not hard, not soft. I had the feeling he was doing his duty as asked. When done, he put the rod back along the sofa and hurried out. At the door, he turned slightly and said: "I am sorry."

Through my welling tears, I saw his sturdy brown legs and tennis shoes, his white shorts and pullover — a seasoned engineer who commanded hundreds of workers, rode wild horses on his inspections, travelled through dangerous forests infested with wild boars and tigers, struck a Frenchman who had slapped a defenseless worker. My father, my hero, at this time when I was distressed and confused had meekly submitted to Mother's wishes. The door closed behind him, and I murmured: "I love you, Father. I, too, am sorry."

I waited awhile. Nobody came in to tell me what to do. I got off the bed and went to my sister's bed. There I remained until dinnertime. My heart was laden with shame and deception. I felt ashamed that Mother had dragged my father into such a private thing, my dignity—the dignity of a girl.

The next day a horse carriage pulled into the backyard. My mother called me into the dining room. A set of white pants and shirt lay on a chair. "Go wash your face and put these on and get ready to go."

I obeyed. When I was ready and presented myself at Mother's side, she told me to go to the horse carriage. "He knows where to go," she said, meaning the driver.

I went out; the old nurse went with me. Mother looked out from inside the house. So this is the horse carriage they ship me in. Hm, I thought, indignant, although normally I would have enjoyed a ride in the horse carriage. I climbed in the back.

My bag of clothes and one pillow were tucked against the wall of the front seat. As soon as I got in, the old nurse pulled down the shades. Darkness instantly enveloped the cabin. Inside the narrow rectangular box, my eyes fixed through the darkness. It was like a prison. I'm in prison, I thought. I don't even get to sit in a better carriage with a bench in front to see things. Shame. Shame. Shame.

I felt the carriage leave the driveway onto the road. I sat with my knees up, my chin resting on them, rocking in cadence to the dark trunk that carried me. The horse carriage had long crossed the two bridges. My soul was still totally crushed under the weight of injustice, shame, and despair. I wanted *out*. But how? Even Father was spellbound by Mother's judgment.

In the middle of my contemplation, something sounding like planes exploded in the air. My mind leapt with excitement: "Could it be war?" The driver jerked the horse to a stop. I pounded on the back of the front seat, "Why do you stop? Have we arrived?"

"No, Miss. But I think war is here. People who came from Saigon said you have to hide when you hear the planes."

The Saigon scene appeared in my mind. Adults, children, rich, poor, aristocrats, and peasants, all equal, all running together for their lives. I heard the driver ask, "Shall I move on?"

"Yes. Move on," I commanded. "But first, pull up these curtains."

In Thu Duc, ten miles from Bien Hoa, the carriage stopped in a big courtyard surrounded with tall brick walls. A French nun came out to greet me. Her French was fast and fluent, and for some reason I hated hearing it. I hated the place.

The vast garden was shaded by large trees. A wide cool veranda led us to the meeting room. A dozen French nuns and a dozen girls, all older than I were sitting around. I was very surprised to see Bright Moon, happy as a sparrow, among them. So this was where Mother had sent my sister. A nun asked her in French to introduce me to the group. They all spoke French in that place. The girls sounded happy. The nuns sounded happy. Their voices were clear, high, and pure like those of birds in the early morning.

It was three o'clock in the afternoon. Two nuns went with the group to another section of the premises behind a tall brick wall. They went through a large iron gateway and entered a large building with a huge veranda and a huge room without doors opening onto the veranda. I was told that that was the huge kitchen where the girls learned French cooking. After cooking they went back to the meeting room to recite prayers and hear a nun read the book of St. Theresa. Her voice was so beautiful, her smile sweet, her eyes clear, it made me think I was sitting among angels who were listening to a song they were to learn.

That evening, after dinner, we went and sat on the grass. The students each had a French name. They asked what French name I wanted to be called. I didn't know. They brainstormed, giggling, agreeing, disagreeing until they came up with Rosaline. A nun said she liked it, and the rest approved excitedly. So my name was Rosaline. I was thirteen, and they were between seventeen and twenty. I was their little sister and had to obey them all. At cooking time, Rosaline cleaned the potatoes and vegetables while the others did the artistic slicing, marinating and testing. At sewing time, Rosaline threaded the needles with different colored threads for them to embroider, cleaned up the mess, and folded the clothes, all the while singing and praying along with the happy nuns. Day after day, the nuns and students went back and forth from the kitchen to the sewing room, then to the grassy garden, singing and praying, doing the same thing over and over. They never seemed to tire of the place and always looked cheerful and happy like the little lambs from the Indian's herd near my elementary school.

Weeks passed. One day the old nurse came with the horse carriage to take my sister and me home. The nurse said the war was getting worse and our mother wanted both of us home. I refused to go. I had learned that the building behind the wall was an orphanage. I told the nuns I wanted to go there, to live with the orphans. They smiled and said nothing. The next day, my aunt who visited us from North Annam came with my father's Citroën. She cried and insisted that they were all worried about me and that I should go home before the war broke out so we wouldn't get separated. She would not go home unless I left with her.

We all went home. Before the front gate of my house, I looked for my tree on the other side of the street and saw the vacant lot now fenced up with barbed wire and sandbags. Japanese men were all over the field. They were very short, round, and naked, except for a loincloth. I turned away. That was the first time I had seen a nearly naked man.

6

IN OUR BACKYARD along the fence, sandbags were piled up forming the walls of a six-by-nine-foot shelter covered with aluminum sheeting. A jar of rain water one foot high was placed inside with some dried food.

The morning breeze came to my window fresh and cool. Life at home was relaxed and peaceful as opposed to the scheduled pace of life in Thu Duc at the nun's school, where everyone strove to be good and useful every minute of the day until their bodies came to rest in bed late into the night. There, even before I uttered a word, I had had to remind myself of the tense in which it was constructed in French. Yesterday, today, tomorrow, the past minute, the minute before that, the plural, singular, nouns, pronouns—they all crowded my mind, ready to jump at me—present, past, future imperfect, conditional, subjunctive, etc. Life was much simpler back at home.

The breeze felt good. I thought to myself in Annamite, "A little while I eat a bowl of hot cereal, then go see how my tree do." There was no need to conjugate or worry about the tenses in Annamite verbs. I was so happy. "What a bother," I thought, "having to remember all that grammar."

I laughed aloud to myself, "I love my language. It's so simple."

Next to me my sister stirred. I looked at her out of the corner of my eye and saw her also smiling while stretching, her long limbs extended, her arms above her head, and her fair skin shining in the morning sun against her long, brilliant black hair.

She looked pretty and fragile. Suddenly I liked her. I forgave her for what she had done to me with the letter. After all, without her I wouldn't have known what a nun's life was all about.

At the breakfast table my mother looked preoccupied. The usual

54

table formality was followed, but there was a rushed feeling. As soon as we finished breakfast, the cook's assistant hurriedly cleared the table. Everybody went to their little corners: I to my *Livres Roses* and my sister to her usual window bench, only she wasn't listening to her music this time. Instead, she gazed out of the window toward the sky.

Somewhere from deep in my daydream came the piercing sound of the siren. The siren had always blown at precisely twelve noon. I was surprised to hear it at this time. "Nine, ten? We just had breakfast!" I looked up from my book across the rooms. My sister was still there on the window sill, though one of her legs dangled on the floor. I put down my book and went to the middle room, the activities spot. The nurses were there; each carried a bag, my brothers and sisters at their sides. My mother saw me and simply said, "We are going to the shelter."

We followed Mother. My sister appeared in the shelter a little while later.

In the distance, beyond the river, airplanes filled the sky. We stooped to get into the shelter and arranged ourselves on the two benches placed along the walls. I was at the end of the bench by the shelter's opening. My curiosity commanded me to stick my head out to see a formation of planes the shape of a bird's wings. There were no Japanese "sun" flags on the planes; these must be the Allies. They quickly passed and then passed again closer to the ground. Then they were gone. "Mai," I vaguely heard my mother order from the opposite bench.

I pulled myself back inside. We sat and waited. The smaller children started making noise and crying—it was boring, hot, and stuffy. Luckily, the sirens shrilled off. We got out of the shelter and resumed our activities. The cook prepared dinner with her helper, and the old nurse even joined in to help accelerate the process. Some time later I was called out to lunch, but at that point, the alarm sounded again. The cook and her assistant rushed to take the tray of food and bowls, and the nurses grabbed their bottles of milk for the children who still drank from them at the ages of four or five—together they ran toward the shelter. We continued our meal in the shelter, each with a bowl piled with food. My mother was served first, then my sister, myself, and my brother. Then came the turn of the nurses. The cook's team preferred to dish out their food and go to the kitchen to eat. Those who remained in the shelter took their siestas in a sitting position until the sirens announced the skies clear again.

The scene repeated itself the next morning. The second warning siren came immediately after lunch, short and repetitious, giving a note of urgency. Everybody dropped what they were doing and rushed to the shelter. The nurses ran with their heads low, their shoulders hunched, using one of their hands to push down the heads of the children they were carrying. They planes sounded close, as though they were directly above us. Awhile after the planes had passed, I excused myself, "May I go ... to ..." I looked at my mother, who nodded her head. I went to the back of the servants' quarters, all the while hating where I was going—that terrible stinking toilet. I hurried in, quickly washed my hands, and instead of going back to the shelter I went to the study room. There I wandered around a bit. My mother's room was open, so I went in. A magazine was spread open on her bed. Normally the door would have been locked and the magazine locked in her armoire. I looked at the magazine, the *Paris Match,* and saw a horrible picture of a dead woman in rags left half naked on the ground, a stick pierced through what used to be her secret spot. My eyes moved to the subtitle, then the whole story telling what the Japanese did to the Chinese during their invasion. I flipped the pages and saw a few more pictures of the same nature but smaller in size. My mind was numb with shock.

I heard my name called. I returned to my seat in the shelter. A moment later I thought I heard swearing in the corner at the end of the shelter where the cook's aide was telling a story.

All eyes were directed at Chi Sau. She was saying something about the Japanese cutting off one woman's hand a week ago for stealing their canned food; she heard this from her son who collected all rumors from the market. "Me, cha tui no" (Their mothers and fathers), a young nurse swore. This was a strong curse. Parents were to be respected, their names never called, their beings never mentioned disrespectfully. To use such terms was to provoke a fight or to bring about hatred in a man's lifetime.

Chi Sau said that the man next door said he heard that in Hue they had opened an old woman's stomach and stuffed hulls in it. The woman had been in charge of feeding their horses. Her own family was starving, so instead of feeding the horses with the rice grain, she had taken out some and replaced it with husks. "Do Troi danh" (May God strike them), the younger nurse swore. "May the bombs blast them dead." Then the northern cook timidly voiced: "I received a letter from my uncle. He told me people fell dead in the streets every day because there was not enough rice to feed them. The Japanese used our rice to make fuel to run their trucks."

The group fell into silence. My eyes ventured over to my mother and found her still sitting straight in her seat, eyes closed, head tilted backward in a sleeping position.

The sirens repeated their warning on my third day home. Again we were just through eating breakfast. Instead of following everybody to the shelter, I disappeared into the living room. Cautiously unlocking the door to the veranda, I sneaked out and carefully reclosed the door behind me. I hitched myself up to the veranda and looked over the empty field now occupied by the almost naked Japanese. They looked the same this morning as when I had first seen them three days ago that afternoon coming home. All naked except for their loincloths. They were busy immersing their barrels in the water. I wondered what the barrels contained. Later I found out from my little brother, who had become friends with the Japanese through his classes, that the barrels contained fuel to run their trucks. They had to hide them in the water each time they heard the arrival of planes.

My father returned home to stay and teach math to us, the three older children who no longer went to school because of the plane raids. One day, Father stopped in the middle of our math lesson and told us what was happening. "The Japanese took over the government during the night while you girls were in Thu Duc. I went to work one morning and found Japanese at all the desks, no French to be seen. I went to town for coffee and saw trucks of French families being transported away. It was a swift, smooth change of administration," he said with a seriousness that I had never seen in him. "I resigned because of sickness." He seemed to want to tell us something and yet reserved all detailed thoughts to himself. In fact, this was the first serious adult matter he had ever spoken to us about.

That night, lying with my brother Spring Field, my eyes wandered to my mother's blue rattan chair in front of her large desk. Mother did not stay up late today because Father was home. I remembered the conversations of the maids in the shelter and the timid complaint of the northern cook. The poem that I had heard my mother recite while I was hiding under her desk one night made sense now (I liked to pretend I was invisible or living in a cave). She was composing an appeal in poem to the people. It read something as follows:

> Our country Nam is our country Nam.
> Divide it into Central, South, North,
> It is still our country.
> We came from the same ancestor,
> and were born from the same ovary.
> Our Northern brothers and sisters
> are dying of starvation,
> God gives us food in abundance in the South,
> Let us share with our brothers and sisters.

She often cried and wrote long letters or poems at her desk late into the night. I thought it was just something she liked to do, the way I liked to sneak out late in the dark to play hide and seek.

I always had to guess the meaning of what my parents did by myself. I remember one night being awakened by whispering when I was sleeping on the wooden bed in my parents' room. I heard Father tell Mother about the problems he had had with workers the previous day: "A group of about twenty, thirty workers refused to work. They sat in the middle of the street and would not pick up their shovels. My assistant was very troubled when he reported this to me. He thought they were rebels and suggested that I carry my gun if I went to meet with them. But I went out to see them on my bicycle. We discussed our problems a bit, and I urged them to go back to work, and they did. Their spokesman said that they listened to me because they knew I was honest and just. 'I was one of their countrymen,' they said. They are good and simple people. I don't think they know what it is to be convicted as criminals, tortured and exiled to the far-away island for life." Mother sighed with relief. I could hear Father turning his body—his way of concluding a conversation. Soon after he was snoring.

A while later I heard my mother waking him in the middle of his snoring. "Daddy," her nails scratching his back. (Father never wore a shirt to bed.)

"Ho!" surprised—the snoring stopped.

"Listen." She recited the poem she had just composed.

"Hm," the snoring started again softly. I heard the springs squeak under their bed. Father had turned to the wall again, resuming his snoring loudly. Mother continued reading her poem, this time louder so she could hear herself while Father accompanied her with his rhythmic snoring and, I imagined, the raise and fall of his bare belly.

My parents never discussed their affairs in front of us, even at the dining table when nobody seemed to have anything to do or think of, except for eating and watching their manners. One day though, we were sitting around the dining table at lunchtime watching for the food to come. The cook's aide brought the meal out on a large, round copper platter carved with a dragon around the rim. She stood at my mother's side, about to put the steaming hot dishes on the table, when suddenly my mother raised her hand, knocked the copper tray sideways, and brought the antique plates and bowls flying to the ceramic floor, making a broken mess of the antiques which she had always ordered the maids to take good care of, to make sure that nothing got chipped. Everyone froze. My mother stood up and walked away. A moment later my father got up from the other end of the table, his square jaw protruding, showing a slight smile. He walked away, his broad shoulders straight, his stomach flat, his large hips moving slowly in a defiant manner to follow Mother to their bedroom.

7

DAYS AND WEEKS flew by fast. The town's attention converged into waiting for the sirens, the planes, and the Japanese activities. One bright morning we all arose awaiting the sirens, but they did not sound. We waited anxiously until noon. Lunch was served, hot and formal as always.

In the middle of the meal, Sau ran up and said excitedly, "The Japanese in the vacant lot are gone. Only a few still are loading up their trucks." We all looked at her in surprise. After a second of reflection, our faces brightened with a sense of relief. Then my father quietly announced, "I heard on the short wave radio that they've surrendered to the Allies."

My mother nodded her head. She looked happy. After lunch my father skipped siesta and rode his bicycle to his branch office near downtown (his car had been confiscated by the Japanese the day he had resigned).

Two days after the Japanese left town, a classmate of mine from the seventh grade, Minh, visited me. She told me about an organization called Women Save the Country, to which she belonged. I went off with her without asking my mother's permission, walking halfway to my elementary school. "I won't be long. Nobody will miss me," I thought.

On approaching the long building adjacent to my father's office, I saw girls of different ages in the yard and the corridor. My friend walked to a long room called the office. A plain bureau was in the middle of the room, a chair behind it. A small red flag with a big yellow star planted in the center was tied to one bar of the window. In a corner, at a beautiful white piano, a girl was playing a song that sounded sweet, like running spring water. She wore a long white dress and white pants. Her black shiny hair was set in an unusual bun that fluffed loosely behind her head.

She was singing and playing at the same time. I approached her and saw her big, sad black eyes through her long curly eyelashes. Her white plump fingers ran smoothly on the ivory keys. Our eyes met; she smiled shyly. I fell in love at once with this beautiful woman. My friend took my hand and pulled me to another room which was filled with girls in black pants and white or black shirts. They looked about my older sister's age.

Minh whispered in my ear: "Sister Hon, our leader." Sister Hon was a mature woman, maybe twenty-five or more. She had a pretty oval face and a fair complexion. Her teeth were very even; her eyes direct and friendly. She was asking the girls to stay for lunch: "We have plenty of food, and if you need a siesta later, just go to that room over there, spread the straw mats on the floor, and have your siesta." Then she said cheerfully, "While waiting for our lunch, let's sing our song."

She pointed to a girl kneeling on the floor by a low table, "Shall we?"

"Bac, Trung, Nam cung la mot nha" (North, Central, South all are one house. Vietnam, our country we shall explore).

My friend sang with them. I stood there, puzzled. These words were all new to me. When I was in elementary school, I used to go around repeating things with my friends, saying the people in Annam, the central region, and the northerners (French Tonkinese) were different people, no racial relation to me. The central people were all poor and had a king that didn't amount to much. They were so poor they had to pretend that wood fish were live ones so that they could swallow their rice mixed with corn. They were hypocrites, fake like the artificial mountain and shallow river that their king had made them build. As for the Tonkinese, they called one another "Cu" (Old Dignified One) when they were still young brats just because their parents or they themselves had a title. I had heard my mother tell her Cochinchinese friends (southerners) that her people in the north considered the southerners as "Nam ky cuc" (Weird southerners) since, in the South, cyclomen, car and horse carriage drivers, and maids all ate in the same cafés, at the same time and place as those who hired them.

"Vietnam" was also a new word, a new name for me. "Cochinchine" was the name I knew for my region in the South, "Tonkin" was a different country in the North, same as Laos or Cambodia. These four, plus the center or "Annam," formed "l'Indochine française." the French-given name, "Annamites," applied only to the people of the three regions of Tonkin, Central and Cochinchine. Together these three regions had one name: "Colonie française." I had known these names as clearly as a math formula, never asking why or what made it that way. Now I heard Sister Hon's group singing that we were all one people, like in my mother's poem!

61

Sister Hon stirred the group to another song:

Who loves Uncle Ho more than us children.
Our Uncle has a big forehead, a lanky body.
Our Uncle's brown skin is weathered
by cold wind and heavy fog.
Our Uncle swears he'll revenge for our country.
Long live Ho Chi Minh (Ho, a very just man).

I found myself reciting after them. I stayed for lunch. Afterwards, I went back to the room with the piano and poked at the keys. A while later the pretty lady came in. I asked her to play a song. She gave a sweet smile and said in her northern accent, "It will be a sad song."

I nodded. The music sounded sad, and the lyrics were about a broken love—a woman knitting and waiting for a man who travelled far away. After a song or two the pretty woman left. I went to the kitchen and saw Sister Hon, the leader, sitting by herself at the table used as the dining and writing table. (A few weeks ago, I would have had to call her "Ba" or "Mrs." Now, from this time on "Chi" and "Anh" [Brother and Sister] were used among all Vietnamese in the occupied Communist régime, as opposed to the old hierarchy which reserved the same appellation only for siblings or for masters addressing their inferiors and servants in "corrupt régimes.")

She looked up from her writing and gave me a big smile.

"Come and sit down. What's your name?"

"Mai."

I sat on the chair opposite her.

"I'm working on a schedule for martial arts lessons. Would you like to join us for the lessons?" Sister Hon asked.

"Do *you* teach martial arts, too?" I was curious.

"Yes. My husband and I used to teach it, along with Vietnamese language. We travelled a lot, and when we were not teaching we practiced martial arts with each other." Her face became serious. "You see, in the old times, before 1930, martial arts was something respectable men were proud to learn. A few women also learned it from their fathers or husbands. We used to call up competitions in villages and towns all over the country from north to south. Overnight we would build up platforms and pass word to meet and compete in the market places of villages and towns. That was how we selected our leaders. After the thirties, when there were a few attempts to revolt against the French, the French forbade martial arts people to meet in public and tracked them down in

62

private. Many leaders were imprisoned in Ba Tu and Con Son, and the movement died down." Her voice now became dreamy, and her eyes wandered somewhere in the distance.

"Con Son," I recalled. There was a song I used to sing about Con Son. It told about bad people who stole mangoes at night and were caught by the French police and imprisoned on the island of Con Son. No wonder when Mother heard me sing that song she used to stop me abruptly and sternly: "Mai, I told you not to sing that song. Do not sing it again." I didn't know why then. It sounded very Catholic to me. The music was taken from one of the Christmas songs, and the lyrics had a moral lesson to them.

After a brief silence Sister Hon asked, "Where does your father work?"

"In the building next door."

"I know some people there. What does he do?"

"He's an engineer."

"Oh." A pause. "Do your parents know that you are here?"

"No, not yet."

"I'd better talk to your father . . . after a while." Another pause. "You like the piano, it seems."

"Yes."

"It is not good to listen to sad songs. Weak, crying love songs. There is so much to do, so many things in life to enjoy. Many deserving people need you to give a little of your time," she said, smiling. She closed her book and stood up. "Let's go see what the girls are doing."

I understood what she wanted me to do.

When I got back home that evening, Mother showed no signs of having missed me. Sister Hon must have talked to Father.

Within the next week I learned many songs, martial arts, and marksmanship with a pistol, a shot gun, and a bow and arrow. I seldom was home. I lived with the community and forgot myself in it. Father and Mother did not seem to mind.

One morning as I was standing at my gate about to leave for the community, I saw a bus overflowing with army people. They hung from the doors, out the windows, over the rooftop. The bus was rolling noisily down from the direction of the two bridges. There was a great commotion of yelling, calling and singing. Suddenly I heard my name called repeatedly. I tried to identify where the call was coming from in the bus. A familiar face appeared from among the many crowded in the rear doorway. I saw Minh in army pants and a man's white shirt. One of her arms was hooked to the door frame. The other waved up and down with a pistol.

"Mai! Mai! Mai!" Her face was red with the effort of yelling above the other voices. "I'll see you this afternoon."

The bus rolled away, carrying with it the male voices, loud and incomprehensible, like the noise of thunder exploding and diminishing before the rain, leaving me standing alone to wander.

Tam appeared at that moment and told me that Mother wanted me. I knocked at the door to Mother's room and entered. She told me to close the door. On her bed there was a market basket, the one the cook used to go to the market with. It was all covered up with green banana leaves. I barely had time to puzzle over the abnormal situation before Mother said, "Take this to the Chinese medicine man. I already talked to him. Leave the whole basket as is with him. He is going to keep it in a safe place for us. Now, Mai, this is a very important matter. Our jewels are in there. Go straight to him. Do not stop to talk to anybody. After you give the basket to him, take this fabric to our tailor and have him make you two pairs of shorts." The blue cotton fabric was placed on top of the leaves, and off I went. I caught Mother making the sign of the cross on her forehead.

I did as told with the basket. The Chinese man was sitting at his medicine counter. He gave me a big smile, rubbed my head, and said, "Good girl. Run home and tell your mother that I said I will do as she asked and not to worry."

I took the fabric to the tailor at the other end of the market. Upon seeing the tailor and his wife, a new thought flashed to mind. When they asked me what Mother wanted to do with the material, I told them: "Please make me a sport jacket, one like my father's only with long sleeves." It would look like the jackets of the men I had seen on the army truck this morning. I told them I needed it quickly. They said to come back the next morning.

My friend Minh didn't show up that day. The next morning, I stopped by the tailor to pick up my jacket before going on to the women's center. They knew my mother would pay for it later. Unlike other days, I had nothing to do. The number of girls had dwindled down to a very few. Sister Hon was not around. I just walked around, busying myself with my own thoughts. Then I saw Minh.

"What happened?" I asked.

"Come with me. No time to explain now." She saw the new jacket that I had on. "Hey! You look like you are ready," she said, pulling my hand. Her pistol was in a holster on her waistband. I followed her to a house which was quite a distance away in the east part of town near the plantation and airport. Once or twice, during my elementary school years,

I had visited Minh's house, which used to be on the island between the two bridges. Minh didn't wait for me to ask.

"This is my father's house. He got drunk all the time so my mother brought us back to live with grandmamma." Minh took some of her father's shirts and stuffed them into her cloth bag.

"OK. Let's go," she said.

"Go where?" I asked.

"To your house for you to get some clothes. Then we'll go to Lien's house, and then the army," said Minh assuredly. Minh was one year older than I. She had stayed back two years in the sixth grade and two years in the seventh then dropped out. I hadn't seen her since until she suddenly showed up to invite me to the women's group. I mused about what Minh said on the way to my house. There I saw the gate open. In front of one corner of the veranda, a large group of neighbors and some strangers crowded around my father's big Phillips shortwave radio. They were listening attentively to my father, who translated the news from French into our language. Minh joined the crowd and told me to go get my clothes. "Hurry," she added.

I went to my mother's bedroom, thinking I should ask her permission first. At her door I saw her and my sister sitting face to face on one side of the bed. I moved in softly and stood at the bed rest almost as tall as myself. I hadn't seen Bright Moon for days. I had heard she had joined the Youth Avant Guard and had been sent to the hospital along with her girlfriends to learn nurses' aid. One of them, a close friend, came from a family of doctors, and she herself was in her first year of medical school. There were many young men in my sister's group, but my mother didn't seem to mind.

Standing now by the headboard, I saw my mother putting two, three gold bracelets on my sister's wrists and a gold necklace around her neck. Then she performed her usual blessing, bringing her thumb to her lips — giving it a kiss, I imagined — then pressing her thumb on my sister's forehead, drawing at the same time the sign of the cross. Tears ran softly down my sister's cheeks. Standing behind my mother, I could imagine her with her eyes closed, her lips slightly moving to recite the Hail Mary prayer, which she did whenever she worried.

"Reverend Mother, I'm leaving," my sister said, with tears in her eyes and voice. She stood up, walked backward for a few steps, then turned abruptly to the door.

"God speed," my mother said in earnest, then resumed her usual silent manner. She made little movements with her right hand to wipe her eyes. I stood there a long time, it seemed, not knowing what to do.

Finally, I threw my mother a kiss over the air the way I had read valiant princes bid farewell to their mother queens and slipped out through the door behind the bed. There was no need to break mother's heart once more by asking for her approval and blessings which, I was sure, would be given the same way they had been for Bright Moon. I would let Father know, though.

I went to my room, took my shorts and shirts, and went out looking for my father. I saw him sitting inside the veranda, listening attentively to the radio. The crowd was still there outside the veranda, looking up to the radio and trying to follow my father's expressions to guess the news. I hesitated a moment, wondering if I should interrupt him. In the crowd I saw Minh frowning and nodding at me urgently.

"Anyway," I thought, "I'll be absent only for a day or two. Father is so busy, he won't miss me at all."

I walked around the house. Minh was already by the fence hiding behind the veranda. She crawled through the dog hole and made a sign for me to follow. "It's safer this way."

Already I missed home and my parents, but I didn't know what to do. I had to be brave. We walked across one bridge to take a sampan ride to Lien's house. It was the first time I had ever been on a sampan. It was full of people sitting in the middle and on both edges of the long, thin wooden boat. Minh and I had to squeeze into one side. The crossing was wide, the waves were high, the boat was loaded, and there was only one man to keep it moving forward with two long oars he used to stir one at a time in and out of the water. From my seat it looked like the sampan floated a mere four to five inches above the water. More than once the water leapt up and wet my shorts. At first I thought that I would keep cool. The third time this happened I got jittery and jumped up, imagining a crocodile was trying to snap at my bottom or the boat was about to sink. "Take it easy, would you?" Minh said, giving an embarrassed look to the other passengers. "I ride it every day. I'm still alive, don't you see?"

She glanced at me angrily, and I reseated myself. On shore, we took off on a dirt road packed with white clay soil, very white and very clean. There were fences on both sides of the road sometimes; other times just on one side. Sometimes the road just wound between houses, flowers, bushes and fruit trees: hibiscus, jasmine, pink climbing roses, goyaves, soft prunes, yellow ice plants. After a while, we came to the middle of a yard. A woman of thirty or perhaps forty was standing under a prune tree.

"Good morning, Aunt. What are you doing?" Minh greeted her.

"Oh, I'm just looking for some ripe prunes to pick and serve at our altar. And what are you doing here?" she asked good-naturedly. "I haven't seen you for a long time."

"We came to see Lien," Minh said evasively, her eyes turned to a branch.

"She is in the house," Lien's mother said and returned to her business of looking for ripe prunes.

Minh and I, a few steps behind her, advanced to the house, a cute cottage built on tall wooden pillars. The staircase was decorated with a large purple bougainvillaea bush which stretched high along the pillars and down across the bottom of the house. Another yellow bougainvillaea branched out from the other side of the house to meet with the purple flowers under a large window.

We climbed the stairs and found Lien and her little sister in the living room. The room had two wooden armchairs, a low table, a large wooden sofa and an altar elaborately carved and inlaid with seashells. Lien, looking like a little girl with her hair tied up in two pigtails that hung loosely on her back, saw us first.

"You guys! What are you doing here?" she said gaily. Her cheeks were very pink. Her eyes were clear brown, and the whites were actually blue. I had not seen Lien since seventh grade, almost two years ago. Minh pulled Lien out of her sister's earshot and said, "Come. I have something to tell you."

Lien, bewildered, followed. They were now in the corner of the back room. I sat down on the wooden sofa. My eyes wandered to the altar, and I noticed a large plate of bananas, grapefruits, and oranges. An oil lamp was lit in the middle where there stood a drawing of a woman Buddha. To the side there was a picture of a man. He looked like Lien's sister. "He must be their late father," I thought.

A phonograph was quietly playing a "Vong Co" (a style of singing reminiscing the past). The smooth quiet song attracted my attention. It was the voice of a mother telling her daughter what to do, how to behave when she reached puberty and crossed the threshold of her husband's house. Each sinking sad note at the end of each phrase pervaded the still midday air and seemed to linger on the branches and flowers before fading into the distance. I felt as if I had truly just heard echoes from the past.

"Let's go," Minh called out.

I turned and saw Lien, ready, with her grey embroidered bag at her side. She went to her sister who stood near the wooden sofa and laid her bag down on it. Her white hands, dotted with clean pinkish fingernails, pressed against her sister's cheeks. The latter looked up, surprised.

"Stay home, little one, and take care of Mother. I'm going to fight for our country and will be back in a few days. That's a promise," she said cheerfully, her eyes glittering, her rose lips quivering.

We walked down to the garden where Lien's mother was still standing.

"Mom, I'm going with my friends to the army." Lien put it so naturally and amicably that it made me admire her composure, that of a daughter of a peasant.

Her mother looked shocked. After a moment she asked, "When will you be back?"

"In a few days, I'm sure," Lien smiled reassuringly. "I'm leaving," she said and turned away.

"Daughter, be careful," her mother called after her.

We walked to the shore. We did not stop at the same place we had landed. But I was determined not to give Minh a chance to make her arrogant remarks again. We were about two or three hundred yards above where the other sampan was unloading. We sat on the edge of the boat again. A boy pushed our sampan forward out of the mud for the oarsman to singlehandedly and seemingly effortlessly steer us across the dark threatening waves. Now that I was used to sitting on the edge of the sampan, I no longer worried about the water lapping at my shorts. Instead, I concentrated on figuring out how one thin man like the oarsman could row a sampan loaded with no less than twenty people across such a fierce river. By the time we got to shore and saw the other landings, I discovered that he used the current to carry the boat and only needed to guide the direction with his oar under the water. "Who said peasants were dumb?" I thought with admiration.

Lien looked pensive. Her eyes lingered on the waves as if trying to absorb the familiar scenes for the last time. An echo of the past seemed to have sadly invaded her cool composure.

8

WE GOT OFF the sampan onto a muddy shore near the Bien Hoa town market. In silence, Minh led the way toward the Sens Unique, then to the boys' school. There, we saw some army trucks and soldiers milling around in the schoolyard. I was mindful not to be seen by the director or his wife, who was my godmother. Their villa was directly behind the school. Minh told us to wait in the hall; then she disappeared. After a moment we saw her head sticking out of a classroom upstairs, nodding at us to come up.

We entered a room empty of student benches. A man in uniform stood behind a large teacher's desk in the middle of the room. He was lean, tall and had a northern accent.

"Minh told me that you want to join the army." His loud, warm voice vibrated in the empty room. "I commend you for your bravery." He smiled kindly down at us from behind the desk where he stood. "But you are very, very young. We would not know what job to give you. Our soldiers have to carry guns and . . . sometimes . . . kill. Sounds new to you, hm?"

"We can do anything you want us to do. You need nurses, too," Minh said eagerly.

"A team of nurses are already here, waiting for us to contact them. Besides, we would have to talk to your parents if we take you. Do you think they will approve?"

Minh, looking ready to back out, begged for the last time, "Please Brother Vinh. We promise we will be useful."

Brother Vinh reached out his hand and rubbed my head which was closest to him. "Be good. Run along home. You will be useful at home, too."

Minh reluctantly led us out of the room and down the stairs to the courtyard.

She asked the soldiers where they were going. They didn't tell us much. One man, another northerner, shrugged and said, "We just follow whoever is ahead of us."

Minh got an idea. "Stick around," she ordered. We stayed close to the man. Soon, two more soldiers joined him, their *ba-lô* (backpacks — a word I learned from them) on their backs, a long rifle similar to my father's in their hands. An army truck left the schoolyard. The men started walking in the same direction as the truck. Minh didn't move to follow. When they arrived at the Sens Unique, Minh nodded for us to go. Ahead of them there were groups of three, four, and five all moving toward the train station about two miles from the school. I thought they would turn in to ride the train, but they walked on toward the deserted landscape, in the middle of the asphalt road, still hot from the dying sun.

I was hungry and tired — I hadn't had lunch, hadn't even had a drink since I met Minh in the morning. I wished they would stop to rest. It was getting dark. We stepped up to close the distance between them and us so as not to lose sight of them. Finally we caught up with them. They were now sitting on the thorny grass by the roadside.

"Little sisters, you are still here?" One of them asked in surprise. "Yes," said Minh, "we are going to the same place you are going." "Oh?" they responded. Minh made a sign for us to go forward. I understood what she meant. She didn't want them to suspect us of anything. One of the men was the one Minh had asked for information.

The second group we met up with consisted of five men, two in uniform, the rest in civilian clothes. They were a mixture of men from the North and the South, and they were noisier. They talked loud and sang a bit. Now and then, we giggled at their jokes. One man finally turned and asked, "Are you our little nurses?"

"Soon we will be," Minh toned in proudly. They laughed, probably thinking it was a joke. But knowing Minh, I knew she was serious. We were going to make it to the army and be their nurses, too. We walked in the dark for a while, then the moon appeard. At the bottom of the sloping road ahead loomed an ox cart. One of the men said, "Wouldn't it be nice if we could ride on it?" "That's a good idea. My legs are tired." "Let's try." They stepped up the pace, almost running. We followed suit. I was delighted with the blessed idea.

When we came near, we saw an oil lamp rocking underneath the bottom of a very tall and wide ox cart. In the middle, between the two huge wheels that raised the cart some four feet above the ground, a man lay in

70

a hammock which was also swinging with the tempo of the oxen. Leisurely walking behind was his dog, also swaying in the same rhythm. The cart was empty except for a jug of water. A pair of shorts hung on the wall as well as some dried food and cooking utensils. Nobody was directing the two large, dun-colored oxen. One man asked whether the owner would mind if we sat in the cart. The owner lifted his head up from the hammock to scrutinize us then said, "It's all right. Just don't overload the oxen."

Two men climbed up, while the oxen kept on walking. They asked us if we needed help to climb up. "Please." "Give us your hands." They pulled us up one by one. Then they spread themselves out on the cart floor, and we sat in the back, legs dangling in the air.

In this position I slept until I heard: "Let's get off here and eat." I opened my eyes and saw all five of the men in the cart and lights and people nearby. We jumped down to make room for them. They thanked the cart owner and walked off toward a café. Minh called after them: "Big brothers. Is the army nearby?" "Yes. But aren't you hungry? Don't you want anything to eat before you get there?" "We have no money." They looked at one another. "Well, come with us anyway."

They were very nice. They told us to order what we wanted. One southerner ordered *hu tieu* (noodle soup cooked with pork), another ordered fried rice. The third southerner got a sandwich with chicken pâté. The northerners contented themselves with two eggs each, sunny side up, eaten with freshly baked French bread. It was the first time I had seen such a copious breakfast, and for me to choose! I had a hard time making up my mind. Finally I decided on the egg dish. Eggs were something we had been eating every day for breakfast at home, only those eggs were made into a big omelette to be eaten with rice soup and shared among the entire family. The bread smelled delicious, especially with the French canned butter (*Beurre Bretel* made in Normandy). At home I could only eat this on Saturday nights when Father was present. I had never eaten fried rice or *hu tieu* before, but since I had never had them I did not miss them. After breakfast, one of the southerners and a northerner smoked cigarettes. The others did not smoke. They all drank coffee.

Many army men had come and gone around us.

It was mid-morning before we left the café to head for the army headquarters. Cool, brisk air filled my lungs and freshened my dirty face, which had not been washed since the day before. The ground around us was rich with red soil. Trees grew tall and green, the rich color of seaweed. The grass was soft and bore colorful flowers. The morning fog lent a mysterious beauty. We were in a place called Trang Bom, about thirty miles from home.

71

After a while, we arrived at the headquarters which was in the French administration complex (a huge, elegant villa in the middle, with long rows of annexes on each side). The regiment was still sleeping. We saw men lying scattered in the rooms and on the verandas of the low buildings. Our outfit of men went to a veranda to stretch out, using their *ba-lô* as pillows. We went with them.

The sun was already high when I woke. The soldiers leisurely moved about in the spacious court. Some soldiers and civilians busily walked up and down the steps of the huge villa. In the distance, a man was petting a beautiful brown horse, saddled and ready for riding. He led the horse in our direction. He was a young man in his early twenties, fair skinned and student-like. When he approached, I said: "A beautiful horse." "Yes," he agreed in his northern accent. "It reminds me of the horses on our ranch."

"Why don't you ride it?" I asked. "Oh, no," he said. Later I found out that he was a student in the university. When Ho Chi Minh had appealed to the Hanoi public to join his force and fight the French, he had been among those chosen to stand on the first greeting line because he was tall, handsome, and educated, a perfect picture of elite youth. To own a horse was a very exceptional thing for an Annamite. He looked and acted rich and educated, like few I had met so far. From my sweeping glance over the yard, I thought I could distinguish two classes of soldiers: the educated and the uneducated. We were told that independence would bring better life to the poor. A good educated person should not let himself stand out arrogantly, but should mix and blend in with the others. At that moment, I was probably one of the very few who knew that the handsome student owned horses.

The horse tapped its hoofs on the red dirt. "Could I?" I asked eagerly.

Had the scene of my first ride presented itself at that moment, I would not have even dared to stand close to a horse, let alone ask to ride one.

About half a year before, my mother had taken us to stay with her northern friends. The husband was the director of the mill, the only sawmill in the province of Bien Hoa. The people of the town were called "the people of the mills" because most of them worked there and were inhabitants of the neighboring villages. The friends of my parents had a big weekend house that was built of wood and stood on pillars.

The house was located at the end of a dirt road hidden by fruit trees, among the homes of peasants. Behind it was a narrow river. In the middle of the river was a small vacant island. Recently, they had brought home a dozen beautiful riding horses. I heard they belonged to some Frenchmen who had asked them to keep the horses while they were away on a long trip. This was during the time the Japanese were in Bien Hoa. My parents' friends had constructed low stables of straw for the horses and a wide dirt walking trail for them. A village boy was hired to take care of them.

On one of our overnight visits, I saw the boy walking one of the horses. I asked him why he didn't ride it. "I don't know how. Besides they wouldn't allow me to."

"Don't know how to ride it? Such a simple thing," I thought. I had seen my father on one when we visited one of his inspection stations in a forest near Bara—he had not allowed me to ride though. Men and women in the *Livres Roses* rode horses every day around castles, in towns and in forests. It was a normal thing to do. I ventured aloud: "Let me ride it."

"No. You don't know how to ride. Do you?" he hesitated, a ray of hope and admiration in his eyes. "It's simple," I said.

He wasn't sure what I meant but added, "Besides, I'm not allowed to let anybody ride them." I could see he wanted to know whether I really could ride. He had never seen a mounted horse.

"I will ride him for you. You'll save a lot of time. Walking all those horses!" I took the reins from his hand and estimated the height of the horse. I had to make sure he didn't think I couldn't do it. "This horse has no saddle," I commented expertly.

"Yes?" he answered with surprise. He had never seen a saddle in his life either. I led the horse to a bar in front of the stable and attempted a clumsy mount. My bottom had barely dropped onto the horse's back when suddenly my whole body was thrown backward. The horse had reared up.

Snorting madly like a ghost horse, forelegs fiercely kicking the air, off he galloped. I didn't know what kept me from falling off—my body was practically flying in the air, only my fingers were clenched tightly to the horse's mane. He raced down the dirt path, threw himself into the orchard, and zigzagged among the trees and low branches. I clung to him, my body pressed flat to his back. Luckily for me he ran with his head up because he needed to avoid lower branches. Then, suddenly he dashed sideways out to the clearing and before I knew it, jumped across a well. I only felt myself raised up by a strong jerk while my eyes caught sight of a round wall with a big black hole in the middle. The next moment that I was conscious of was when I saw the horse in the stable and found myself hanging onto a pole that extended across the thatched roof. I closed my eyes to rest, to absorb the shock.

Needless to say, the shock must not have been very great for I now found myself eagerly waiting for my new acquaintance to readjust the saddle and shorten the stirrups for my sandaled feet. He helped me into the saddle. Suddenly my bad experience came back to me. I braced myself. But the horse started off nicely. Gently he walked on his familiar ground. We made it halfway to the end of the court in a leisurely manner, then I began to feel bold: "No, you can't be sleepy at this time, horsy. The day is brand new. Let's gallop." I kicked my legs and pulled on the reins. He galloped.

Bouncing in the air, I heard hands clapping around me. "Good. Good. Beautiful ride." Passing the villa, I saw Brother Vinh walking out to watch. Already I felt it natural that I should know how to ride!

After the second round, I got off the horse where Minh and Lien were standing. The young man was there. He took the reins and praised my performance. Minh said, "Let's go eat. They are serving free food in the other building."

We crossed the yard and were about to enter the gateway when, from a distance on the road, I saw the outline of a familiar form. It got closer. I recognized the "casque" hat, the white tennis shorts and pullover, and the bicycle. My father! He was pedaling toward us. Minh pulled me down. We crawled on all fours to the fence wall. There, the three of us hid ourselves and waited. My father arrived at the main gate. He pedaled on toward the villa and parked his bike at the bottom of the steps. He talked with a man who was passing by, and the man pointed up the steps to the open door. Father walked toward the open door, then out of sight. My heart beat fiercely. I could hear it pounding loudly. He reappeared on the steps, descended, his head lowered, his eyes downcast. Slowly he mounted his bike, and pedaled painfully toward the gate. My head screamed: "Run! Run! Run!" My eyes were blurred with tears. Something was tugging tightly on my shorts. My wrists were held firmly to the ground.

The heavy form of my father, limp with pain, pushed slowly toward home. My eyes followed my dear father until he became a speck. "What must I do? Quick. Quick. What must I do?" No answer. The dot on the road transformed itself into the picture of my father fondly handing to my mother a paper on which I had written my resolution.

It was the morning of the first day of the Lunar Year. We children had put on our new clothes and were sitting at our desks to write or do anything related to our studies, in order to start off the new year making good use of our intellect in school. This was done following the strict instructions of Mother the night before. She did not want to risk starting off the new year displeased. The maid had had to stay up late, but not beyond midnight, to clean up everything. The house had to be clean to receive the new year, but sweeping on New Year's Day might brush away the first entrance of good luck to the house. Besides, nobody should start working on the first day of the new year. Food for New Year's Day was cooked the day before, and at midnight, all the cooking ceased. Ong Tao (the spirit of the stoves) had to leave for heaven to report to the supreme one on the activities of the household during the past year.

We waited around for our parents to come out of their bedroom into the modern living room so that we could recite our best wishes to them. They would in turn give (*li-xi*) each of us a red envelope with money inside for us to spend at our will. That year, I did something different. Instead of doing my math or writing my composition as part of the school assignment for the holiday, I had written a resolution having to do with the maxim Father had written on the blackboard: "Look up. Seek always to elevate yourself." I don't remember what it said specifically, but it must have been good for my father to have handed it to Mother saying proudly: "Look Mamma. Look at what Mai wrote. She said she will make one resolution every year. Just one resolution a year, and she will see to it that the resolution works."

Father vanished over the horizon. I wished I could have made another resolution that would have pleased him as much as that one had. I wished I could have abandoned what I was doing to return to my parents. But I wasn't sure if that would have made them proud of me the way I was proud of them—Father defending his driver or explaining to the neighbors what was going on in the world as they gathered in front of his radio; Mother sending my sister off to save our country. Would my mother be as proud of me seeing me doing little chores like carrying the jewelry basket to hide at the Chinese medicine man's as seeing me join the army and being a brave soldier? Mother had shown no regrets in seeing my sister go. She had even given her jewels to wear and kissed blessings on her forehead.

All these arguments made me confident that I was doing the right thing. When I heard Minh say, "Let's go," my eyes were already dry of tears. We passed the villa. I saw Brother Vinh on the top step. This reassured me further. Brother Vinh must have thought our presence no longer objectionable since he had seen me riding the horse but hadn't told Father.

That afternoon, while taking our siesta, I saw two men and a boy walking towards us. A man with a row of gold teeth talked to us in a southern accent: "Greetings to our little sisters. Brother Vinh sent us over here to talk to you. I am Tran. They call me Captain Gold Teeth. This is

Brother Hai, he is our Japanese advisor. This is Captain Nhan. He looks young, but he knows four languages: ours, of course, French, English, and Japanese. He has a team of nine boys. With you three included, he will have twelve all together. You are to do what he tells you. Brother Hai will train you all on the operation. That's all that I have to say. Captain Nhan, why don't you tell them when to start."

Nhan was about a head or two taller than me. He looked about sixteen. His complexion was the pinkish white color of the French. He had a high nose. He looked *métis*, half Annamite, half French. He talked with a southern accent and the voice of a male duck — a boy who was changing from boyhood to manhood.

"Tomorrow we will all meet here at ten. Have your breakfast beforehand. Other instructions you'll hear tomorrow. That's it." He turned to the Japanese advisor: "Right? Brother Hai?" Brother Hai smiled and stood at attention, "Hai!"

Captain Nhan and Captain Gold Teeth saluted him in soldier style. Captain Nahn then turned around to us and said, "This'll be your first lesson. Salute." We obeyed, saluting automatically. Nothing to it. We had learned it from school, from the girls who were selected to hoist the French flag every day before classes.

"Good," Nhan said. The others seemed to be surprised at our efficiency. They turned around and left us to resume our business. Lien combed her hair out and redressed it into two pigtails while Minh lay back to sleep again. I lay down along side her. We ate dinner and went back to sleep again.

The next day, precisely at ten o'clock, a line of boys, paired off, stood in the yard in front of us. Captain Nhan whistled and made a sign for us to join them. We ran toward them and were told to line up by size. While we were marching, the boy next to me told me that he had been in two battles at the Gia Dinh Bridge — battles against the French. It was pretty fierce he said. Before that he had been a student at Petrus Ky High. His parents were merchants. He sounded phlegmatic as he talked about the war. I admired his experiences but did not ask any questions. I was used to listening.

When we met the Japanese advisor again, Captain Nhan translated that we were going to learn how to spy on enemies. Our first lesson started right after the meeting. Captain Nhan took the three of us to a field, showed us how to look for signs of enemy installations, how to get to enemy camps, and how to send information home. All that time I pictured the "enemy" as being those having white skin, big noses, and tall bodies — the French.

76

That was our only lesson. That night, when it was still dark and the moon had not yet appeared, we saw the soldiers gathering up their belongings and walking off into groups with rifles on their shoulders. They exited the gate in the direction of the forest. Then Captain Gold Teeth came to tell us to get on an army truck and go where it went. Our truck ran in the dark without its lights. In the dim light of the night we could see only a few feet ahead.

We arrived at a big building in the middle of a forest. Our truck pulled up in front of the steps to a large rear entrance of the building. After having crossed a huge hall, we were directed to a room. The door of the room was open. We peeped in and saw girls scattered all over the place, on the tiled floor and on the shiny copper bed with huge curlicued round tubes of copper decorating its headboard. The girls were much older and bigger than us. We walked in hesitantly. Nobody seemed to notice our coming. We sat on the floor near a large window. An electric light from the bed kept the whole place softly lit. I fell back to sleep again, sitting with my arms around my knees.

Time passed slowly with the occasional interruption of murmurs and soft footsteps. Suddenly I was awakened by a loud commotion from the hall then directly at the door entrance. Opening my eyes, I saw Brother Vinh standing between two uniformed men, one of whom was Captain Gold Teeth. "We need a volunteer here. Someone to go get some information for us," said Brother Vinh in his usual loud voice. Dead silence fell in the room. "Is there anyone among you who could take up the mission?" He repeated. Still dead silence. I looked around to see if any hands were raised. I hated to look like a hero. The three men stood still. Embarrassment reigned in the room.

I raised my hand halfway, timidly, ashamed to have to stand out, "Could I?" Brother Vinh looked in my direction. A big smile came over his face. "Come with me."

I stood up, arranging my *ba-lô* to go. "Leave your things here." I followed the three of them to a room. Brother Vinh was brief. "There is a truck stopped in the street. I want you to find out who is in it. Be careful on the way. If somebody calls 'Lang' you must answer with 'Son.' That's our code. Do not forget. He might shoot if you don't give the right code. Here is a pistol for you to use. Here is how it works. It's loaded. All you need to do is flip the security down and pull the trigger. They're real bullets, so be careful."

I had learned how to use one at the women's center.

Minh had a similar one, but bigger. I took the gun. "Thank you. I'll go now." I walked out the front door and down many large steps into the gravelled road which slowly faded in the electric light that shone from Brother Vinh's room.

I tried to find my way in the dark, following the engine sound of the truck I assumed to be the one I was supposed to get information on. By and by, I could hear my heartbeat and my footsteps — so loud were they that I feared they might attract the attention of the enemy around me. I moved toward the grass which I discovered was taller than me and full of sharp blades. It cut my feet and bare arms, but I had to move fast. When I got closer to the sound, I lay down flat on the ground and started crawling on my belly, holding the gun in front of me in my right hand. All of this I had learned at the women's center and from Captain Nhan that morning.

The truck's lights shone full blast onto a huge tree trunk that had collapsed across the road a few meters from where I lay. I found myself a short distance from the back of a commercial truck.

I crawled up toward the front and saw the forms of some people sitting in the front seat. "What do I do now? Tell them to get off the truck? Ask them to give information from where they sat. What if they won't? I must not show them my face. That was what I learned from the army. But I must never attack a person from behind. That was what I learned from home. What to do to compromise?"

I crawled toward the tree and placed myself behind it. With my gun pointing at them, I sprang up erect into the flood of lights. I figured if something happened I could drop back down behind the tree trunk and crawl away. The faces inside the truck jerked forward and made themselves seen behind the front windshield. "Drop whatever you are holding and slowly get off the truck, all of you."

The truck driver put his head out, raised his hand, and implored, "Please. We are ordinary rice merchants. We have a truckload of rice to take to Phan Thiet. This has been our regular route for years. We got stuck here because of the tree. We meant no harm. Please spare us."

"Get down, anyway. How many are you?"

"Only me, my wife, and my six-year-old daughter."

"Have them get down and show me your I.D."

They all got down while he kept saying, "I am telling you the truth. I'm just a poor merchant." He walked toward me with his driver's license in his hand and my gun pointing at him. I had forgotten to flip the security. No matter. He looked scared enough. "I must take this with me," I said, taking his license. "Show me what's in the back." He walked with me to the back. Half of the trunk was filled with rice bags. "O.K. You may return to your seat and wait there."

I walked with his I.D. in my hand back into the tall grass. I had to make sure he did not know where I was going. Once in the grass I started crawling again. Then, suddenly it occurred to me that I didn't know where I was going myself. I moved straight ahead, faster and faster, hoping to see the lights of the headquarters somehow. "Hang on to the I.D.," I kept reminding myself.

I was completely absorbed in the maneuvers when from the tall grass, I heard a quick, nervous: "Lang." The word sounded familiar . . . I had to answer. But what? I had forgotten the answer. "Lang" what? "Lang" . . . I heard the cocking of a gun.

"Wait! Wait!" I shouted in panic. "Brother Vinh told me, but I forgot. Wait. I'll remember, right away."

"Ah. You are one of us," he said, relieved. A second later, "What are you doing crawling like that? You are in our territory."

I jumped to my feet, bitterly ashamed of my cowardice. The building stood not far from me. The light from Brother Vinh's room shone brightly through the large glass window. "Thank you," I said running toward the steps of the building.

Brother Vinh was there talking to a few men. I gave him the I.D. and told him what I had seen. "Good job" he said, rubbing my head. I handed him the pistol.

"You can keep it." I wondered what Brother Vinh was going to do with those merchants and their I.D., but I didn't dare to ask until the next morning when I became very concerned about them during the shooting. They had begged me to return their papers, but I had not promised them anything since my assignment was to obtain their I.D. only.

After my mission that night, I returned to the room with my friends and dropped back to sleep until I heard something about eating the next morning. We went out to get our share of *chao* (rice soup). Then we were each given an aluminum container of *chao* to take to the soldiers who were posted in the field. We were to take our *ba-lô* along too. While distributing the soup, I passed Brother Vinh who told me to follow him. We arrived at a rubber plantation. "Run behind the trees," Brother Vinh told me, "and join the soldier in front that carries the machine gun." I did so. Brother Vinh was behind me when I reached the man. "Brother, let her help you with your round of bullets."

The soldier looked up from his kneeling position and saw Brother Vinh. Without a word, he gladly slipped the bullet belts off his shoulder and handed them to me. Ooff, I thought. The pair of belts were extremely heavy and were pulling down on my shoulders.

"Mai, from now on stay with the man and feed his machine gun."

"Yes Sir."

We ran forward from tree to tree. Gunshots sounded ahead of us. I remembered my promise to the merchants. "The merchants were waiting for me to return their papers," I said, so that it didn't sound like I was questioning Brother Vinh.

"They can't go anywhere anyway. Didn't you say their truck was blocked by a tree?" Brother Vinh snapped at my question then disappeared among the trees.

Brother Vinh returned to us a while later and was talking to the machine gun man: "The Japanese tricked us. Our men in front saw them going down the hill wearing the same uniforms they had given us. They waved so our soldiers thought they were on our side. When our men came near, they pulled their triggers." I saw then that there were two of our men lying dead by the rubber trees.

This was confusing to me. I had understood from the boy marching next to me in our "spy" team that we were going to fight the French. Later, I found out that Brother Vinh's group had been armed by the Japanese on the last day of their rule in Saigon, before they were declared defeated after the bombing of Hiroshima. With the pretext of helping the Allies to dislodge the Japanese, the French and the British had moved back to their respective colonies, Indochina and India, to reestablish their dominion. On the morning that the Japanese were to be disarmed, they offered their ammunition and army supplies to the Vietnamese. That day, some Japanese officers committed suicide, some joined the Vietnamese fighting groups—such as our Japanese advisor—and some withdrew with their men into the countryside and continued their fight against all the rest. Thus we were to consider whoever did not speak our language our enemy, and I was to carry out my "spy" missions against *all* foreigners.

Sometimes our group stayed in town and sometimes in the forest; sometimes we were copiously fed, and other times we treaded for days in the continuous monsoon rains, with empty stomachs and leeches sucking stubbornly on our limbs. When we would be reunited in a town, Minh, Lien, and I would stay at the headquarters with Brother Vinh and his officers. We would then all sleep on the floor. Sometimes we would be taken to eat at restaurants. Most times we ate the food cooked by village volunteers.

Every day there were changes of either location or assignment. My life in the army was to me not much different from that at home. I did the army assignments as I used to do my schoolwork. Before it had been the duty of a student, now it was the duty of a soldier. We lived like a large family and did things together more often than I had done with my siblings at home. Brother Vinh was like a father to me. I did not miss home at all, except now and then when some soldiers would shock me with their crude behavior.

One day I went with a group of soldiers (these soldiers were mostly uneducated city dwellers), and we discovered a huge villa made of stone deep in the forest among plantations of rubber and coffee. A French owner had deserted it a long time ago. A beautiful chestnut-colored piano sat intact in a large room that looked out on the morning flowers, the jasmine and roses which climbed all over the stone wall. We ransacked the basement and found a cache of weapons. One soldier found a small navy jacket and a navy blue beret, both made out of wool, which he gave me to keep. We returned noisily to the living room after the soldiers had emptied a few bottles of wine they had found in the cellar. They started getting rowdy. Having nothing else to do, they pushed the piano out to the balcony.

"Wait. Wait. What are you doing with it?" I said running after them. "You'll see. You'll see." They were laughing and pushing, and they pushed me out of the way. They pushed the piano to the steps. Then "Cling . . . Cling . . . Clong . . . Clong . . . Br . . . om . . . Br . . . om," the piano went tumbling down the stairs and landed sideways on the red ground. I ran down to inspect, touched the ivory piano keys, and cried out loud, "You ruined it!"

"Look at silly little Mai," someone said laughing. "Mai. Hey Mai. You want to see something funny?" a guy said and ran back into a room. He took out a record player that looked similar to the one we had at home, the Victrola—the Dog and His Master. Another fellow ran out with records. The one holding the gramophone threw it crashing down onto the balcony. Then, pulling out his pistol, he reached over for a record, tossed it into the air, and shot at it while laughing hilariously. A few soldiers copied him. Those who didn't have a pistol used their shotguns. They bent over laughing at each performance. The rest of us stood there looking, helpless. I felt very disappointed with them, my "oppressed" countrymen for whom the first Vietnamese songs I had ever known were written. Songs expressing such great love and devotion that they had moved so many people—from my parents to Sister Hon, the Women's Club leader, to Brother Vinh and his friends, my commanders and "brothers"—to believe in them and be willing to sacrifice for their cause.

Not too long after this incident, we were caught in a fierce battle with the French. Their weapons were far superior to ours. Their mortars shot at us beyond our guns' reach, so that we were forced to retreat. We escaped through a forest, walking along a muddy track, one behind the other, each holding onto the shoulder of the person in front. After what seemed an eternity, with no food in our stomachs, my torn-up sandals long since thrown away, we came upon a meadow. I heard a baby crying. I looked up from my treading and saw a naked baby, crawling to his mother's breasts which lay open on her still torso in her unbuttoned black *ao ba-ba*. The mother was dead. She was shot in the ankle, and red ants were eating around the wound creating a large hole. I started to run toward the baby. A hand behind me grabbed me back.

"It's a baby. He is hungry. We must feed him."

"No. We can't stop. We have nothing to feed him. Get going."

"But we must not leave him here. Who will take care of him?"

"Somebody will. Not you, move on."

"What's holding you back up there?" somebody shouted behind me. "Move." The man behind me pushed me violently. I jerked forward. I had lost track of the guy in front who disappeared behind a tall bush at the bend of the muddy track. I had to rejoin him fast. Several times in the past, from sheer exhaustion, I had dozed off, dropping my hand from the shoulder of the fellow in front and causing much commotion in my trail when I suddenly jerked away to find my frontman. They had warned me: "You can be shot if you cause us to lose track of the front guy. Worse, you could lead us straight to our enemy."

Thus, in spite of myself, I moved on. I could regret. I could feel guilty. I could wonder about my patriotism. I could ask why I was there to save my country but could not and was not allowed to save just one little baby — what was a country then? But at the same time, I knew the crying of a baby could get us all killed. Like always, I had to keep my questions to myself, for me alone to answer.

Some nights, I had problems with the soldiers themselves. Once, when I had to share a blanket with a few soldiers while we lay on the wet ground, a soldier attempted to touch my body. My first reaction was to turn to the other side so that he would be aware that I objected. But I knew I had to come up with something better and fast. I didn't think it was a good idea to alarm the others by protesting loudly, for it would only expose them to dirty thoughts while I would still have to find my own solution. Besides, similar situations would happen again, and they did not happen only in the army — this I knew.

Once when my family lived in Kratie, near the border of Cambodia, where the heat was intolerable and everybody's skin was dry and had a burnt brown look — even my mother looked very tan — I ran into a similar situation. I was six and went to a public school which was near a cemetery.

82

One day during recess, I was roaming alone among shady trees in the graveyard when I saw a group of four or five boys a little older than myself, behind a tombstone. Against the flat stone stood a boy struggling to pull his briefs up while the others were wrestling to push them down. The boys saw me, and before I knew it, they grabbed me and pulled me to the stone with the other boy. They shouted, "Pull her pants down!" I felt their hands attacking me. I kicked and hit violently. They had a hard time fighting the two of us. The drum sounded, and we all ran to resume classes. I didn't know if the boy said anything to anybody, but I certainly did not. I kept silent and told myself not to wander in those vacant places again.

While I was recalling this scene, an idea came to me. It jerked me up from my prone position between the two soldiers. Quickly, I rolled over the sleeping man on my other side and soon was able to drop back to sleep myself.

God saved me, as he had saved me on the first ride on the wild horse with no saddle. The way I figured it, after a first experience, it was up to me to store the information for later use when a similar situation occurred. Of course, the more people involved the more complicated it would be. But most of the time I just had to keep silent and observe, to buy time and to memorize. Somehow I didn't consider these bad experiences a loss for me. I felt they were part of life and might be useful to me someday. It did sadden me though that such things happened, for I liked to think of my fellowmen as my "soul" brothers striving for the same ideals.

Had life in the army been that bleak all the time, I would not have lived to tell about it. My army friends gave me many memories that, in the future, would often cheer me up and help me in my continued belief in a good cause.

During one of the big battles that we engaged in, Minh followed the soldiers to the field. When I returned to camp, Captain Nhan said Minh was in the Red Cross room. I went in and asked for my wounded friend. Some soldiers who were sitting around started laughing. "The wounded soldier? Go see for yourself." I went to her bunk and saw her lying, sad looking, with no bandages but with a handful of money. She told me that she had been running behind a soldier with her Red Cross box. They came to a grave and hid behind the gravestone. Then the soldier stood up about to run forward, she behind him. Suddenly she heard a big *boom*. He fell backward, and she passed out. "The soldiers carried me here. They said I got scared, so I passed out. I wasn't scared. His head hit my chest hard like a stone. See that man over there with a bunch of bandages on his head? That's the soldier. They said he won't live till tomorrow."

"I believe you," I said. "What's that money in your hand?" "Brother

Vinh gave it to me. He saw me arguing with the soldiers, so he told them to quit teasing me. He said it's a reward for my courage."

We left together and went to find Lien. The three of us went off to the village to celebrate with the reward.

A few days after that battle, I was sent to spy on the Japanese army which occupied the town. In that mission, I had to threaten a girl my age, telling her if she didn't go with me I would kill her with my gun. I pretended I had a gun hidden in my *ao ba-ba*. I needed to report on the strength of the Japanese army up the hill: the only plausible reason for me to give them for going up there was to tell them that I lived on the other side of the hill, but I needed to know what lay over there. I met the girl in a deserted garden while she was digging potatoes. She said she knew what was on the other side, but she wouldn't go with me for fear the Japanese would catch her and maybe rape her. The gun had convinced her to cooperate. At the foot of the hill, a Japanese appeared from a bush on the sandy slope. He pointed a gun at me and said something in Japanese. I knew then that the Japanese were actually posted there. I told him in Vietnamese that my house was across the hill. He yelled back something else in Japanese indicating for me to back up. I insisted I had to go forward. Finally, he handed me the butt of his rifle and pulled me up with my new friend. I walked through their camp, trying to absorb as much information on their number and the size and quantity of their big guns as I could. Finally we reached a street on the other side of the hill. We walked past empty houses. I felt there was a Japanese soldier following us. I told the girl to drift into a house. We sat on the balcony, I pretending to look for fleas in her hair (a common pastime among the poor). The Japanese stood behind a bamboo tree awhile, drawing something until he lost interest and left. We split up. She went back to town, and I went back toward my camp by way of the hot asphalt road.

When the hill was out of sight behind me, I saw in the distance ahead a horse carriage. Two men were waving at me. I was very glad to see Captain Nhan and our Japanese advisor, who were so glad to find me alive, I supposed, that they ended up scolding me for going on a mission not ordered by them who were the heads of the spy section: I could have been killed; a million things could have happened to me; next time only go upon their personal order. They then gave me boiled eggs (a delicacy we rarely had) and fresh rainwater. The Japanese advisor also taught me how to sing a Japanese song praising the beauty of Peking where he had once been a captain in the Japanese army.

Two days later I had a fight with Captain Nhan. Brother Vinh had decided that the whole regiment could go treat themselves to a restaurant meal with their first salaries (it was also the last salary we received from "up-high")—we always got fed by the peasants and slept in school buildings when in town. I was supposed to march with our group of twelve "spies" to town. I was dragging my feet, objecting to the idea of marching. I wanted to enjoy our day of good luck. I didn't feel like disciplining myself in such a show-off march. Captain Nhan drew my attention twice. The third time, he called me out of the ranks and made me walk in the last row as punishment. I dragged my feet even slower. Finally, I dropped out of sight and ran back to our camp, with Nhan screaming orders behind me.

Back at camp, Brother Vinh and his colonels were just on their way out to the restaurant.

"Why are you not with your group?"

"Captain Nhan punished me."

"Why?"

I explained to them what had happened.

"Well . . . You cannot miss this occasion! There will be plenty of good food," said Captain Gold Teeth.

"Come with us. We'll talk about your punishment later," said Brother Vinh. At the restaurant, we passed my group which was still waiting to be assigned to a table.

I had the best food and the most fun eating with our big brothers who encouraged me to help myself to as much as I wanted.

After the feast when we were back at camp, Nhan asked Brother Vinh to make me apologize. I didn't want to. I insisted that he had already punished me for whatever he thought I did wrong by making me walk alone in the rear.

The next day he called up a few friends to witness a court-martial in which he said he intended to shoot me dead for disobeying his order. He made me stand against the stone wall then raised his gun about fifteen yards from where I stood and pulled the trigger. I heard a blast by my left ear and a shout from Nhan at that same instant. Then Captain Nhan flew over to me, grasping my head, touching my chest, all the while asking, "Are you hurt? Where are you hurt? Why didn't you duck down? I didn't mean to hurt you!"

"I felt nothing. I'm not hurt anywhere!"

Still disbelieving, he kept asking, "Why? Why didn't you duck down?"

"I didn't think you really wanted to shoot me."

His friends were laughing. "Hey, you're lucky Nhan's not a good shot!" Nhan started laughing with them, too. I bet he never felt so good missing a target.

9

1947. MY YEAR and a half of fight-
ing in the volunteer army of Brother Vinh ended abruptly one afternoon
when our group stumbled into the clear hot sky of a green valley after
a week of trudging in the damp forest. The villagers welcomed our arrival
with a banquet befitting that of a rich landlord honoring the memory of
his deceased father. The celebrants, numbering about eight hundred,
gathered in the vast front yard of the wealthiest man in the village. Rows
of soup bowls and plates of pork and chicken meat, prepared with corn,
eggplant and melon leaves, were spread out on colorful straw mats.

Minh, Lien, and I got to sit next to our commander and his colonels.
The landlord sat next to them. Delicate antique rice bowls and ivory
chopsticks were made available for our use. After having walked seven
days and nights, under dark dripping foliage on an empty stomach, I was
immediately revived at the sight of food, which I swallowed in large
chunks with delight. I gorged myself until I couldn't blink anymore and
I was staring blankly ahead into the faces of those sitting opposite me.

It was then that my commander, Brother Vinh, asked me to sing a
song, to thank our generous host on behalf of our comrades-in-arms.

I made an effort to sing, but nothing came out of my throat. I then
tried to say that I couldn't sing. Still I could not utter a word. I was frustrated with myself and with my commander. What made him so sure that
I knew how to sing? I jumped up, nodded at the audience, hoping my gesture would be understood as an apology, and ran back in the direction
of the forest to find a bush where I could empty my stomach while
violent, twisting movements in my intestines almost took away my breath.
I sat there for a long time quietly. The shock passed. I guess it was the
reaction to my vulgar eating, or rather, my stuffing food into a shrunken

stomach which had gone seven days without it. When I returned, the unit was clearing out. I followed.

We walked until late that day into a town called Quang Ngai where we found ourselves welcomed by another army unit. There our commander was gone for a while. I spotted him when he returned. Brother Vinh was flanked by two new army men. Hesitantly, he stepped forward and, in his sad northern accent, said, "My friends. General Nguyen Son of the Viet Minh army has asked me to tell you to surrender our guns. Our unit has been dissolved. We've been asked to split up."

Dead silence fell on us who stood staring blankly at our commander.

After a brief pause, perhaps to recover from the emotional shock, my commander continued, "You may choose to join the new army, the propaganda team, or the radio station of the new Viet Minh government. The girls may go with the women's group." He lowered his voice on the last word. Then raising his right arm as if to chase away dark thoughts, he said, "I'll leave the army today, to have a medical checkup in Hanoi. I would like you to know, comrades-in-arms, the times we've had together were the dearest, happiest moments in my life. They will continue to be the most beautiful moments in my memory. You are my family, I have not known a more united family." He gave us his benign, loving smile. "By the way, you may take a month vacation before joining your new unit. Check with our friends here for the facilities and allowances. Chao cac ban [Farewell my friends]." He turned and walked abruptly away with the two strangers. I never saw him again.

I felt very sad. What did Brother Vinh and our whole company do wrong to be treated this way? I was very much at a loss — the same feeling I had had the day after the love letter scene when my mother ordered me to lie down on the punishment bed, awaiting her spanking without knowing why and when she would punish me. Looking down at the pistol hanging loosely at my right side, I whispered, "Good-bye my gun!"

I unbuttoned the belt and slipped off the holster and gun — my special reward — to end my time in the army. Our army consisted of volunteers like myself who did not have a uniform. Our guns were given to us by our commander and his assistants, who in turn got them from the defeated Japanese. We had fought the French and the Japanese for almost two years. We had survived through the courage and good sense of organization of Brother Vinh and his officers. We had lived on food supplied by compatriots who sympathized with our cause.

I felt it was unfair that we had to surrender our guns to these strangers. Nevertheless, I stepped forward to give mine to the nearest uniformed man of the other army, which was supposedly trained and supported by the government of Ho Chi Minh. Later on, I learned that General Nguyen Son had been in the small group which had led the Long March with Mao Tse Tung. But I still felt that Brother Vinh could have been just as great if he had been given the same opportunity.

Minh was behind me as I turned around. She already had a plan. "Let's go to the North to visit my sister. After than I'm going to join the radio unit." I took up the first suggestion without hesitation. The decision of joining another unit could wait until I returned.

Minh, Lien, and I were now on a train heading for Hanoi. We were sitting on a long bench alongside the wall of a wagon. The train was not crowded, except for the floor, where all kinds of commercial items in rattan baskets and bags of personal belongings were placed pell-mell in front of their owners to ensure that nobody walked away with somebody else's. An old lady smiled at me and reached into her pocket and gave me some money. I shook my head, also smiling. She frowned and pushed the money into my shirt pocket before Minh turned to us. I didn't know what to do, so I nodded and looked away. When I turned back, the lady was wiping tears with a folded brown handkerchief. She must have had a daughter who became a volunteer like me. The travellers were dozing away, their heads bobbing back and forth in harmony with the train's rhythm.

In my dream, I heard my name called, "Mai, Mai. Wake up. We've arrived."

I hardly had time to open my eyes when Minh pulled me out of my seat and began tumbling around the baskets to the open door. At the door I saw a sea of water, shining threateningly under the soft moonlight.

"See the bridge in front of us," Minh said, pushing my shoulder out of the door, her eyes indicating the grey gloomy form of a bridge which loomed ghostlike out of the water. "Soon we will approach the bridge. We don't want to go on it because my sister's house is on this side of the river," I nodded my head understandingly.

"So we're going to jump off the train."

"What? Are you crazy or something?"

"We have to do it quick. The bridge is coming near."

I looked at the dirt slope that made up the foundation for the railroad tracks — a narrow steep strip that extended to the boundless water. I was seized by a violent shudder.

"What if we can't stop and roll off down into the sea?"

"What sea?" Minh asked impatiently, her eyes following my eyes. "Oh that? It's just flood water, dummy."

I didn't want to show my ignorance. "Still. I'm not going to jump into that water, whatever it is."

"Hurry up. The bridge is here. Tell me if you have any better ideas. I'm jumping."

No sooner said than done.

"Wait!" I looked in front. The bridge was now only a few feet from me. I hung on tightly to my cloth bag and executed a clumsy dive-somersault. When I got to my feet, I found myself a mere half a foot from the edge of the water, with Lien pushing on my back. Lien always followed us so quietly that I never noticed what she was doing. The only time I heard her protest vehemently was the time Minh tried to extort her savings from her so that we could go to a café shop and eat something we liked.

That was when our unit was posted by the seaside in the rich town of Phan Thiet, known for its famous fish sauce. Minh and I had taken a walk in the marketplace. We had seen many things we wanted to eat there. We returned to base, and Minh told Lien all about it. "Let's have some fun, Lien. What do you save money for?"

"No. No. We need this money for when we get sick." There were no nurses in Brother Vinh's group. Lien always carried a tiny bottle of analgesic called Nhi Thien Duong (Second Heaven) to smell, or rub on herself or us whenever we had headaches or stomachaches.

"Who cares about your medicine anyway. We have to eat now. I promise you it won't cost us more than two pennies." But Lien wouldn't give in. Minh then walked over to the mat of Captain Gold Teeth which was spread just three feet from us. Captain Gold Teeth was having a nap.

Minh bent down and unsheathed his sword that hung at his side, awakening him. Captain Gold Teeth had barely opened his eyes when Minh placed the point of his sword in front of his nose. Minh said, "Captain Gold Teeth. We need to eat something good. Lien won't lend us the money. Give us some money or 'Whish, whish.'" The sword flew in front of Captain Gold Teeth's face. Then its point landed right at his throat.

"Enough! Enough!" Captain Gold Teeth pretended to cry out loud. "How much do you need? Don't kill me." All the officers sitting around were laughing.

"Give what you have," Minh said, smiling. He emptied out one of his pockets and let a bunch of pennies roll on the mat. Minh picked them up and slipped his sword back into its sheath. Then off we went. We spent almost all the money except for the pennies Lien had grabbed from Minh's pocket saying, "I'll save these for the Second Heaven bottles."

Lien and I were now standing at the edge of the water. Minh called us to come. We walked along the slope for what seemed a long time until finally we came to a dirt road that barely emerged above the murky sea of water. We followed the road and a long while later arrived at a village. Out of some houses, dogs ran and barked; others just came out to look at us then turned away. Minh zigzagged about in this unfamiliar land without a moment's hesitation. She walked in front, silent like a leader preoccupied with her important project of saving our lives. The road had no landmarks. Even if we had gone back three times to the same place, I would not have known — everything looked alike. At a large opening in a fence, Minh hurried through to the front of a house and up the steps onto a veranda. "You two wait here," she said, leaving us standing barefoot on the cool tiles.

A moment later I saw her walking back with a woman, naked from head to toe. Her young, full body stood erect on the steps; the milky moon waved its soft light along her shiny black hair which touched her knees and made the water spots on her body gleam gently. "My sister, Ly," Minh introduced. "I called her out of her bath in the pond."

"I didn't know you were coming," Ly said quietly. Somewhere on the other side of the veranda a baby cried. She hurried to it, with us behind her. She raised the baby up to her left breast and applied the nipple to the baby's mouth, which sucked greedily as if it had been starved for years. A man in the kitchen directly below the balustrade brought his oil lamp above his head to check in our direction. I saw drops of milk trickling out of the other nipple.

Turning to the light, which was quickly brought down, I caught a strange expression in the man's eyes — one of contempt and at the same time shyness. Apparently the peasant was one of the poor relatives who got to live in the kitchen to guard the house of Minh's parents and grandparents. Of course he was not accustomed to seeing naked women running around in public. In the old times, they could be sent to be "stampeded by elephants" as the people in North and Central Vietnam would say.

"Brother-in-law is not going to come home," Ly said. "He has some important job with the comrades north of here. So just spread out a straw mat and sleep next to me. It's prettier out here with the moon." Ly had a northern accent, although she had lived in the South most of her life. She asked Minh about news of their parents, whom Minh confessed not to have seen since she and Ly had left to join the army — each going to their favorite unit.

When morning came, we left the house to catch the bus (free for army people) to Hanoi, the old capital of Vietnam. We got off at a residential corner, and Lien and I followed Minh to a villa where we entered and saw a man whom Minh called "Comrade" busy writing on the blackboard. He turned around to answer Minh who introduced us as her "comrades" and asked for a place to stay for the night. He seemed pleased and surprised by our southern accent and quasi-army clothes. "Little sisters, greetings from Hanoi. You can go upstairs, and take any room that you see empty or just push aside what you see on the bed and make yourselves at home."

We got up late the next morning and heard from a young man who stayed in the bedroom opposite ours that we could have free breakfast in the villa next door. We each had a bowl of *pho* (rice noodles with beef in hot spicy broth topped with fresh leaves of basil and cilantro) for the first time in our lives. The delicious aroma filled our nostrils the minute we walked in the door.

A man came in and said to the group of guests, "We must hurry. Uncle Ho is going to be at the meeting in the square a block from here." We arrived late to the spectacle, so we had to watch from afar, perched high on a fence on a street corner. What I heard that day was not clear to me, but I saw Ho Chi Minh, a tall lanky man in khaki uniform, his long beard reaching down to his chest. The wind blew his thin beard to one side and carried his resonant voice across a sea of city people, handsomely bundled in smartcoats. I was immediately moved by the warm, eloquent voice. Uncle Ho was standing all alone, tall and thin, on the huge platform in the huge open Ba Dinh Square.

On that fall morning, Uncle Ho, with his long white beard, had the look of a venerable grandfather, a look which inspired love and trust. His simple military jacket reminded me of my days of walking in the rain and cold, with leeches that crawled up to my bottom and armpits. I remembered how they itched and hurt, but I could not stop to get rid of them. The line of guerrillas had to keep moving in the dark to escape detection by French troops. Ho Chi Minh's deep-set eyes, when they looked in our direction, gave me the feeling of a desperate man with a big heart, appealing for love and sympathy from his countrymen, our countrymen. "Share, share," the eyes seemed to call out. "Give, give; your people need you; your country needs you. Your land is being devoured by the savages. Give, share, save your suffering motherland."

With my deep-rooted French education, my heart began to sing "La Marseillaise" while listening to the anti–French exhortations of Ho Chi Minh's speech: "Allons enfants de la patrie..." In my mind "la patrie" became Vietnam, and Uncle Ho, with his weather-beaten yet respectable look of a Confucian scholar, appeared to blend in well with my vision of a traditional Vietnam. Suddenly my reverie was interrupted by the thunderous wild applause that greeted the end of Ho Chi Minh's speech. Women took out their handkerchiefs to wipe their tears. Minh turned, and we looked at each other's red, wet eyes. Empty milk cans were passed from hand to hand above the people's heads. Arms were raised, and gold bracelets, rings, earrings, and other jewels were stripped off by their owners and dropped into the cans.

After the demonstration, Minh, Lien, and I walked towards the market. On the way, we saw corpses on the curbs and piled up in carts pulled by haggard men dressed in rags. The bodies, dying or already dead from starvation or bitter cold during the night had scarcely a ragged piece of dirty pyjamas for cover. I began to understand what the cook had said in our shelter over a year ago: "The Japanese took our rice to make fuel to run their trucks and let our people starve."

The war among the Japanese, French, and Vietnamese broke out right after that, so there had been no time to grow rice and no means of transportation to bring it from the South. Besides, everybody it seemed had gone into the army or was busy with the national cause. There was no production.

The difference now was that the Japanese soldiers were replaced by Chinese soldiers in filthy uniforms, with guns dangling from their shoulders and their feet dragging while they roamed in groups of threes and fours all over the streets in front of shops and houses. I wondered where they came from.

Before the main entrance to the market, we met with row after row of baskets full of fresh ready-made food. Whenever customers checked the hot pots kept inside the baskets, delicious aromas escaped. We stopped to look in with the customers and to inhale the enticing vapors. In the middle of our entertainment, we were interrupted by a loud voice. We turned and saw a crowd immediately forming in that direction. Curious, we walked over and weaved our way into the inner circle to get a good look. In the center stood a beautiful lady wearing a peach-colored silk dress and white satin pants. In her high-heel clogs, she stood as tall as the Chinese soldier who was holding a handful of steamy cakes. The owner of the food basket — a peasant in a long black dress — was voicing her complaint to the crowd: "He told me to sell him the cakes. Then he tried to walk away with the cakes. Oh God Almighty, can you see my misery. He stole the food of my children. He robbed my livelihood. God who has eyes, please see!"

I almost laughed at the complaint, so lengthy and rhythmic as if she were reciting a poem. A southerner would have just said, "Hey, give it back to me!" then prepared for a fight.

92

The Chinese soldier's tiny eyes peered at the peasant. When she reached out to take the cakes, he jerked back his hand, barking a mean "Ho" to scare her. The peasant dropped her hands. The soldier turned to walk away.

"You. Stop!"

The beautiful lady shouted her order while her hand swiftly lashed at his face and gave it a terrific slap, making a sharp, dry sound. "You dirty scum. Give back her food. They brought you here to disarm the Japanese, and all that you scum do is loot and steal."

The Chinese soldier raised his hand to touch the red spot left by the slap. Then his hand moved to the strap of the gun on his shoulder. Someone in the crowd stepped forward. Then the whole crowd advanced, tightening the circle.

The Chinese soldier looked at their faces, then threw the cakes down onto the basket. He turned around, shuffling toward the crowd which let him pass then dispersed silently a second later. He left behind a pungent odor — the smell of sweaty, dirty feet wrapped too long inside dirty, wet shoes.

We also turned to go. I was full of admiration for the lady. I wondered if I would dare to act the way she did. I had been taught not to resist older people and not to show my emotions so openly. Still, when I grew older, would I be able to fight for someone the way she did? I didn't think so. I was too tame, not as feminine, articulate, and passionate as she. I felt sure her way would never become mine. This brought me to admire her all the more.

Back at the Center, Minh recounted the incident to the man who sat by the door working on some propaganda papers. She wanted to know why the Chinese were there.

"You see," he said, "right after the defeat of Japan, at the request of the Allies, the Americans agreed to let the British go back to India, and the French to Indochina. Also, at the request of Chiang Kai-shek, through the recommendation of the American representative in Shanghai, the Americans agreed for the Kuomintang Chinese to disarm the Japanese in North and Central Vietnam. Chiang gave the mission to a self-appointed Chinese border general — a warlord named Lu Han. This warlord brought in his own troops and their wives, children, parents, and relatives — whoever could make the trip. They descended on North Vietnam like locusts, eating and stealing everything on their way."

"I thought the Americans were on our side," I said, remembering my Viet Minh leader of the organization Women to Save the Country, who called America the "Beautiful Country."

93

"They were when we were fighting against the Japanese. Back then they parachuted their O.S.S. [Office of Strategic Services, precursor of the CIA] men into our *maquis* [the guerrilla areas] of Cao Bang, Lang Son, to train our soldiers and supplied us with weapons to resist the Japanese." He paused and shook his head in sorrow, "It's a long and complicated story. All that I can tell you is that we thought the Americans who had fought the British for their independence would understand our situation and support our cause." He sighed.

"The O.S.S. men were good men. We read and learned their constitution through them. But when the war against the Japanese was over, they told us their government no longer wanted to help us, in order to please their close allies, the French and the British."

"Were you with them in the *maquis?*" I asked. The speaker looked at me without answering. The man in the background said, "Yes, he was. He got wounded there."

The speaker continued, "We learned later that they suspected our leader, Ho Chi Minh, would lead us all into the Communist system. But that was just their excuse. The French were closer to them; they listened to them more often, that's all." He suddenly lifted his chin. His eyes and mouth showed bitterness and anger. "Our leaders were killed or led to be killed one by one by the French or the pro–French governments. No countries supported our cause except for Russia and Communist China. Uncle Ho only did what Tito had done—got the training and recognition from Russia. But even Russia did not give him any guns to fight with. Those colonialists accused us of going with the Communists, but they themselves went in with Communist Russia to make the Allies of Four!" Then, waving his hand as if resisting being forced back, he said angrily, "But what do we care. It's our country. Fight for it. Fight to the last drop of our blood."

"We fought for almost two years!" I thought, catching his bitter mood—the picture of the frail, helpless dead lady and her baby vivid in my memory. Many of us to the last drop of our blood. We got nowhere, only more confused.

For the first time, I realized the meaning of the word problem. Before, a problem had been something like a math problem. Read the question and line up the given factors in the right order, and the right answer would present itself. Not so with this life problem. Now I found out. My life problem seemed to be Vietnam. And I felt it as such an immense problem, so vague, so uncontrollable. Just an hour before, the dead bodies I had seen in the streets were the fault of the Japanese, who had taken all the rice in Vietnam to make gasoline substitutes. But then I remembered our Japanese advisor, who had taught us how to spy on our enemies, including his own countrymen, the Japanese. He was a gentle and sincere person, and only allowed himself to handle the tough jobs.

And now Vietnam's enemy was no longer the cruel, organized Japanese, but these corrupt Chinese who looted and stole and printed their own paper money to force us to sell our businesses, properties, and women. This I heard in the background from a man who sat leisurely at a nearby table.

To fight our enemy, we not only needed people with good will but also with money to buy guns and feed the soldiers. The man in the background was saying that Uncle Ho had not taken the money from the French Bank of Indochina where he had posted his guards. He was waiting for the day he could show to the world, and specifically to the Americans, the dignity of the Vietnamese—that he was a man of integrity—a characteristic trait of the Confucian scholar that the Vietnamese admired and revered. This might help the Americans to change their mind about supporting the French.

"All washed away like water on taro leaves," the man said with a sigh. "But I loved Uncle Ho for that." I thought that was what my father would have done. The collection at Ba Dinh Square this morning was necessary for the Revolution.

To think back, Uncle Ho may have had another reason. The French money would have been of no use to an independent Vietnam, and it would have been of no use to him if the French had returned, because they would have just printed out new money to exchange for the old discarded currency. It would have been hazardous for the Vietnamese to have to identify themselves in the exchange. Any gold in the bank would have been taken away by the French or the Japanese long before we could have gotten our hands on it.

Still, in the eyes of his admirers, Ho was an "honorable" leader, never mixed up in money matters or corruption. He personified the exemplary Vietnamese leader and scholar for the rest of his life.

Minh, Lien, and I stayed at the Center for two days. Meanwhile, I remembered my father had a brother who was a director for the railroads and whose two sons had come to visit us in Bien Hoa some years ago. We asked around for his family. We found their house on a street of two-story homes. My oldest cousin, about twenty-seven, had his dental office in the front room that was supposed to be the living room. He greeted us and told us to move in and stay with them during our vacation.

The first two days were miserable. My uncle was very ill, so I didn't get to see him. We ate at a long table that was placed in the garage, which seemed to have become the family room. There were two other cousins, one a pharmacist, the other, the youngest, a university student. They sat and ate quietly. Nobody talked. They read their newspapers for hours, scrutinizing every word it seemed. Their aunt, my father's sister, would walk in and out of the kitchen and up and down the stairs without a sound.

During the day, Minh, Lien, and I went out to explore the town a bit. On the second evening, after dark, we had just finished eating when my aunt came in and told me that my uncle wanted to see me. On the way upstairs, she added that my uncle might die that night, so I should try to stay with him as long as possible.

Until he spoke, my uncle's face looked like that of a ghost under the dim electric light. He was breathing heavily, but as soon as he began to talk, he became lively. He talked to me as if I were his equal. He told me that he was disappointed with his children—the cousins I had so much respect for. "I would not be surprised if they should end up getting shot in the back by their own people before they got a chance to fight against their country's enemies." He continued with urgency, "You see the way they behave at the table? They either shout at one another or sit gloomily as if they were at a funeral. They eat with their newspapers in front of their faces! Since independence, three months ago, we have had more men assassinated than the whole time we were under the French. Members of one party get killed by another's party members or by their own members. Such a waste." He sadly shook his head, "You may not know that each of your cousins has joined a different party. Your first cousin belongs to the Democratic party. They are mostly young professionals and university students." He shrugged, "Relatively nonviolent. Your second cousin joined the Viet Minh in the *maquis*. He went back with them, slightly wounded, to declare Vietnam's independence." My uncle looked tired and sighed with exasperation. A minute later he continued, "Your youngest cousin goes with the Vietnamese Kuomintang, trained and supported by the Chinese. But the Chinese that you see here now are not from his party. You will draw the conclusion yourself. I don't trust the Chinese. I am afraid for my country! Lucky I have only three children. If I had five more, I would have five more political parties in my house, one pro–Japanese, one pro–Third International, etc.

He closed his eyes again. This time out of disgust, I thought, for quickly he added, "They think this old man does not know anything, hm? This old man, their own father!" As in a dream, I heard his voice slowly continuing, "I understand they must do something. The pain of the

96

country is like the wounded heart of a man and the people like parts of his body. A wounded heart threatens the life of all parts, and each must react according to its capacity and liking. But our independence is too young and still not recognized by other countries! Mai, I tell you this because you are young. You're sixteen now, aren't you? They may get killed, but you may survive. Open your eyes. Learn. Don't make the same mistake . . . if you love your country."

When he appeared to fall asleep, I dozed off on the chair by his bed. That night he died in my presence, and I didn't even know it.

10

A FEW DAYS later, Minh and I left Hanoi to go back to Quang Ngai, the town south of Hue, where we had been disarmed. Lien remained in Hanoi and later married my youngest cousin. Minh went to a propaganda unit that sang national songs on the radio and performed plays depicting Vietnamese heroes fighting against French colonialism. I decided to join General Son's army, thinking I might be more useful in the army than in a singing group. A week later, I was picked by the leader of the women's unit to get my first political training in Da Nang with her.

Our training took one to two weeks. We were the only women in the class.

That Sunday morning, I went to a Catholic church near our training center. At the end of the mass attended only by two other elderly persons, the priest greeted me and invited me to his quarters. While waiting for him to take care of some business, I sat at the piano and struck a few notes, those that I had learned from my sister's piano lessons. (My mother hadn't thought I was old enough to spend money on.)

The priest came to me and said, "You must be from a good family of class. What are you doing here by yourself?"

I told him about my training. He was disturbed. He gave me some cookies and told me to stay around for a while. Later he came in and told me with a serious air that this was not a place for me and that I should go home to my family.

"I can't," I said. "I can't walk back there." I thought of all the mountains I had crossed and the dangerous towns full of enemies I had gone through as a spy.

He lowered his voice, "There is a French ship that is due here soon.

I can arrange to have you on board, so stay around and come back to see me now and then." I sat quietly for a minute, then bade him good-bye. I wasn't about to do something as silly as that. Get on a French ship? Get my enemy's help?

On our last day of training, there was a test in which we were expected to illustrate the weaknesses of Plato's philosophy and capitalism versus the strengths of Descartes and communism. I remember ending my analysis based on what I had been taught in the training, but with a comment against Descartes, who seemed to believe in his own power — "I think therefore I am" — rather than in God's, and for Plato, who believed in God and right and wrong in society. I had no idea what these philosophies really meant. I only knew I was not going to let them think that I was already absorbed by their communism. I was a patriot, and that was all.

When I got back to Mr. Son's camp, I was called up to his office to see him. It was the first time we met. (General Son was called "Ong Son," Mr. Son, instead of Brother Son because he looked much older than all of us. Also, there wasn't supposed to be any rank in the Communist régime.) "Oh. So it was you. I got the report from your training class in Da Nang. They said you were not enthusiastic about our party's teaching?" When I said nothing he went on, "But, it's all right. It takes time to understand, and you are young." He then opened his drawer and pulled out a bunch of Catholic rosaries and said, "I received this from a priest who said to give these to a little girl who brought her friends to attend mass at his church some weeks ago. Was that you?" He smiled. I nodded.

He was referring to an incident before my training trip, when I had happened to see a small church, entered, and found a priest saying mass with a little altar boy. No attendants. The priest had stopped the mass to ask who I was and where I lived. I told him I was with Mr. Son's army and asked why nobody was attending mass. "People are scared that they might get their heads chopped off if they go to mass. The people's organizations here think the church is allied with the French and the rich people, who were their oppressors in the past."

He continued after a silence, "Tomorrow is Sunday. If you have any Catholic friends bring them to mass. I'll serve at nine."

I went home and contacted Nhan, my former army captain, and two girls, my new acquaintances who were also Catholics. They came with me to mass the following day simply because I told them that our church was deserted. I guess the priest had sent us the rosaries to encourage us to attend his mass.

Ong Son gave the four rosaries with black beads to me and asked, "What would you want to have at this moment?" I happened to be standing by the window. My eyes looked down to the concrete court one story below. I smiled and said, "Nothing." He went to the window and looked at what had made me smile. It was the food vendor who was selling to the soldiers her steamy hot goodies from her two baskets.

"The food looks good. Makes you want to have some, doesn't it?" I nodded. He pulled out a bunch of bills from his pocket and stuffed them into my shirt pocket. "Go enjoy yourself," he said rubbing my head.

At that time, I wore my hair down, letting it hang naturally past my shoulders. Nobody had cut my hair since I joined the army. One day, mingling in a Women's Center among a group of girls my older sister's age, a girl touched my hair and said in a low voice so that the others could not hear her, "Your hair is very long and nice. Don't you have to cut it short like us?" They all wore very short hair, above their ears, and I thought it was their style.

"We have no barbers in the army," I replied.

"Your are lucky!" she said with envy. "My hair was very long, to my waist. I liked it long, but right after the revolution we were ordered to cut our hair short. The girls who didn't obey were caught by our organization and shaved to look like monks."

"Why?"

"We are supposed to be equal to men, look like them, act like them. No time to waste on combing hair and washing in lemon and *chum-ket* [a type of bean-like fruit that gives suds like soap when boiled; women used it as shampoo to keep their hair shiny]. We belong to the Communist party. We don't like intellectuals nor rich people. They are traitors to Vietnam." Her eyes reddened, and a moist film covered them. She said, "I am surprised Mr. Son lets you have your hair long. I shouldn't be, though. It was Mr. Son and his army that moved in and saved us from massacre among ourselves." She invited me to her house for lunch. Her mother was dressed in peasant clothes, but her manners were those of the comfortable rich. Vegetables and dried fish were served in beautiful antique bowls and plates. The father was not there. In the middle of our meal two men walked in and saluted us with a casual, "Hi sisters."

The mother suddenly lost her natural authority as boss of the house. She politely invited them to stay and have lunch with us, but they declined, stood around, talked to each other, and then bid us good-bye.

"They saw me bring back a new friend, so they wanted to find out who it was. They were surprised to see a soldier, so they left." My new friend shrugged; she looked pleased with the surprise she had brought them. As we left her house to return to the Center, she took me through the backyard to a fence. She pointed to a nice piece of stone and said, "This is in memory of my father killed during the revolution. He belonged to the rich class. We could not take his body back and could not worship him in the house, so we put a piece of uncarved stone here to pray in secret."

As if my long hair had given her confidence and made me closer to her, she confided in me later, "One of the men you met was a helper in our house. He used to call my mother Respectable Elderly. Now he calls her the common name, 'Sister.' I think he was in the group who took my father away."

I was very puzzled but kept quiet.

My mission after my training was to mingle with women's organizations. Later, I was sent to the countryside to organize peasant women. I did my rounds effortlessly: I talked and talked, ate and slept, and moved from village to village. Now and then I wrote or read a speech requested by someone higher up in rank. I followed the pattern of my two-week training to organize women in groups of three called cells, to ask them to report their problems and encourage group discussion concerning all aspects of their lives. I helped them to learn how to read and write, told them about our great women leaders — the Trung Sisters (A.D. 40–43) and Mrs. Trieu Au (A.D. 248) who had led armies of men against the Chinese — and reminded them of the pride and worth of their farmer and artisan classes. All this information had been unknown to me before the training class. For example, at the time of the Trung Sisters, the Chinese called us "Bach Viet." We called ourselves "Lac Viet," our Hanoi, "Co Loa." We made buffalo yokes, scythes, knives, and axes in copper and traded our famous Ngoc Lu bronze drums, sixty-three centimeters tall and seventy-nine centimeters in diameter, artistically carved with the sun in the middle surrounded by sunrays and sixteen circles depicting nature, animals, and men at work and play. We cooked in symmetrical earthen pots, and used decorated ceramics and old bamboo trunks for containers.

After a short period of doing this work, a man from "high up" came to the village where I was working by the seaside and told me to read a speech he had written about me and my joining the army. It was an invented piece, for he had never met me nor heard my story from me personally. But I had learned to identify these *chanh tri vien* or political organizers who promoted themselves through the ranks through works of this type: making speeches, organizing meetings, and advising on political decisions for the villagers who were mostly illiterate and ignorant of the happenings outside of their villages. A "high-up" was an ambitious city man who could read and write and had been exposed to political events. The speech was a piece of propaganda to let the poor peasants know that there were many like myself, of good background, who fought on their side. The peasants came to me after the speech and cried on my shoulders. I was very moved; they treated me as if I were a hero who had saved their lives. Poor people, I thought, they believe in you, they believe in a good cause, they even believe in a piece of paper that they can't read. I'd better not let them down. Then I thought of the helper in my new friend's house, and I felt that they had been betrayed and that I had been betrayed by men like him. I cried with them.

During one of my village meetings I met a friend of Bright Moon who told me that Bright Moon had been wounded in the thigh by the French during an ambush. She was now recuperating in a village with the group of army men who had stayed back to rescue her and had been separated from the rest of their outfit.

The village was only a day's walk from mine. I informed my group that I needed a few days off to see my sister.

There were no maps nor street signs in the countryside. I just followed where the villagers pointed their fingers and the trail on the narrow dirt dam which separated immense rice fields. I arrived at the seashore in the late afternoon. The heat there was unbearable, and the whole place seemed to be nothing but sand and soil which was packed like cement on the fields. The peasants here were very poor.

Finally I located Bright Moon. She was glad to see me. She described how the bullet had been removed. (Although she and her friends were called "nurses," they actually only knew how to clean and dress wounds.) She had suffered with her leg swollen for days before an eastern medicine man came, gave her a large dose of rice wine to make her pass out, and used a long, sharp bamboo stick to push the bullet out through her flesh. She had been crying when I first saw her, and she began crying again after she finished describing her wound. I asked if it was still very painful, but she replied that she was not crying about her injury. She cried for her friend, Hung—"our friend," she said, "because he said he liked you, too. He was murdered this morning by the villagers not far from here. He who had felt sorry for their lot—'Such miseries, such injustice,' he repeatedly said." She sighed. "He hardly talked, but he would often show surprise at the boy who rode half naked on the muddy buffalo under the burning sun or the old man who bent his bony back over the dry furrows."

Our friend Hung, the one who had let me ride the horse, had switched to my sister's camp to be among the students' group. Born to a rich family in Hanoi, he had only seen the countryside when he visited his vacation house and his horses. He had never noticed or heard of hunger, or knew of destitution, until the wake of the revolution when he volunteered with other young northerners to go south in the hope of liberating the poor and suffering South Vietnamese from the French colonialists.

A week ago, he had been transferred to a small town a few villages away. Then, yesterday, someone at the headquarters said he had heard that there would be a people's tribunal in the neighboring village to sentence a young man named Hung. My sister's group was appalled. They tried to send word to their captain who was on a mission so that he could come to Hung's rescue. But they had not heard from him, and now it was too late.

"What did Hung do wrong?" I asked.

"They said he was ordered to guard a building in town where the administration kept their prisoners, but he released the prisoners when the French returned to reoccupy."

"Why did he do that?"

"According to what I heard, the prisoners, some old men and women and some young people like him implored him to release them when they heard the fierce shooting. They all told him they hadn't committed any crimes. They had been put in prison because their compatriots misunderstood them — thought that they had been too close to the French before and that they had land and exploited their poor countrymen. This was not true, they claimed. They were also anti–French and would be killed by the French when they arrived. Since he had been left alone to guard the prison, there was nobody to consult. He opened the prison door to let them run for their lives. After the French ransacked the village and took some followers with them, the peasants returned to their village. Some gathered to accuse Hung of being a traitor: 'A traitor must die as a warning to his fellow men,' they said."

A friend of my sister's, a former medical student, walked in just then.

Absorbed in the story, I asked, "Do you think Hung was a traitor, doing what he did?"

His face turned from joy at seeing my sister to pain. "We tried to tell the people he was a good man and that he must have thought that was his best and most patriotic deed. But the people voted him guilty. We didn't know what was involved in the tribunal court and what was going to happen after the verdict until they buried him alive this morning."

My sister shrieked, then dropped sideways, fainting on the wooden bed. Her girlfriends, two other nurses, rushed in and asked us to leave the premises. My sister was the youngest among them and they babied her a lot. They blamed us for upsetting her. Apparently Bright Moon had not known that Hung had been brutally buried alive. In any case, she had always been pampered at home, too. I was used to it.

Her friend Tam and I walked to the haystack in the front yard. I could see he was very much shaken by the morning scene and wanted to talk some more. He told me that he had gone to the tribunal place "incognito." A peasant had turned to look at him. He remembered the man's ruddy face. It was in his house that they, including Hung, had been invited to stay and recuperate some weeks before. The man's normally dull eyes suddenly emitted a strange coldness mingled with hatred which froze him for a second. Then he quickly turned his gaze to the center of the crowd and his eyes met Hung's, who furtively averted them. The three men and woman who stood behind Hung had the most expressionless faces he had ever seen. The averted look of his friend warned him of danger. He followed his instincts and backed away from the crowd.

He could still see Hung standing stiffly in his white shirt and black pants. The villagers had taken away his uniform in order to justify the jurisdiction of the people's court over him. An expressionless voice rose from the group of "judges" behind Hung.

Tam saw Hung begin to shift his weight from one leg to the other. Then he looked up to the sky, bit his lips, and said, "I wish. . ." he stopped, then said louder, "I wish to thank my friends who have come here today. If they ever meet my parents, please let them know I died while serving our cause."

His head dropped at the end of the sentence. The man behind him had struck him with a spade. He fell into the hole in front of him. Then the gathering villagers were called to help shovel dirt over him.

"I don't understand it," I said, after recovering from the shock. "What are we here for? Aren't you brothers supposed to be the ones who came to help them, to enlighten them? How is it that now they are in control over you?"

"Brother Sang," Tam called out to a man who was about to walk into a hut. "He is the philosopher and a party member. He is a good man. I'll let him answer you."

Brother Sang slid across the court. He was thin and tall and seemed to glide over the ground. We greeted each other, and he plopped down onto the hay beside me, his legs extended leisurely.

"Mai has a question for you. What are we here for? We who thought we were fighting for the poor, the oppressed! We were wondering who were really the oppressed." His voice sounded sarcastic.

"You're referring to this morning," Brother Sang said, then silence.

I felt that Tam was bothered by the same question I had and was using me to get Sang to answer.

With his long fingers, Brother Sang touched my head. "Good girl. I had wondered myself." He changed his comfortable position, drew his knees to his face, and remained sitting huddled that way for some time. Then he spoke in a soft, sad voice.

"Hung was unjustly killed this morning and you think the peasants hate you—they don't deserve to be your equals." His words turned into a stream of thought: "Life is certainly complicated. Sometimes it's easier to accept than to question. Things come so fast one has not time to think out and judge; it would be best then to go along lest one be left alone to fight the lonely struggle." It seemed as if he were trying to solve his own problem while talking. He continued his discourse as if to himself, and I vaguely absorbed it as in a dream. "I don't think those farmers hate us or wanted Hung's life. You see, farmers are simple people. They have lived a life surrounded with nature too powerful for them to understand; therefore they have learned to quit questioning. Suddenly someone comes along. You. Us. We claim to have read books, seen better worlds. The new world we promise them is bright with glory, abundance. Plentiful seeds to grow, acres of land to cultivate, seas of golden rice stems, and schools for their children to give them brighter futures—these our rich and learned compatriots will share with them, for we are equal citizens and are entitled to equal opportunities. It is no longer as it was in the old world where the rich abused the poor to stay rich, the learned profited from the ignorant, and the state of scarcity was due to someone else's abundance."

I turned to look at Brother Sang with admiration. His words flowed like a river, modest yet forceful.

My attention must have interrupted his thoughts, for he broke the regular rhythm of his voice and changed to a loud, affirmative pitch.

"I say it was not hatred that you saw in those eyes. It was a look of confusion, madness mingled with ignorance and powerlessness. Those farmers believed our preachings. But when we came, we came empty-handed and relied on them to work and feed us. And we brought along the French, who stampeded their land, killed innocent people, and created hatred between the pro–French and the pro-nobody. They felt they had been deceived. Before, they were their own masters in the fields, with their ancestors as their spiritual guides and their ancestors' experiences as their religion. To them, their knowledge was as complete and unquestionable as the fact that black clouds bring rain and roosters crow when the sun rises. Out of nowhere came the intellectuals who

105

degraded their knowledge, defied their God, questioned their ancestors' wisdom. Born humble and obedient to destiny, they were not equipped or prepared to react. Obey and go along were their only weapons for survival." He whispered as if to Hung's soul, "Don't blame them for what they are. . . ."

I returned to my village having lost my sense of belonging.

11

SOME WEEKS after my return, Minh came with her propaganda team. She told me that she had just been to Hanoi and had accidentally met my father. "Your three sisters were there. They looked poor and unhealthy. Your father said he had come all the way from Saigon to look for you."

I thought about it that night, and when morning came, I went back to the town of Quang Ngai to see Mr. Son. "Sir, I wish to ask your permission to visit my parents." A pause.

"You are able to contact them?"

"Yes sir. My father and my sisters are in Hanoi, staying with my cousins."

"I could arrange for you to come with us. We have a meeting in Hanoi in a few days," he said, touching his beard pensively.

Two days later, a chauffeur drove us in an old Citroën. I sat in front with the chauffeur. Mr. Son and two "comrades" sat in the back. I had with me a pair of grey trousers, a blue shirt, and the navy blue jacket that the soldier had given to me from the ransacked French villa—a souvenir from my army days. Except for Saigon, the cool mount of Dalat, Cap St. Jacques, and Nha Trang with its blue Cam Ranh Bay, our countryside and cities were now temporarily "independent" from the French and other legal administrations.

After two days of travelling, we arrived in Hanoi. The streets of Hanoi were now clear of Chinese soldiers. Shops were reopened, and there were no hungry, dying people lying around. I walked from Mr. Son's office to my uncle's house. At the gate I saw my three sisters playing inside on the concrete backyard. They had grown very fast. I walked toward them with a strange feeling of joy as if I was holding something fragile and dear against my heart. But what had happened to their eyes! — they were swollen and red. They told me that they had been on a French ship a long time without much water or proper hygiene. I looked through the window into the house and saw my father walking toward me, thin in poorly fitting clothes.

A feeling like something sharp caused a pain in my heart, a feeling intense and deep, unlike what I had experienced when I saw my soldier friends killed or wounded comrades suffer — a helpless feeling that sank deep into my being and stayed locked within. I sensed it in my father: despair. I had read about it in my *Livres Roses* stories, but now I felt it for the first time. My mother was still in Saigon with my three brothers. I decided right then and there I had to quit the army and go home. My family desperately needed my help.

When I did not return to headquarters as I was told, Mr. Son sent a friend of mine from the "spy" group in the army to give me a train ticket to return to Quang Ngai if I could not catch him in time for his return to the South. I returned the ticket and told my friend I had quit the army. Helping my sisters and being near my father was more useful than making speeches and organizing women. They would immediately send somebody else to take my place anyway.

That Saturday, my sisters and I strolled to the Lake of the Returning Sword (Ho Hoan Kiem). The northerners seemed to know their history far better than the southerners. I had once heard my mother telling her friends about this lake in the old capital (named Thang Long at the time). She said that the legend of the Returning Sword was connected to the history of the revolt of Le Loi. In the early fifteenth century, when Vietnam was under Chinese occupation, which lasted on and off for nearly ten centuries, there came from the mountain region of the province of Thanh Hoa a peasant leader, Le Loi. He rallied around him the best scholars and strategists, among them the genius of Nguyen Trai, and after ten years of fighting drove the Chinese invaders out of Vietnam once and for all. Le Loi founded the Le dynasty in 1428. It was said that a golden turtle surfaced on the Lake and brought Le Loi the magic sword he used to expel the Ming Chinese troops from Vietnam. Then the turtle reappeared and reclaimed the sword which was returned to the lake.

Pedestrians crowded one side of the lake walkway. From afar one could see a flow of colorful dresses floating on the cement walk laced with trees in full blossom, white, pink, and yellow. A wide strip of green lawn separated the rows of flowering trees from the dark green water. Willow trees and purple orchid-like flowers embroidered the lakeshore. Walking on the six-foot-wide curb, I could see a line of elegant shop windows across the boulevard.

"So pretty," Kim Van (Golden Cloud), my nine-year-old sister, said, giggling and picking up the tiny flowers that fell on my six-year-old sister, Blue Water. "Like confetti," Soft Breeze, my five-year-old sister, wriggled with delight. "Tickles! Tickles!" cried Blue Water. (Being a poet, my mother named us after the sceneries of nature.)

Two girls, tall in their thick wooden clogs, were approaching from behind. One wore a long velvet cape over a long velvet dress of reddish brown color; the other a silk dress of egg-yolk color (hand-woven in Ha Dong, a province near Hanoi). They sauntered by. The girl with the velvet cape had black hair down to her waistline, clipped with a small tortoiseshell bar halfway down its length. The girl with the Ha Dong dress wore her hair a few inches past her shoulders. They were smiling.

Walking about three feet behind them were two boys in navy blue trousers and dark pullovers. I heard one say: "Beautiful like flowers! Flowers on her hair, flowers on her shoulders, flowers in my hand." He lifted his hand to catch a flower dropping off the branch above him. "No flower is as pretty as the one in front of me."

A glow of affection and embarrassment filled my heart. I turned and headed for the lake with my sisters at my heels.

On the way, we came across a group of three girls trying to reach an orchid-like flower hanging over their heads. They were reaching, laughing, and pulling back and forth. "Oh, please let us help you." I turned to see two men, smartly dressed in Western clothes, smiling and running across the lawn toward the girls. The girls changed their laughing to shy giggling. One man picked the lowest flower; the other tried to reach another branch. "We'll get three flowers for the three pretty misses." They all laughed, and the men led the conversation about the flowers, the willows, the autumn water.

"We are fortunate to have flowers all year around," one girl was saying.

"So you like flowers, I see," one of the men said tenderly.

"Very much," another girl said. At this time I was already away from the group and could only hear the rhythm of a poem being recited by one of the men. I wanted to lead my younger sisters away so that they could not hear the romantic conversation, which I thought might plant wrong ideas in their innocent heads. It was something I did out of impulse, without knowing why. As for myself, I experienced the pleasant feeling of one who had just heard and seen gentle affection in person. People in the South expressed their affection mostly with short, simple, direct words

109

or childish teasing. As for my family, everything there went by the rules, rules that my mother seemed to apply quietly and relentlessly, regulating the interactions between husband and wife, parents and kids, masters and servants, and the dealings between people at home and outsiders.

I remembered an incident that happened when I was eleven. I used to hide under the huge desk where my mother sat late into the night composing poems and crying quietly, blowing her nose into her handkerchief. I assumed she was writing poems, because I heard her read and correct them now and then. My father was stationed away in Saigon at the time, and my mother was expecting her seventh child. She looked heavy, couldn't do much, and didn't see much of her friends. She must have missed my father, and I guess she wrote the poems to entertain herself.

Weeks passed, but my mother continued to be sad. One Thursday afternoon, she went to Saigon for her medical checkup. Having no school, I was playing in the living room where Chi Sau, the maid, was dusting the furniture with the front door wide open. She said she liked plenty of light when she dusted and polished so she could see the bright shine brought forth by her work.

Suddenly, a woman appeared in the doorway and sat down in the armchair closest to the door. She told Chi Sau to bring her a cup of tea. Chi Sau took a second look at the lady then quietly disappeared behind the side door. From the corner of my eye, I noticed that the lady had shoulder-length curly black hair. Her face was ivory white, like my sister's, but older looking. She wore no makeup except for red lipstick. She looked tall and pretty in her white embroidered blouse and long black satin pants. The lady looked around at the sofa, the ceramic vases, and the thick, glossy books — my father's collection of picture books on Napoleon and French royal families. A swift turn of her head brought her gaze directly to me. She frowned and ordered, "Take me to your mom's dressing table."

My eyes opened wide in shock, while at the same time I was considering what to do. Fortunately for me, at that moment I heard my father's voice coming from the same place the lady had stood.

"No, you can't go in there."

The lady looked around, perplexed. "Why not? I need to clean up, to comb my hair." My father answered cooly, "You cannot go into my wife's room."

He walked past her and through the swinging door. I heard the clicking sound of the lock on his bedroom door.

"Bring a brush. I need to brush my hair," the lady said to me, more a request now than an order. I didn't know what a hairbrush looked like. Everybody in our house had straight hair. We didn't brush our hair; we combed it.

"We don't have a brush," I said.

"What a house! Go find me an adult that I can talk to." I felt relieved. I hurried out of the room to fetch Old Nurse. Old Nurse didn't seem surprised to hear about the visitor. Chi Sau must have told her. She even looked glad to take part in the scene, for she went off in a hurry.

I stayed behind, trying to figure out what was going on while swinging playfully in the hammock where Old Nurse had been napping. It was Old Nurse's hammock. She had it hung across the garage whenever the Citroën was gone (this happened quite often because my father was always away during weekdays). Old Nurse had a rope attached to the wall opposite and used it to swing her hammock. Nobody dared to use her hammock, even in her absence. Perhaps everybody was afraid of her loud mouth. But today I used it, and I didn't even pay the slightest attention.

In the middle of my nap, I was awakened by sounds around me, voices saying that the lady had attempted to commit suicide. She had gone to the pharmacy with Old Nurse to buy something then went to the bathroom to drink it. I opened my eyes and saw the maids helping the lady walk from the bathroom behind the gargage. Six of them were supporting the lady, holding on to her sides and back, up the steps, into our house. I saw my mother standing by her desk, still wearing her long travelling tunic. The maids laid the lady on the wooden bed, next to my mother's desk.

"All of you get out of the house, the children, too. Except for Tam and Trung (my mother's adopted children)." My mother gave these orders in a soft, controlled voice. She told Trung to go fetch the doctor and Tam to sit with the lady. I and everybody else went out to the neighbor's yard. We looked very conspicuous, standing silently in a group in the middle of the dirt-packed court. The neighbors slowly came to join us, yet nobody uttered a word. It was getting dark.

I was tired of standing around. I decided to sneak back into the house.

In the middle of the room where the lady was lying, I saw my mother, my father, Tam, and the doctor. This was the first time a doctor had visited our home. Through the mosquito net, in the light that shone from my mother's electric desk lamp, I saw the lady lying unconscious, her back to the group. They opened the net. The doctor took the lady's pulse, then said that he needed to give her an injection. "Could somebody pull her pants down, please."

My father stepped forward, about to bend over. "No, Tam, you do it," Mother said sternly. Father stepped aside. Tam moved up, reached across the lady's waist to untie the string that held up her pants. The doctor gave his shot. The mosquito net was reclosed. I heard my mother tell me to go ask the rest of the group to return home. She had noticed my presence but chose to ignore it until then.

That night, dinner was served but our parents were not present. Old Nurse was told to sleep with the lady. The next evening I went straight home from school. I was urged by my instincts to look for Old Nurse, but the maids told me that Old Nurse had left with the lady on the bus. "Old Nurse travelled first class to Saigon. There were only two first-class seats. She took one, and the misses took the other," they told me in their sing-song tone, delighting in sharing their secret.

Sunday night Old Nurse came home. I was doing homework when I heard Old Nurse say to Mother, "She is all right now. She sent me home. She said to thank you. She told me you are a nice and good lady, and pretty too. She said she was ashamed of herself and of what she did. She gave me a letter for you." With two hands the Old Nurse held up a crumpled letter that she retrieved from the pocket of her *ao ba-ba*. My mother turned away from the sight of it and told Nurse to leave it on her desk, "Go have dinner, Old Nurse. You must be tired." Old Nurse probably repeated the story down in the maids' quarters. The doctor came back to our house a few times after the incident to take care of my father, who was running a very high fever. I heard the maids say that the fever was so high that it could make him crazy. Sometimes I would see my father standing listlessly, staring out of the living room window. "Poor Sir. Mister has gone mad," the maids would say. Nobody talked about my mother, but everybody seemed to apply themselves more seriously to what they were doing, especially when she appeared on the scene.

The handling by my mother of the southern lady friend of my father left a deep impression. It illustrated to me the meaning of "propriety and love" as my mother tried to teach us. So complicated and subdued were these feelings in me that even now, as I watched the scene of gentle courtship between the young men and the girls near the lake, a vague sense of guilt came to mar whatever enjoyment I might have felt.

I led my sisters across the wide asphalt boulevard to the opposite side where the shops were located. Along one side street were boutiques selling silk. Here, roll after roll of silk was lined up according to color — each color having a dozen shades — on shelves which filled the walls from the ceiling to the floor. I had never seen so many shades of colors in my life.

Where did these silks come from, I wondered. A few months ago, when the Chinese soldiers were here, the shelves had been empty.

Another street, much less crowded, was lined with jewelry shops. Here gold was sold in the form of rings, necklaces, bracelets, and other jewelry. Designers molded and carved the pieces behind their shop windows. On and on we walked past these specialty shops. Each street sold a particular product: Sugar Street, Brass Street, Basket Street, Pottery Street, etc. They seemed endless to us.

"I'm tired and hungry," Blue Water said. "Let's go home."

"Yes. Let's go home," I agreed. "We'll never be able to see them all anyway. I once heard a song about Hanoi and its thirty-eight streets like these."

"Thirty-eight streets like these?" Cloud exclaimed.

My uncle's front room, my cousin's dental office on my last visit, had been converted into a bedroom. Lien, who had married my youngest cousin, now had a child. My two older cousins seemed much more relaxed than before. One took us around to visit all the girls in the neighborhood. The girls loved us and fed us homemade cookies and preserved fruit.

My cousins dressed in the latest French fashion: wool slacks and sweaters. I loved to be with them in their apartment on the top floor. They bought their snacks by lowering a basket to the vendor with their money in it to exchange for fresh-roasted peanuts, fried potatoes seasoned with a few grains of sugar, spicy beef jerky served with pickled papaya, fresh shrimp fried on the spot in a mixture of thinly sliced yam and seasoned flour served with minced pickled cabbage and carrots—all North Vietnamese delicacies.

Not many days had passed when one morning I was suddenly awakened by a loud noise. I looked out of my bedroom window from upstairs and saw my two older cousins, the dentist and the pharmacist, busy hammering at a spot in the wall separating their house from the neighbor's. I ran down the stairs to them, "What're you doing, cousins?"

"Making holes so we can communicate from house to house."

"Oh! That'll be fun." They had original fun ideas, I thought.

"The French are returning." My cousin brought me back to the present.

"Oh, already?"

"Yes," the elder cousin said. "Mai, you go with our aunt and the kids to the countryside."

"What about my father?"

"He said he'll stay here and fight with us."

"Oh, God. Not again," I thought. I had hardly seen him, had had no chance to talk to him since our reunion over a week before.

That afternoon, my aunt took us and the children of another aunt to the countryside. We walked, each with a bag on our shoulder, three miles from Hanoi to a village where patches of lettuce, cabbage, and cauliflower spread out on acres of square fields separating the street from the village. Small patches of chrysanthemums and pink, red and burgundy roses colored the entrance to the village.

The following mornings, I took my sisters and my aunt's two children to the slope by the dam, the only spot which was not cultivated, to make them exercise – the way I had learned in school. When lunchtime came, I would help my aunt with the cooking. She taught me to cook our simple meals in a day or two. A meal with fresh cabbage and fresh pork was the easiest thing in the world to learn. Fresh cabbage newly picked from the field did not need any seasoning. I quartered the heads and dropped the pieces in boiling water. The minute the water bubbled again, it released an aroma like green grass, sweet like pure honey. The boiled cabbage and its sweet juice, combined with slices of pork meat from the morning butchering, boiled with freshly picked onion and seasoned with salt or fish sauce and pepper, made a delicious simple meal – so I told my little sisters and cousins who stood around to help me speed up the cooking process. I spent the evenings telling them stories which I had read in the *Livres Roses*.

Not much time had passed when my aunt received word from my mother that she and my three little brothers had arrived on a French ship from Saigon. As soon as they had landed in the port of Hai Phong, now reoccupied by the French, they had left for the house of my mother's father in the countryside.

In took us half a day to get to our grandpa's house. My aunt was walking in front, when through the thin fence I saw my mother standing on the veranda. She walked quickly down the steps to meet my aunt. They looked at each other, their hands touched and locked.

"Chi" (Sister). "Mo" (Brother's wife). My mother then turned to look at me. I came to her. She held her arms out, and I leaned my head against her chest. Her arms pressed my head tight against her, "Daughter." My eyes were wet, "Mother." She stroked my hair gently. A few seconds later she started talking to the rest of the children, "My children look so healthy, red cheeks, white skin, plump."

"We ate lots of cabbage and rice and did exercise too," Breeze twittered. "Sister Mai said they're good for us." I looked at them and was surprised to see that their eyes were no longer swollen, and they did look fatter. It must have been the combination of fresh air, fresh food, no fuss, and no worries.

My mother's hand reached out and touched each head. She then said to my aunt, "You must be very tired from the long walk. I have prepared some warm salty water for your feet. If I may be excused." I felt my head pressed and released and heard my mother say, "Children, go play."

My mother then walked to the back and brought out a copper sink, dark brown on the outside and bright gold on the inside. She put the sink under my aunt's feet and sat down next to it. "Let me help you," she said, pulling off her sister-in-law's knee socks. It was like a feet cleansing ceremony. My mother's expression was very solemn, her hands pampering the feet as if they were delicate, fragile objects. They had been until the revolution. My aunt was married to one of the highest ranking mandarins, who supervised a regional school district. Like Mother, she had never had to work in her life.

My aunt sat straight, her face expressionless, her red eyes moistening. Looking at my mother, my aunt, and the scene, I felt like crying. Oddly, I had the feeling that that moving scene, showing restrained love and mutual appreciation and respect through symbolic gesture, would never take place again—that the good family traditions from our 2000-year-old civilization were coming to an end. Perhaps what I had seen during the revolution had given me this sad, intuitive foresight at the age of sixteen.

We took the bus to Thanh Hoa, north of Central Vietnam, near Ha Tinh and Nghe Tinh, the birth place of many revolutionaries and leaders, including Ho Chi Minh. But unlike poor and dry Ha Tinh and Nghe Tinh, Thanh Hoa was a province rich in water and known to produce the best oranges. In the whole northern region, Thanh Hoa was the only province that had no mosquitoes or lice. It was the only province where women did most of the labor in the fields while men babysat their children at home!

Having lost the battle to the French who reoccupied Hanoi, my father, my cousins, and other patriots retreated into the countryside to continue their struggle. Father came and visited us for a few days before he joined the engineer group that moved wherever the "country needed them." We didn't see him again until almost three years later. My mother was left alone to take care of the seven children, with no savings, no income, and no skills. But her situation was not exceptional. All "intellectual" Vietnamese who had some pride and love for their country left Hanoi to contribute their work force to whoever could lead them in the fight against the French. Others moved to where they thought there was safety.

Rumors of the French return, the sight of young professionals organizing the resistance in their own homes, the enthusiasm of students running around in groups of threes and fours trying to find a leader to start their resistance cells—these were signs warning businessmen to close shops and families to find refuge in the safe countryside where homes were open wide to welcome people from the city. Food was shared or sold at a minimum price. The new evacuees and the peasants who welcomed them thought the unsettled situation would be over in a matter of days. They had high hopes following our recent history which had been full of surprises: Within a year and a half they had witnessed the eighty-five years of French colonial rule swept away overnight by the Japanese March 1945 coup, then the Japanese disarmed by the Chinese—after their defeat by the Allies in their own country—then our own people taking over for a few months, only to have the French return again. Who knows! Something might happen to make the French leave again.

To earn an income, Mother imitated the other city ladies who resold medicines in a box spread in front of them on the curbs leading to the entrance of the marketplace. The peasants trusted these city folk who they thought understood French and knew what medicines were for what sicknesses: aspirin for acute headache and arthritis, quinine for malaria, cod liver oil for constipation and tiredness, etc.

My mother added her special "wind" medicine, an oily liquid she had brought from the South in a huge bag—a liquid that one used to rub on the body to cure all kinds of sicknesses which were believed to be caused by bad drafts. We made good money considering. Mother used me as an errand girl to fetch the medicines from other city ladies, her new acquaintances, and to calculate the price so that she could resell them at a profit. Within the hundred hard trips, I had to figure out the total amount based on the percentage of profit—which varied from about a third to one-half mark-up, depending on the rarity of the medicines (as described by the sellers). I would make these calculations before handing the products to Mother who I assumed would be confused, if not consider it degrading to make a profit on the poor villagers, especially when this involved only a short trip to her friends.

Mother looked very happy where she was, among her northern friends who read her poems aloud, putting the accents in the same way she did, laughing about and sharing in the similarities of their own situations with those described in the poems. For once in her life Mother had the chance to earn respect for her own merits. Her clients loved her for the conscientious way she treated them and their sicknesses. Her friends respected her for her rich mind and the noble motivation she inspired through her poems. Above all, she lent dignity to this "low-class merchant" profession, while using it to serve her country, proudly and openly.

Now and then in my free time I would ask my sisters to recount to me what had happened to them during my absence. Cloud and Clear Water told me that before they went with Father to Hanoi, Mother and Father had a small restaurant in the reoccupied Saigon where their friends, the engineer group, cooked *pho* (a special northern soup) to make their living because they had decided not to work for the French anymore. (Later I learned from Father that they had used the place as a "contact" post to meet with revolutionaries and pass messages for them.) They had moved to Saigon because they had been expelled from the rented house in Bien Hoa after their return from their evacuation in the countryside. The French had told Father to go back to work with them; they would pay the salary for the whole year that he had missed. But Father had refused. They then confined the whole family to a room in a nearby hospital, guarded by their soldiers. After three months, they released the family and ordered my father to return to work. When he refused again, they again sent the French police to evict the family from the rented home.

My sweet little Breeze said: "We saw a boy your age standing out in the street in front of the hospital. He had bandages all over his head and belly. He was yelling at a French soldier, saying: 'Look here . . . dan [people].'"

"No. No." Blue Water took over, "'Thuc dan [Cannibals]! You think you hurt us and we will stop fighting you? You are wrong.'"

"Yes. It was scary," Cloud broke in. "The people crowded behind him. Mother stood behind us in the window. He pulled off the bandages from his belly, then from his head. Blood gushed out from his wounds. He kept yelling: 'Look. Look. Thuc Dan. I'll prove it to you.' Then he fell down in a pool of blood."

"Mother pulled us inside and said crying, 'Pray for him. Pray for our sisters,'" Blue Water said with tears in her voice.

"If not for Brother Spring Field," Cloud said, "we would all have starved in that camp. He brought us canned food from his trading. The Indians and the Chinese wanted favors from the French; Brother Field used his French to get favors for them. Then both sides gave him food and toys."

Cloud laughed suddenly. "I hated him sometimes though. Whenever he took me to the cinema, he would wait till after the movie was due to start for the lights to be switched off. Then a group of his friends would start a fight in front of the ticket man to distract him while the rest of us would run inside to watch the movie free. We not only went in illegally, Brother Spring Field also made sure that we sat in the 'loge' [first-class box]. I don't know if it's because he liked first class or because loge seats had huge, tall backs that hid us. Whatever his reasons, in the middle of the show, they would spot us, and I would feel this hand come up from behind to pull my ears and throw us out of the theater. He was really terrible." All of us giggled.

We stayed in the city of Thanh Hoa for a few weeks. Then news that the French had reoccupied Hanoi started pouring in with the medicines brought in by black market merchants. Many city ladies, including my mother's new friends who were not used to the "patriotic" way of life, left their refuge to return to Hanoi, to reestablish their businesses under the new French régime. With Father away again to join the revolutionaries, us cooped up in a room of a businessman's house, and her two good friends gone—back to Hanoi with her enemy the French—I guess Mother felt disillusioned again. She had us pack up, and we moved to Da-Ne, another countryside, where she had heard the French would never be able to invade. There she awaited Father's return.

In Da-Ne, the rent was cheap and the children had more room to play. Until the arrival of the refugees, the peasants in North Vietnam used to reserve the main house for the cult of their ancestors and leave it unoccupied. The influx of refugees caused them to rent out the side house where they had lived and move over to the main house. It was as if these farmers had united and unanimously decided to rent only the side houses no matter how much the refugees were willing to pay for them. It was a question of face and also of family honor that they kept the main houses for themselves.

Things settled down rather quickly in the countryside. City people brought with them their urban lifestyle which they somehow had to improvise in order to cope with the new circumstances. Country folk continued with their usual chores in the rice fields and in their craft-work, using the skills handed down to them by their ancestors. Unlike the extremists of Quang Ngai, Central Vietnam, the peasants in North Vietnam did not involve themselves in persecuting the rich. They were only vaguely aware of the existence of the Ho Chi Minh administration and did not really seem to care who was at the head of the government. The maxim "Lenh vua thua le lang" (The King's order comes second to the villagers' customs) fitted well with the mode of these peasants. Economically independent from their neighbors, they were very set in their ways and confident in what they knew, what they had to do, and what they could do.

To entertain themselves, the city people organized plays and musical gatherings. The village children came to look and join in. Young city people who had joined political organizations in the city now joined the fight against illiteracy among the peasants. They stood in groups of three and four at the entrances of markets with bold letters written on cardboard and taught the peasants how to read them: "'i,' 't,' both have hooks on the bottom; 'i' is short and has a dot; 't' is long and has a stroke." Young peasants, shy at first, didn't mind repeating the cute rhymes they were taught.

With my sister Bright Moon still in the army, my adopted sister Tam leaving the family to live with a rich city lady so as to earn pocket money in return for housekeeping, and my adopted brother Middle staying in Saigon to take care of his future, I became the oldest in the family. I now had to work to help my mother feed my five younger brothers and sisters. Spring Field was sent to a Redemptorist school away from home. Middle and Tam, though not having official schooling, being overaged at the time Mother adopted them, were now considered educated among the peasants thanks to Mother's persistent pounding of simple math, reading, and writing.

For some kind of livelihood, I would sneak across the French lines to buy aspirin and quinine to sell at black market prices in the small open village markets where farmers from surrounding villages came to buy food and household articles. A person could make better profits selling rare items such as Western medicines, good quality rice, and incense sticks in those remote places. My trade varied between these items and the rubber sandals called Ho Chi Minh sandals which I sold to students in the big towns.

My regular schedule was to rise before the cock crowed and prepare baskets for the market. I would dress as my father had described the northern women to me years ago, except I wore my black pants instead of a skirt. Walking in the dark on the narrow dirt lanes dividing the fields, with a little lamp on the front basket to light the way, I would balance myself and the two baskets (hung on the ends of a bamboo pole by bamboo ropes) and chew a tonic-like mixture of betel leaves, areca nuts, and lime like the rest of the women to keep myself warm and avoid having bad breath. Sometimes I would walk for miles without seeing another soul.

North Vietnam had very chilly winds and cold, humid fog. This lent

119

a mysterious calmness to the atmosphere. Cold as it was, without warm clothes and with bare feet, I loved to walk in those early mornings.

The betel and nut mixture that I chewed kept me warm inside and excited my brain. Some nights when there was moonlight, I would make a trip on a large wooden boat on the Giang River to buy a two hundred-pound bag of quality rice grain which I would pay the boat's "porter" to carry to my home. I would divide this rice—using an empty condensed milk can as a measuring cup—into smaller portions to take to sell in remote villages.

On those river trips, most women would sit under the bamboo roof of the large wooden sampan that could transport about a one-ton load. I liked to find a place on the deck where I could enjoy the fresh air. This usually was where the male merchants gathered. From there I could watch the moon. The other passengers would observe me with curiosity, but I didn't care. I was used to being independent from my army life.

In the total darkness, the clear silent moon would slowly appear. It would shine through the thin cold fog hovering over the immense rice fields, spotlighting the shapes of the houses from which previously only little warm yellow lights could be seen. At the sight of the moon, the silent merchants would stir softly in their places. The black water would turn dark green. The waves, unseen a moment before, would jump playfully on top of one another, their tips splashing the moonlight and spreading its magnificence over the wide, swift river.

With light came life. Out of the dark into the powerful moonlight the oarsmen would come to their posts opposite one another and begin dipping the long oars into the water. All was orderly, as if it were synchronized by the cold, silent command of the moon. Seconds would pass, and then a deep sound would echo from the hollow wood beneath the oarsmen's bare feet: "Ho," a low, rich sound. "Thump. Ho. Thump. Ho." They rowed harmoniously. The rhythm created by their bare feet and breathing, the swishing of the water escaping from the uplifted oars, and the bending of their bodies was like a ballet which floated smoothly over the moonlit water.

The moon began to evoke in me a feeling of love—a love coming from my soul, escaping through my body to evaporate into the universe then return to me with touches of deeper feelings. "Is this Love?" I had asked myself the first time that sensation had come to me. "I feel like I'm missing somebody or something, and yet I feel so full and complete." Over and over I would muse at this feeling whenever I saw the moon.

Occupied with my duties of trading, cooking, bathing my five brothers and sisters, and washing their clothes, I grew attuned to this regular, flowing lifestyle. On the way back from my trips to markets, I would roam across hilly lanes to mysterious caves and deserted temples where domesticated fish serenely gathered by the hundreds at the drop of a piece of cake. Oftentimes the still vastness of these places, the quiet soft air, made me feel weightless, as if I could float into space and mingle with the universe.

One late afternoon, returning from a long market trip, I heard a violin playing in our living and sleeping quarters. I left my baskets in the kitchen and walked in. There I saw a young man, tall and large boned, his back towards me, playing the violin. Beyond him was my father lying still on my mother's wooden bed! What a wonderful surprise! Father finally was home after two years in the revolution in Hanoi.

Mother, sitting at his bedside, saw me and said, "Your father is very ill. Brother Pham came to lighten his head with music. For that I'm grateful."

My father opened his eyes slightly and smiled when he saw me. "Why don't you sing a song with the violin?" said Mother.

The young man was a complete stranger to me, but somehow it all seemed like something that had happened before. Later I heard he was the son of the rich lady my adopted sister worked for. Somehow the mothers had gotten together and devised a plan for marrying me to the lady's son, whose father was also a revolutionary like my father. I tried to make things look as natural as I could. I sang with him a national song praising the compatriots who, like the birds, flew over the country to spread their love and music to their suffering people. Mother liked this song very much. She had embellished it with verses of her own.

The following day, I took Cloud, my nine-year-old sister, to the market with me. We took a sampan across the river and walked two or three hours towards the town of another province where there was a university for refugees. I carried, with the support of a bamboo yoke, two baskets of crudely made Ho Chi Minh sandals to sell to the "rich" students and their professors.

On our way home, we stopped at one of my favorite spots at the foot of a rocky cliff. I set the baskets down and led my sister halfway up the slope to the top of the huge rock that served as my "look-out cave." I liked to take naps and daydream on this black rock, three times the size of a bed. I used to think not even a king could have such a nice cool bed, and this perfect view at his feet. To the left was the view of the province from

121

where we had just come, and to the right that of the swift river and our own home hidden under shady trees.

Somehow my conversations with my sisters always ended up being related to the time when Bright Moon and I were absent from them. I asked Cloud to tell me more about the family's activities while I was gone. She looked sadly into the vastness and said, "Daddy is very sick, hm, Sister?"

I nodded.

"Poor Daddy. He went through so much!"

"Yes," I agreed thinking she was talking about the last two years of his absence.

"After you and Sister Moon left, we all went to live in the weekend house of our parents' lumber mill friends. They were gone, back to the North. We had fun for a while until one day some strange men came with their guns, hoes, and spades. They took away all the animals. But Mother pleaded with them, and they left us one milk cow so she could feed our little brother."

The story sounded familiar, like the one I had heard from the girl with short hair in Quang Ngai about her rich father being put to death by their former house servant. I could still see her rigid face trying to hold back her sorrow and hatred and her eyes red with tears that didn't dare fall lest they betray her feelings in front of those cowards . . . And Hung's death. . . .

Cloud's words transformed into vivid pictures. The group of cowards came and searched the house, saying that Father was a traitor for having worked for the French. They could find nothing to incriminate him. At the end they picked up a miniature of a ship in the living room. They lifted it up and saw on its bottom a drawing of the French flag. They said that proved that Father was a real traitor.

Father said, "My two oldest children are in the army, and I could have stayed and worked for the French, but I am here to join our cause."

"Ach. You're lying. You came here to spy on us." They confiscated the ship and dragged Father away with them. The next day, they returned and found Mother with the children on a float made of banana trunks. Some villagers on it were helping to push it out to the deep water. They were trying to leave the village by way of the river so that they could go find Father. The men ordered Mother to get back and shot at the float which kept turning round and round. Finally the float was carried away by the swift water.

Two men took Father to Binh Da, out to a place by the river away from the village. They tied his hands behind his back and weighted them

122

with some bricks. They blindfolded him and pushed him aboard a small sampan. They said they were going to drown him since there was no use wasting a bullet on a traitor. It took them a long time to get out to the deep water.

Suddenly they were yelling to get back to shore. The water was very rough. Father heard thunder. A storm had arrived. It began to rain. "Get back. Get back!" "Dump him first." "No. That will tip over the boat." "He will talk." "We'll take care of that after the storm."

They struggled back to shore and pushed Father down on the ground by a tree trunk. Father was saying the Hail Mary prayer the whole time, even though he hadn't been much of a Catholic before. He remembered Mother saying to repeat nine Hail Mary's when in trouble. While Father was praying, he heard the men greeting someone, a woman. Her voice sounded familiar. They were asking her about her husband, Brother Hon.

The minute Father heard the name, he knew that she was Sister Hon, the leader of the women's organization in Bien Hoa.

"What do you plan to do with this man?" Chi Hon asked. "What did he do wrong?"

"He is a traitor. He is very rich, owns horses and cows. He exploited the blood of our people to build his weekend house. A traitor, working for the French, now come to live with us to spy for them."

Father said angrily, "I am not a traitor. My daughter Mai joined the army. My daughter Bright Moon joined the army. The house I lived in was my friend's house. They took away my friend's cows and horses, and then they took me away. They tried to drown me."

Sister Hon didn't say anything. They sat in silence waiting for the rain to die down at which time Sister Hon said, "We better get back on the road." She paused. "About this man, I think we better bring him to our people's tribunal; that's what they are there for." Then she said, "Shall we. Before it gets dark."

They pushed Father up, pushed him forward. "Go, traitor." His eyes were still blindfolded: "Walk. Faster. What's the matter. Can't you walk, traitor?"

The morning after, Father was taken to a yard full of peasants. They took the blindfold off. He saw a man sitting behind a desk and two men next to him. Brother Hon, who presided, said, "Cac Dong Chi [Comrades with Same Ideal], we have here a man, an engineer, accused of being a traitor. Before we sentence and execute him we'd like to prove to him that our judgment is fair and that, even though we're not educated like him, we are decent, good people." Then he asked Father to tell them who he was, how he got rich, and what he had been doing while his poor compatriots struggled to free all from "serfdom."

Father explained to him about the house, told him that he had quit working for the French and was waiting for a chance to serve the revolutionary cause and that his two daughters were in the army serving our country. "Can you prove it?" Brother Hon asked. Father looked in the direction of Sister Hon who was standing in the first row, a few steps from Brother Hon. "The lady there knows me. My daughter Mai was a member of her 'Women Save the Country' organization."

Brother Hon looked at her, "Is he telling the truth? You recognize him?" "Yes. His office used to be in front of our building. Both of his daughters did work with the revolution." Brother Hon then turned to the crowd: "What do you think. I think he's a good citizen. Don't you?"

There were whispers. "Those who favor releasing him please raise your hands." A hand was raised; then everybody slowly raised their hands. "Praise justice. The court is dismissed. Someone untie him and let him go." An old man walked up and untied Father. Father looked for Sister Hon, but she was already busy talking with a group of women, and Brother Hon had turned around to go with a group of men.

Cloud's voice stopped, but my head continued recreating the terrible scenes. My eyes, full of tears, strayed to where Cloud sat. She looked like a frail, helpless little bundle, like the poor baby tiger my negligence had led to be strangled to death. Weakly I raised myself up. My thoughts were terribly dark. I wanted to clear this darkness. My eyes searched in the distance for what had been to me the perfect view, but what I saw was a discarded painting lying amid torn-up images of war, death, and the distorted faces of dishonest men. I moved to the dark crack of the rock leading toward the way down. I wanted to be alone, in the dark, not to see again.

That night, I dreamt of a girl named Thu whom I had met some time ago while still under the service of General Son. She had told me of her pitiful story, which somehow until now I had managed to keep buried deep in my subconscious.

Like many of her friends, Thu had joined the national movement and participated in various training programs organized by the Viet Minh when they arrived. Not long after she had joined the party, however, the French returned to her town. Everybody was urged in advance by the nationalist organizations to take refuge in the countryside. Some left, and some were not sure what they should do.

124

Unable to decide on such short notice, Thu's family stayed behind. Thu let her party know her family's decision. The Viet Minh did not want to lose the golden occasion. They gave her a hand grenade and instructed her to throw it at the French when they arrived. Thu saw her opportunity to serve her country, took the grenade, and hid herself behind a tree near her house when she heard news that the French were coming. The French marched nonchalantly up the street. A few Vietnamese traitors followed them to indicate the houses of the pro-nationalist organizations or those to whom they had sworn to take revenge on someday.

Thu waited until they were near, pulled out the pin as instructed, and threw her only hand grenade at the "imperialists" and their "hound dogs."

The grenade rolled slowly on the street, and the group stopped, panicked. The grenade stopped rolling; Thu watched it, surprised not to hear the explosion that she was told would follow. The group recollected their courage, and in the confusion Thu started running. Behind her somebody shouted in Vietnamese: "There she is! Shoot! Shoot!

A chaos of shots, footsteps, and shouts in French and Vietnamese followed. Thu ran through her house, into the backyard, zigzagging among the thick trees and ditches and out to the rice fields.

On and on she ran until she heard no more shooting or shouting. She stopped, her heart pounding as if about to burst. She sat there on the dam separating the rice fields thinking of her next move. She would have cried if she could, but no tears came out. She sat there with dry eyes, wondering why she didn't cry, while staring at the immense steamy fields. A huge tree appeared in her view; she ran over to it, dropped into its cool shade and slept for many hours. When she awoke, the sun hung low on the horizon. Exhausted and hungry, she looked at the disappearing golden rays. Extending to the horizon was a sea of golden rice stems forming little waves at the slightest touch of the crisp evening breeze. A sweet perfume scented the place. A white stork took off into the blue sky, drew a big circle, tilting its snow white wings as though relunctantly waving farewell to the creatures below. Then, with a sudden jerk, the stork flapped its long wings, stretched its elegant long neck upward, dropped a painful call into the silence of dusk, then quietly vanished into the distant sky. How peaceful and calm, almost pretty, but Thu had no mind to admire this serene beauty any longer. She was hungry, and she had to go back home.

It was already dark when she approached her backyard. She crossed the ditches and crept among the shady trees, unconscious of the change which had come over her. A few days ago, she had still been scared of ghosts and shadows. Even in broad daylight she would not have entered the shady garden without the maid.

Now she moved carefully, ready to duck at the sight of her mother or maids. She was surprised that there were no lights on in the house. Perhaps they had changed their minds and evacuated, she thought. She crept up the steps and crossed the tiled terrace leading to the dining room. The door was wide open. Thu flinched, moved cautiously along the balustrade until she reached the open door, then peered in. Far away, it seemed, in the living room, stood a short candle throwing its shifting dim light on the shape of a woman, stooped on the floor, holding in her lap a small bundle. Next to it lay a much larger form.

The woman, whom Thu recognized as her mother, bent to the bundle on her lap, caressed its face, kissed its tiny hands, repeated in a hoarse voice, "Oh, my son, my darling little son, my baby, my poor baby." Over and over she repeated the words, rocking the bundle. Then she reached over to the big bundle, shook it as though to wake it, crying, "Husband, don't leave me, please don't leave me . . . Oh, God, what did I do wrong to deserve this." On and on she lamented, caressed, and embraced one bundle after another. The yellow flame projected her shadow which moved like a ghost half on the wall, half on the floor stained with black blood spattered around the mutilated bodies. The chairs and tables shattered by gunshots added to the ghastly aspect of the frail shadow.

Thu stared aghast at the scene, her mouth and eyes wide open. She backed up behind the door, stumbled on the steps, fell over, gathered herself up, and plunged into the garden. Falling and struggling out of the ditches, her hands clenched into fists which plugged her mouth and forced back the scream rising from her aching heart. Out in the open fields, she kept running and beating her chest until her tiny body could no longer hold her sorrow. She dropped onto the dirty field behind some peasant's yard.

"Mamma, Mamma . . ." the faint voice died away as she collapsed.

Suddenly, in the dream, I became a stork. And as the incoherent state of dreams would have it, I was soaring naturally and gracefully somewhere over "My Quoc" (The Beautiful Country), the country I had first heard about from Sister Hon, referring to the United States of America.

Shaken by the strong sensation "My Quoc" had created in my dream, I awoke in the dark crying, crying because I could not be there! No matter how I told myself that it was a ridiculous dream—an unreal place like those in the *Livres Roses*—my head persisted in hanging on to that dream and made me frustrated for days. I just didn't see how I could ever get there.

My mother's income as a medicine lady and mine as a vendor were barely enough to buy rice and a bundle of vegetables to eat. Nobody had money to buy. Now and then, if I made a good profit, I would buy a fish to celebrate, but that was rare. The children had no school to go to. Only Spring Field, my brother next to me in age, had been sent to stay at a Catholic school.

A few days after my dream of My Quoc, my mother told me to go with her on some errand. Father was still sick. He stayed home with the kids. As we left the village gate, Mother told me that we were going to find somebody that could give us a permit to rejoin Grandmother north of here. She said that Father needed care and we had no money to take care of him or to pay rent.

We walked on in silence, I half a step behind her as our culture required. She walked very slowly, as was also demanded of her "nobility" class. Bored, my thoughts turned to her. In the back of my mind I concluded that she was tired of this kind of life and was finding a way to get out though I knew she would miss what she was doing. "Ba Lan" (Medicine Lady) was a dignified title and a suitable occupation for Mother. In addition to the French medicines I brought from French occupied territories, Mother also sold her own concoctions which she made of edible herbs. She steamed the herbs and caught the evaporated essence in peanut oil so that she could rub it on the backs and stomachs of her patients, who faithfully waited for the miracle to work. Normally, they would pay for her treatment with a dozen eggs, some vegetables from their gardens, or nuts and betels.

One afternoon, however, we were sent on a rare mission to collect dues from one of her clients. This particular client had not paid Mother after several house visits; she even let her dogs out to chase us. Somebody was in the house, but nobody answered our calls.

"Ungrateful," Cloud said, "and Mother made us sit with her for hours while she rubbed the baby and said her prayers."

I shared Cloud's feeling, but when we told Mother she became sad and said, "I wondered if the baby would survive. I had to baptize him without his mother knowing it. Maybe the baby died. I wish I had the pharmaceutic books of Lan Ong."

"Who is Lan Ong, Mamma?" I asked.

"He is the ancestor of the medicine men. Le Huu Trac, his real name, was a mandarin, who later became famous as a medicine man. He died at the age of seventy-one, in 1791. In Grandpa's time and before, the majority of Vietnamese died between the ages of forty and fifty. Lan Ong was the first known Vietnamese to have done medical research and keep records of his studies on the properties of plants and herbs under different conditions. He was the first to emphasize the importance of preventing diseases through hygiene, nutrition, and clothing."

"Where are those books now, Mamma?"

"At that time, we still wrote in Chinese characters, so the books were not popular among the masses who could not read, and no governments after Tay Son cared about the people enough to spread his teachings. Only a few literate medicine men recopied parts of the books for their own use. But, there is still one set of books kept in the Royal Records. My mother told me Lan Ong said 'Medicine is a human art, the noble art of preserving life, taking charge of the worries and joys of Man, and not worrying about the interest or honor it brings.'" Upon hearing this, I felt a little ashamed of myself for having been angry at the woman for not paying.

In my daydreaming, Mother and I walked from village to village searching for the authorities to give us a permit to leave Da-Ne and travel north towards Hanoi. Nobody knew where the authorities were. One person pointed to a temple and said, "He may be in there." We found nothing but an empty desk. Another person directed us to a school which was closed for the summer. There we saw a boy playing in an empty classroom. We explained to him who we were looking for. "Oh, my uncle. He closed the office to go to my cousin's wedding. He won't start working again until a month from now."

Finally we gave up. Then one day my cousin the dentist turned up, dropping in to see us from his trip south of our village. We had not seen him since we had left Hanoi over two years ago. Mother told him about our problem. The next day, before he left, he handed us an ordinary piece of paper on which he gave us permission to move to Rua due to my father's illness after having served the revolution from the time it moved out of Hanoi. He gave his seal—the illegible signature of a doctor. "Anybody could have written that," I thought.

It took our family five months to walk from Thanh Hoa to Rua, having to settle here and there so as not to look conspicuous and arouse suspicion and also to find food and shelter on the way. Father went separately and joined us at Rua.

One bright afternoon at the end of our fifth month of migrating, my mother pointed at a clump of green bamboo in the distance and said, "Rua is over there. We're going to visit Grandmother. She lives there."

I just happened to hear Mother mention our grandmother for the first time ever when we were trying to get the permit. It was very characteristic of Mother not to tell us anything until it became a necessity. Like magic, upon hearing the word "Grandma," the children increased their

128

speed. They shifted their little clothes bags on their shoulders and merrily pushed forward.

Like all the villages in this northern region, Rua was separated from other villages by an immense rice field and surrounded with tall, thick bamboo trees. From afar the bamboo resembled a circular wall. Each village had a small brick temple built at its entrance, which people used as a resting spot.

Two hours after first sighting Rua, we arrived at the entrance temple — a square grey structure about eight to nine feet long. It had a ceiling, one wall facing the windy side, and two pillars. The floor was lined with red tile as was the roof. Mother told us to sit at the temple and relax in the cool breeze and refresh ourselves with some of the rainwater in the big earthen jar, free to passers-by. From this spot, we had a nice overall view of the village. This particular village, like a few of the rich ones we had just recently passed, had tile pathways ranging from three to five feet wide which wove in and out between fences that defined property lines.

The day before, we had passed many villages, each having its own trade: ceramic pots, copper pots, bamboo baskets, lacquerwares, wooden toys, silk, and so forth. The villagers in this area sold and exchanged their products across the "borders" in French-occupied cities. They did not talk politics, did not go to night meetings, did not participate in opinion sharing. The majority did not read or write and did not care that they did not.

Phat Diem and Bui Chu on the other hand, where my family had stayed for several months before coming to Rua, were different. The villagers there only knew one leader, their Bishop Le Huu Tu, who spoke against Ho Chi Minh and had his own Catholic army, equipped by the French.

We met our grandmother. I didn't know her age, but she looked old to me. (I learned much later, after my mother and father had passed away, from my mother's half-sister, that this grandmother was not our real grandmother. She was a close friend of our grandmother who had agreed to take care of my mother so my real grandmother could remarry. Soon after my mother was born, my grandmother's first husband, who was a grand mandarin, died (at a very young age). A young man of stature then came along and wanted to marry my grandmother, but his family would not permit him to marry her unless she came to his house alone, without her child.

Grandma gave each of us a pat on our head and a few candies stuffed with peanuts and sesame. We ate a big hot meal of boiled chicken, boiled bamboo shoots, and fried *rau muong*—a vegetable which was planted in ponds and believed to have much iron. Afterward, we enjoyed a good sleep in roomy wooden beds without having to fight off the mosquitoes that used to interrupt our dreams in certain villages on our trek.

Father arrived while we were asleep.

Very late the following morning our mother awakened us to eat breakfast. We hurriedly washed our faces in the warm water poured out from the huge earthen pot on the earthen stove. That was another luxury, for wood was expensive, and we used to have to save it for Mother's warm water. Then we went out to the front yard to watch a woman in a long brown dress with a long black skirt making *banh cuon* (rolled rice cake) by thinly spreading the liquid rice batter onto a piece of cloth tied across the large opening of an earthen pot steaming with hot vapor until the batter formed a delicate, moist wrapping. (The high degree of transparency in the wrapping told the art which the woman possessed and guaranteed her success in her craft.) The transparent wrapping was then spread with a bit of onion browned in pork grease. The smell of the browned onion mixed with the fragrance of the rice cake steaming in the cold air was enough to entice the pickiest of connoisseurs. We ate and ate and ate. For the last course, my mother called in a woman who sold steaming cakes of special corn mixed with pork and special seasonings.

In that hour I felt like we—my grandmother and the rest of my family—were the richest people in the whole world. That was my mother's style. Mother could scrape and save, work hard and suffer much, but she would always appear rich and distinguished and was extravagantly generous.

But the pleasure was short lived.

We were about to unpack our clothes and utensils when my grandma called from across the threshold, "Stop unpacking. The French are coming."

The children were called in from the garden. The doors were closed. The family sat bunched up in a corner. Grandma and Mother took out their rosaries and started praying. I took my rosary and went into the dark kitchen where I thought I could sit alone and watch the activities without being seen. The whole family was settled in, and my father had just noticed my absence and called, "Mai, get back here!" when half a dozen soldiers in French uniforms walked into the yard. They were running after the chickens and pigs.

"Hey there," a Vietnamese soldier pointed to me. "Get out here."

I put my rosary in my pocket and walked out of the kitchen toward him.

130

"Hurry up. Catch that pig," he said pointing to the running pig which was being chased by two other soldiers.

I attempted to catch its hind legs, but it escaped. I ran after it and tried again. I caught its legs, but again it ran away, pulling me flat on the ground. I got up and said, "I can't catch it. It's too fast."

"Catch it!" another soldier screamed. He pulled the bolt of his gun. At that moment I heard a French voice asking, "What's going on?"

"She no obey, Captain," the soldier answered in broken French.

I turned and saw the French captain walking toward us. I said in French, "They wanted me to catch the pig, but it was too fast. It ran away."

The French captain gave me a curious look, then asked, "Where do you live?"

"There," I said, pointing to the house. "My father, mother, and the whole family."

"What does your father do?"

"He's an engineer. Would you like to talk to him?"

"Yes. Please."

I went into the house and asked my father to go out.

The French captain and my father spoke softly, away from the soldiers. A few minutes later, my father came in and said a few words to my mother, who turned around and told us to pick up our bags. We said good-bye to Grandma then left with the French captain and his Vietnamese soldiers.

I carried a bag on my shoulder and pushed my father's bicycle with my little brother on the lateral bar and a basket tied to the luggage rack. We left the village and went into the open field. The French captain, no older than twenty-five, saw me pushing the bike with difficulty on the bumpy dirt lane. He came to me and offered to help. He slung his gun over his shoulder. Then he took the bike with my brother on it and walked a few steps behind me on the narrow dirt road.

After a while, he started asking me questions about my schooling in the South and told me about his school in Paris. He said that he had graduated from college and that he came from a military family. He had heard many nice things about Cochinchina and wanted to join the army to help the "Cochinchinese" fight the Communist rebels. I listened, admiring his eloquence and good manners. He looked handsome and idealistic. Too bad, I thought, that I could not tell him my side of the story.

We enjoyed each other's company so much that we forgot we were in the battlefield. The soldiers had spread out, mindful of Viet Minh surprise attacks. Walking separately on a narrow dam trail across the small field, my family was having a hard time following the soldiers.

That afternoon, we arrived at a school used as a refugee camp inside the French lines. The French captain came to our "camp" in an attempt to talk to me again that evening, but my parents refused to let me see him. I understood Father's position, who to be consistent with his principles and culture, considered all French our enemy. I only hoped that my new friend did not feel offended and consider it an act of unfaithfulness since he had helped me to push through the bumpy and narrow trail the bicycle with my little brother and our belongings on it. I never knew if my parents regarded the Frenchman's act as a rescue or a forced journey against their will. But we moved on to Hanoi in a bus and settled in a villa provided by a distant uncle of my father.

Top, left: Nguyen Trung (paternal grandfather of author's husband), governor of Nghe An province at forty-six, 1903. *Top, right:* Maternal grandfather of author's husband, Dao Thai Hanh (born in Sadec, South Vietnam). Died in 1916 at forty-five while governor of Quang Tri province. He started his career as a mandarin in 1902 as an imperial interpreter in French for Emperor Thanh Thai. Self-taught, he wrote many articles in French and was a founding member of the famous French review, *Bulletin des Amis du Vieux Hue.* *Bottom:* Vietnamese delegation sent to Paris in 1889 by Emperor Thanh Thai. Seated from right to left: Nguyen Trung (grandfather of author's husband), chief of imperial staff representing Central Vietnam; Prince Mien Trien, delegation leader; Governor Vu Van Bau, representing North Vietnam. Far left, standing, French-speaking School Principal Petrus Truong Vinh Ky representing South Vietnam (a famous high school in Saigon is named after Petrus Ky).

Top, left: Author's father-in-law, Nguyen Thuc, accompanied Emperor Khai-Dinh (father of the last emperor, Bao-Dai) to Paris in 1922. He was deputy governor of Thanh Hoa Province when he retired in 1945. He and Ngo Dinh Diem (who became the first president of South Vietnam in 1955) served together under Catholic Annam Chief Minister Nguyen Huu Bai. *Top, right:* Author's mother-in-law, Dao Thi Xuan-Huong. Although her father was "progressive" for his time, she was married young, at sixteen, according to traditional customs, and handled all domestic chores in her domineering mother-in-law's household. *Bottom:* The author with her student volunteers, sewing clothes for poor children and giving free haircuts to poor orphans.

Author's father, Nguyen Pham Phuc, a public works engineer, in Western suit. He represents the "modernizing" new generation of Vietnamese born in the first decades of the twentieth century. He was not schooled in traditional "classics" in Chinese characters, but he studied French and engineering. He worked for the French federal public works service in Indochina which was responsible for building roads and railroads not only in Vietnam, but also in Laos and Cambodia. Author's mother, Nguyen Thi Ti (1905–1970) in North Vietnamese attire. She was a gifted self-taught poetess, a member of the well-known Quynh Giao poets' society. She had three books published—two novels in verse and a book of poems entitled *Chin Nam Loan Ly* (Nine Years of War), depicting important family and political events in Vietnam from 1945 to 1955.

Top: Author's husband (youngest pictured) with mandarin family circa 1932. *Bottom:* Temple of the indigenous Cham people of Southern Vietnam.

Author's maternal grandmother in North Vietnamese attire and hairstyle of the time (early 1890s). She was a native of Bac Ninh Province (about twenty-five miles northeast of Hanoi).

Top: The author in 1959 during the electoral campaign for the National Assembly of South Vietnam. She was in conference with the commander of the Seventh Division stationed in Bien Hoa and the incumbent assemblywoman, both notorious servants and protégées of the Ngo regime. (See Neil Sheehan's *A Bright Shining Lie,* 1988 Random House, N.Y.). The incumbent assemblywoman, who was an unpopular protégée of the famous Mrs. Nhu, sister-in-law of Ngo Dinh Diem, actually lost the election in Bien Hoa but was proclaimed "reelected" by the Diem government. *Bottom:* The author's husband with other University students from abroad. Kalamazoo, Michigan, 1951.

Picture of Ngo Dinh Diem as exile at Maryknoll Seminary in Lakewood, New Jersey. This rare picture of Ngo Dinh Diem (never before published) was taken by the author's husband in late 1952. While staying at the Maryknoll Seminary, Diem often invited the author's husband to Lakewood for consultations. In July 1954, Diem cabled the author's husband, urgently asking him to return to Vietnam to help Diem's new government. He did, with a group of five other U.S.-trained Vietnamese.

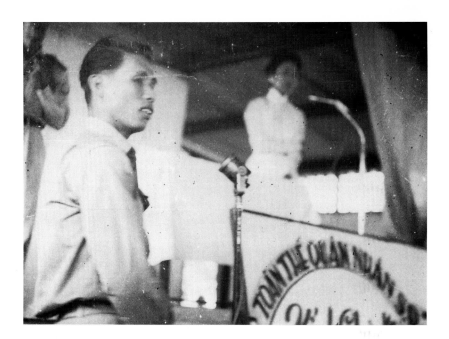

Top: The author in 1959, speaking to soldier-voters serving in the Seventh Division of the South Vietnamese Army stationed in Bien Hoa. The author was then running for election as an independent candidate to the National Assembly, against the incumbent deputy who was a protégée of the unpopular Mrs. Ngo Dinh Nhu. *Bottom:* The author in 1956, reviewing troops during an official visit to South Korea.

The author in 1955, working in a slum area in Saigon. With her group of student volunteers, she was clearing up an area to make a playground for poor children.

Top: The author in 1956 at the christening of her first son with parents and friends in Saigon. *Bottom:* The author in 1960 with her husband's parents and her sister-in-law (a Catholic nun teaching at Regina Mundi School in Saigon).

The author, with her new husband (they were married on July 3, 1954), at the Washington, D.C., airport in early August 1954. He was about to board the plane to return to Vietnam, as requested by Ngo Dinh Diem.

Top: The author with the 1952 president of the Vietnamese Catholic student association in North America and its chaplain, Father Emmanuel Jacques, a Belgian priest who was the representative in the United States of the Council of Vietnamese Bishops in Vietnam. At the time, the latter wanted to send more Vietnamese Catholic students to the United States for advanced training. *Bottom:* The author in 1959 with husband and two oldest children.

Top: The author and husband in Paris in 1972, during the Vietnam Paris Peace Talks.
Bottom: The author, with relatives, back in Bac Ninh in 1990. They were searching for
their ancestors' and grandparents' tombs which had been neglected during the war years.
Among the relatives she relocated was her cousin (standing to her right), a professor of
dentistry who had been the personal dentist of Ho Chi Minh.

Top: The ferry across the famous Bach Dang River in North Vietnam, where in 1288 the Chinese Mongolian troops suffered a decisive defeat and ended their invasion of Vietnam. *Bottom:* The author in 1990 in the North Vietnam Hon Gay area, which produces high grade coal (anthracite). She is chatting with North Vietnamese veterans in the small boat they used as living quarters and as fishing boat.

In the cemetery where Colonel Thao was buried, the author met a fourteen-year-old girl who was wandering around the tombs, offering to clean up the weeds around the tombs, trying to get small donations to help her family survive.

The author, 1992, visiting the famous monument in North Vietnam of patriot Nguyen Trai. A brilliant strategist, he helped Le Loi, the founder of the Le dynasty (1418–1427), expel the Chinese occupation troops from Vietnam. After defeating the Chinese, Nguyen Trai wrote the famous appeal to the people entitled "Binh Ngo Dai Cao" (engraved on the stone the author is touching). In that early example of psychological warfare, Nguyen Trai exhorted all Vietnamese to defend their national independence at any cost.

12

I RETURNED to Hanoi with no hope, no dreams. I didn't know what to think after three years of living in the countryside devoid of traffic, luxury, reading materials, radio, music (except for national songs), money, and crime. As the bus passed through the crowded streets, I could feel the rush of passers-by and smell the polluted dust. The crowds disturbed my view with their different clothing and nationalities — Vietnamese, French, Senegalese, military, civilian — riding bicycles, cars, army trucks, jeeps. We passed the Redemptorist church where a huge group of Catholics were singing outdoors in their Friday procession to worship the Eucharist of Christ. Then we passed Kham Thien, the famous section of the *gai lang choi* (the village of play girls) with a long line of shut doors and windows. Nothing in this town reminded me of my life in the countryside except for the name "Vietnam" — in place of French "Annam" — and the word "independence." These new epithets had appeared together at the time of our 1945 revolution and were now used by both governments: the Viet Minh's and Bao Dai's.

Father returned to his regular job as an engineer with Emperor Bao Dai's government, which had officially declared itself independent from the French, but whose actual budgets and directives were French. Father had no choice. It would have been too risky to recross the borderline; he would have been going back to the pit again, and no way out. We had seen it all. Our family had lived under both governments, and we couldn't approve of either. The administrators in non–Communist Vietnam were either those working for the court of Hue or the "Dan Tay" — the Vietnamese who were granted French citizenship. The Communist régime was a complete anarchy where ignorant opportunists took advantage of

133

the hesitant and confused state of mind of decent people and made themselves important through wicked maneuverings. For the moment, we had to accept this fact of life and store away our idealism.

The villa we lived in was a nice two-story house at a street corner; it faced another villa that had a little red light at the front door which would turn on at night. My mother gave me a room upstairs next to hers. Both rooms had access to a balcony that looked out onto the street intersection, but Mother forbade me to open the door to the balcony. From the living room downstairs, I often looked forward for the red light to switch on; the dim light gave a very soft and mysterious look to that villa.

One evening in the middle of the hot humid summer, I had to open the forbidden door to let in some air. As the door opened, my eyes landed on a French soldier holding a naked Vietnamese woman by the bedside in the red-light villa. I immediately jerked the door closed as if somebody had just pulled a switch on my arm. Nevertheless, the scene remained forever after in my memory as vivid as on that split second of unsuspected sight.

It had not been clear to me before why Mother condemned and called some girls "bad girls." And it seemed the priests, my spiritual mentors, did not even want to hear anything slightly related to the matter. One day, in a confessional of a remote village, I had asked a priest whether I had committed a sin in having a heated desire and confused sense of "sex" in me. Suddenly, I heard him utter something loud and unintelligible; then his confessional door slammed. I saw the back of the priest rushing out to the side door. I didn't know what had possessed him. I went on saying my prayers of repentance and considered myself forgiven by Jesus, who had himself looked at and attracted the famous prostitute Magdalene as he was carrying the Cross. In church, a special station was devoted to this scene out of the twelve Stations of the Cross, in front of which we had to kneel down and commemorate the death of Jesus every Friday. I myself associated sex with love, and love had become to me a thing of beauty, like the purity of the transparent moon that I loved to watch on those nights on the sampans. It tantalized every fiber of my body, making me more desirous of it, yearning to give more of my love. Like the moon, I felt love was above all material things. Yet, at the same time I was conscious of the sexual instincts in me, which made me yearn to be touched, to give my whole body to something that felt like a vacuum in the universe, sucking me up inside, making me melt within myself. A surge of such tantalizing feeling had rushed through my body at the sight of the scene in the red-light villa, but was immediately followed by a sense of guilt, shame, and cheapness. I realized then that that was not sex associated with love, but just sex using "love" to barter. I felt bad to have let this scene taint my love-sex feeling.

Apparently my mother condemned love and sex the same way she condemned and forbade me to go to a coed school—she condemned all things unusual and uncustomary. With Father working, we no longer had to worry about an income. I decided to prepare myself to return to high school in the fall. I could review math by myself, but I needed to learn English, which was a new requirement in school. The one and only school that taught English was coed, but of course Mother said no to it. Without letting her know, I found a job tutoring French and math (wives of merchants paid well for their children's education) and used those earnings to pay for my English classes and violin lessons. My days consisted of going to school, violin lessons, and tutoring other people's children and my brothers and sisters. Like in the countryside, Mother left me alone with my plan once she saw I had already gone ahead with it.

On the big school entrance day, I went and applied to be a junior at Hai Ba Trung (The Trung Sisters), the only public high school for girls in town. I was refused. They said I was too old, three or four years older than their students in the same class. I went home and told my father. The next day he took me over to the school and requested to see the directrice. When they gave the age reason, and the lack of school records, Father became furious. He told them they were unreasonable for not giving me credit for my service to the family the last three years while he was away doing public work.

He said, "You may not care to hear this, and I don't care to know where you've been, but I can tell you one thing: if the French accepted me back after my revolutionary activities, you can't be more French than the French. Let my daughter continue her education. Give her a test if you wish. We are not asking you for a favor, we are asking you to carry out your duty as a citizen. I shall take leave now, trusting that this problem will be resolved by the commencement of classes."

A few days later we received a note admitting me to school. When summer came, I took and passed the national examination which one must pass as a prerequisite to go on to college.

My mother rewarded me with a handsome bright yellow woman's bicycle with wide white tires to match my yellow dress which I had interchanged with my black dress to wear during the school year. This memorable purchase was made with extreme care through the expertise of a male cousin of mine I had not met before. He brought my mother and me to what he considered the best bike store in town—a small, dark, obscure shop where after careful, lengthy examination, testing, and

135

comparison among a dozen shiny bikes, he finally settled on the yellow one.

The following day, Mother treated me to a restaurant specializing in broiled fish. I was very impressed, for it was the first time we were "tête-à-tête" alone together.

Hai Ba Trung opened its first math class for first-year college students, and I and two other girls were the first to join the class. Later, one of the girls became a doctor and the other a pharmacist, but presently, one of them, Powder, became my best friend. Mother had changed her mind about coed schools and paid the tuition fees for me to register in one so that I could prepare myself for the baccalauréat in math, skipping two years of university.

It was the happiest time of my life in Hanoi. Powder and I made friends with two other girls, and together we all represented the female sex in the crowded coed classes. Each of us had a bike. We would race from one end of town to the other to meet one another, share our small desks, do our homework together, then squeeze ourselves in bed together to recoup from brain exhaustion. My friends, whose parents were in business (meaning rich), rented sculls for us to race on the wavy waters of the Eastern Lake and bought all kinds of goodies — shrimp patties, French potatoes — for us to nibble on while we did our studies on the hillsides surrounding the huge lake.

They bought me my first ticket to the movies to see *The Four Daughters of Dr. (something or another)* when it had just come to town. There we met all the boys that were in our classes, and from then on they called me Elizabeth Taylor and my best friend, tall and svelte, Esther Williams, whose pretty picture, the size of a playing card, was sold in the booth at the entrance to the theater. Seeing the picture of Esther Williams, I could see why they associated my friend with her, but I was puzzled, even upset, that they compared me to Elizabeth Taylor who acted like a spoiled, coquettish girl in that movie.

Powder joined me in taking music lessons. She rented a piano and asked Mother's permission to put it in our house, which was roomier, she said, so that we could practice together.

The school year ended with the much dreaded national exam lasting three days and covering all the subjects — the level of difficulty depending on your specialty. On the second day of the exam, as I copied down the chemistry questions from the blackboard, I was exceedingly delighted to see that they were from a chemistry lesson I had just reviewed before entering the room. But after five minutes of looking at the problem, I thought I spotted something missing. I raised my hand to communicate my thoughts to the examiner. He looked at me with disdain and ordered me with mocking eyes to sit down. I felt thoroughly embarrassed. After a few minutes passed, a messenger brought in a small piece of paper, and the examiner erased a portion on the blackboard and recopied the new equations from the paper he had just received. He then told us students that there was a change in the problem. I revised the new equations as I had remembered them to be, and the answers to them happily hung in my head. Yet, when I started to put them on paper, they seemed to all become confused like a giant cobweb with no outlets. By and by, my whole body turned into a heap of nerves, and my head spun until I thought of nothing else but getting out. I forced myself to sit tight for an hour or so. Then my nerves forced me out of my seat toward the examiner's desk to deposit the empty paper and out to the grassy court. As soon as I stepped onto the lawn, the whole lesson came back to me in a flash. Too late.

I had panicked because of the intimidating supervisor and probably from sheer exhaustion — too much cramming in such a short time. Learning in Vietnam consisted solely of committing everything read to memory; using one's eyes as a camera to register the text word for word. A teacher on the exam committee could always recognize his students by the way the text was interpreted, because it would be his own interpretation. It was a plus for the student whose text was recognized.

Nothing was really lost. I just had to review and study two more months for the second test. My friends and I didn't see one another for a while. I didn't ask myself why, but I think we probably felt sorry that we had deeply disappointed our families. In the meantime, I discovered the English language classes organized by the American Consulate, where a few girls and thousands of boys were attending. It was very embarrassing to have to push your bike into the midst of boys milling about and humming: "One day when we were young . . . You loved me and I loved you when we were young one day." The boys were very poetic and seemed to love learning.

About a month after I began the English classes, my American teacher stopped by our house on his bicycle. My father received him, and I was told that I had a scholarship to go to America. Things always came to me that way — unexpectedly. I was very surprised and very excited. So the trip to America, which I had considered a silly dream coming to me deep in the hopelessly remote countryside, was now a reality.

Mother resisted vehemently at first the idea of sending a girl off to school so far away from home. My aunt told me it was because Mother already had picked out a couple of candidates for me to marry. One was the man who had played the violin for Father during his sickness in the countryside, and the other my English tutor, a son of her very close friends. My father, on the other hand, was very happy about my going to America. He bought two sets of forks and knives to help me practice with and red wine for me to drink at every dinner.

"You must show them you are sophisticated and know their manners and their customs, and you must not get drunk when somebody offers you a drink," Father said.

I focused on my table manners, though I had difficulties in holding a knife properly. Half of my right hand muscles had been paralyzed when I was in the army during the intravenous sessions given by the apprentice nurses. I had contracted malaria and run a high fever after several days of marching with my regiment in the forest wet with pouring rain and infested with leeches. Having had a hard time finding my veins, the nurses probably had injected quinobleu outside of them.

After a few weeks, Mother decided to give in. She went and pawned what little jewelry she had left to buy me an airplane ticket for France and a ticket to cross the Atlantic on the *Île de France*.

13

I ARRIVED IN Paris at the end of the fall of 1951. Frost already covered the trees, and people were already wearing their coats. I stood out in my light dress and wooden high-heeled shoes. My newly curled hair, cut from waist to shoulder length at Mother's instruction, was the only thing that associated me with Occidentals. Mother had not worried about the cold; she was more concerned about looks—a new hair-do or an expensive bicycle.

Once when I was nine, I had stumbled across a picture of Mother in a kimono with a geisha hair-do. This had surprised me, for I had imagined her steeped in Vietnamese traditions. Shivering now in the streets of Paris with my curly hair, however, I realized how dearly Mother held fashion. In fact this seemed to be the way of many of us Vietnamese. In my mother's time any woman who was anybody (even very old-fashioned women of the court of Hue) had her picture taken in a geisha outfit. It so happened that for decades near the Truong Tien Bridge of the Imperial City, there lived a Japanese photographer who used to know all the important people—French and Vietnamese—through photographing their wives. When the Japanese invaded Vietnam, this man held the highest position in intelligence, advising the Japanese military commanders in Indochina.

Paris represented to me a step towards paradise. I loved the people; I loved the air; and I opened my very soul to absorb everything. People talked to me as their equal, not as a young girl who had a lot to learn from grown-ups. I was pleasantly surprised that the streets of Paris, its houses and apartments, looked no better than those of the colonial times in Vietnam. Though there were many more buildings, roads, trains, and cars, I found that ours were equal in quality. Their telephones were as complex and unreliable as ours, their roads dirtier than ours during colonial times, and their public toilets as smelly as ours. The only difference was that the facilities in France were to be used by all, while in Vietnam they were reserved for the French and a few exceptionally privileged Vietnamese.

I left Paris for America a week later on the ship *Île de France*. At the port of New York, I barely had the chance to ponder over my first impressions of "My Quoc" when I was met by a Belgian priest and a group of Vietnamese students. As we were introducing ourselves, I saw the two elderly French ladies I had met during the train ride to the L'Havres port approaching. They had occupied the same first-class deluxe compartment that somehow I had found myself in during the four-day crossing. The smiling ladies were followed by a man holding a large bouquet of flowers. They told me that their son (and nephew) had cabled them to give this bouquet to me and to invite me to visit them. This was the first time anybody had given me flowers. And not anybody, but two respectable elderly ladies, and on behalf of a man.

My father had not briefed me about how to handle situations like this. The only time I had seen flowers given were at funerals or in pictures where Ho Chi Minh was greeted by little girls. I felt one thing for sure: I should not accept anything from a male stranger; it could mean that I was engaged to him.

I was overwhelmed with embarrassment. I remembered the young man I had seen in the train with these two ladies. They had sat opposite me, and we had got to talking. I had asked them questions about the surroundings and so forth. The man had only spoken to me once, after the controller had come to ask me many questions about my passport which had been issued by the Imperial government and sealed with a golden dragon. Unlike the normal case, my passport allowed me to go to the United States instead of France, my colonial motherland. The young Frenchman had smiled at me and complimented me for my good job explaining.

I was racking my brain for a proper solution when I heard the priest say, "You're not to take the flowers."

I was shocked. Refusing to take the flowers from the nice ladies meant insulting them. I couldn't do that. They were just being nice to me, and now I was going to hurt them? But the priest looked at me, and the Vietnamese students looked at him. I couldn't hurt his pride either. At the spur of the moment, I went to the lady I assumed to be the young man's mother, who was holding the flowers, and gave a quick kiss on her hand, smiled at both ladies, then turned and walked away. The priest and the students followed me. Out of the busy pier onto the streets packed with snow, I balanced myself on my wooden high heels, touching with surprise and joy the icy rocks and noticing the New York sky brightened with sunlight and a rainbow of striking colors on people's clothing and on the lips of young girls—a contrast to the French atmosphere of somber monuments and people dressed in black or dark grey.

Dampening the enjoyment of my new experiences in "My Quoc" however, was the incident with the priest. So, people still wanted to control me, and they did—whether rightly or wrongly was another matter! I didn't know the people's customs or traditions—how to act sophisticated like Father had told me. How was I to know what sophistication was with these foreigners? I didn't know whether what I did would make me look weak, bad, or worst of all, ill-mannered.

This debate within me went on during my entire stay in America, from 1951 to 1955, in spite of the kind supervision of the priest. He took over the scholarship matter and sent me to different Catholic schools. I missed my short independent period in France, though most of the nuns I met in America were sweet, gentle, and generous. The ones at Trinity College, Vermont, gave me expensive linen, took me to shops, and bought me good coats and shoes. The nurse at Nazareth gave me wine to drink secretly, before dinner, to help me whet my appetite. I received good grades when I deserved them.

Whenever I felt the burden of all these favors too much for me, I would make a move, change schools, and earn my living as a maid or waitress to pay for my daily room and board. The priest was always there to help me make those changes. I didn't know who paid for the school fees, but there wasn't much sense in worrying about that because I wouldn't have had any means to take care of them anyway.

I made many friends, all foreign students though. American girls only talked to me in class but never offered to do things with me or invite me to their homes. I guess my pride told me to ignore what otherwise would have bothered me in their attitude. I told myself that after all I came to their country as a friend, with an open mind to admire and learn. If they did not feel at ease, it was their problem not mine. My duty with them was to behave and dress properly to meet their social standards so that my presence would not annoy them.

I found friendship with men to be easier. I mingled in international gatherings and made friends with young American men so that I could learn about American culture and speak better English. To the surprise of my girlfriends, I felt very comfortable going out with American men. They were to me like any of my acquaintances in the army, in the village organizations, and in business transactions. In fact, I considered myself to be pretty level-headed and my actions quite independent from other people's influence, except for the priest.

One day, however, in one of the Vietnamese summer conventions organized by the Belgian priest and to which twenty or so Vietnamese students gathered from all over the United States, this began to change. I heard a Vietnamese give a fluent speech in surprisingly good English. Hoanh (Splash — I gave him that nickname because I thought it fit his personality) approached me afterwards and asked for my address. I heard his Hue accent and told him that I heard Hue people were phony like their king who built a phony Perfume River and a phony Throne Mountain. Thinking he was a bit too forward, I didn't give him my address.

At that time I was attending Mundelein College in Chicago and exchanging babysitting for room and board with a family in Evanston. When I returned home that evening, I saw the head of my host family, a devout Catholic man, waiting for me in the driveway, his two-year-old son sitting on his shoulders. He said he was waiting for me to walk with him to the subway to pick up Hoanh whom he had invited for dinner. He said that Hoanh seemed a good sort and a very intelligent young man and that I should go out with a Vietnamese.

Again they were arranging things above my head, and I was supposed to go along and observe.

After dinner, Hoanh asked me to take a walk with him. We had walked for about a hundred feet when suddenly he stopped and asked me if I had any boyfriends. When I responded, "Yes," he asked, "Do they mean anything to you?"

I told him that the one in Vietnam was a friend of the family and had been my English tutor. The doctor that I had met through the arrangement of the nuns was also my friend because the nuns approved of his good manners. A university teacher I had met at an international club was a good and brilliant friend; he was one year younger than me. He also lived in Evanston, so he helped me carry my books and frequently walked home with me from school. He took me places so that I could learn about American culture, as I had asked him to do.

I did not tell him about my new friends, thinking it was none of his business. Both men had tried to show me something more intimate than just going out together. But when they had attempted to kiss me I had pushed them gently aside and just shook my head. They understood and no longer persisted. I imagined they had just wanted to show me their manhood, so I did not get offended.

In any case, this young Vietnamese, Hoanh, told me that I had to drop them all because that was not the way a respectable Vietnamese girl behaved. These young men and the American people would misinterpret me. "Our life in Vietnam is a political life. We should be aware of our Vietnamese politics. Tomorrow, come to the park. I will bring a newspaper, and you will learn more about politics and English."

I was aghast at the way he ordered me around. No man my age ever talked to me like that. But then on second thought, he sounded like a leader, purposeful and intelligent. I needed a leader and someone useful for my country.

To be fair to my teacher friend, and to show my obedience to my new Vietnamese leader, I called my friend up and told him that I would no longer go out with him. I told him about this new friend and the English lessons.

"What!? I am an American and can't teach you better English than a Vietnamese?"

"But he does real teaching. This afternoon he will bring a newspaper for me to read, and he will quiz me on my English."

"I can do that, too. You never asked me!"

"You didn't tell me, " I said. "Anyway, I think I like you, but I love him. I must obey him." The word love hadn't been in my heart nor head an instant before. I don't know where it came from.

My new leader also helped me to return the box of chocolates and five dollars that my doctor friend had sent me from Vermont. I had accepted the gift, considering him to be like one of my bigger brothers in the army who had now and then given me money to spend.

At about this time, I received a letter from an organization called the League of Women Voters saying that I was granted a scholarship from the Michigan State University at East Lansing. (To this day, I do not know how and why the scholarship was given to me.) I showed the letter of invitation to the Belgian priest who disapproved of the idea. A coed school was too large and not a good place for a girl. He then went ahead and took care of the letter and found me another scholarship with a Catholic school in Nazareth, Michigan. I complied with his "advice," thinking I knew no better.

In the end I was glad. The nuns, who were strict but loving, intelligent but modest, and reserved but straightforward, gave me a new insight on "dignity." Their way was not the phlegmatic, sometimes cold-hearted, and far too "aboveboard" way I observed of my mother.

For the next year and a half I saw no other man but my new friend, Hoanh. He saw me infrequently, being a student in up-state New York while I was in Illinois, then later in Michigan. For girlfriends I had a few foreign students: Chinese, South Americans, and Island girls, younger than myself, mostly immature, and all too excited about men. But then American girls didn't seem much different in that respect either. I remember the time my teacher friend took me to the university where he taught. The girls, his students, surrounded him in the cafeteria and served him coffee and cookies. They brought me none and even ignored my presence. He told me to go get some at the counter, but I shook my head. So he got up and went to fetch me some. I knew it was embarrassing for him to do that in front of the girls, but rather that than have me think badly about him and his own people. For my part, I didn't think it was proper to serve a man when you were not engaged to him. It was buying affection.

In Kalamazoo, I became very anxious to see Hoanh, to have someone to communicate with. I changed my major from chemistry to history and political science with a minor in economics to have a better grasp of Hoanh's involvement.

My introduction to politics in the United States began when I first arrived in Nazareth, Michigan, and was interviewed by a local newspaper reporter. I was the first Vietnamese to come to Nazareth. The reporter asked me about my country and whom I would choose as leader. Since leaving the Communist countryside in North Vietnam, I had not heard of any Vietnamese that was doing anything exceptional for Vietnam, nor any that fought the French like Ho Chi Minh. The Vietnamese who worked in the French administration were handpicked by the French to collaborate with them and destroy any who joined the anti–French movements. Included among those working for the French were the Dai Viets and Viet Quoc, the Vietnamese nationalists helped by Chiang Kai-shek's Kuomintang, who had used the French to eliminate their Communist competitor in the war for national liberation.

Hoanh had told me about Ngo Dinh Diem, a middle-aged Catholic mandarin in his fifties, who had resigned from the mandarin Annam government to come stay in the Maryknoll Seminary in New York. He said the man was not a good speaker but had been a mandarin in the court of Hue. I had seen Diem in Chicago at one of the Vietnamese student meetings. He hadn't impressed me. He showed no charisma and no revolutionary record except for having resigned from the French government, which was commonly done by all Vietnamese patriots, both young and old.

But there was the reporter, prompting an immediate answer. I wasn't about to name Ho Chi Minh, though his popularity and integrity were great. Why didn't he control the mass in Quang Ngai? They called

144

themselves Communists and went around burying alive rich landlords, Catholics, and intellectuals who resisted their movement. He did not declare any decree to warn or condemn the greedy opportunists around the country who murdered innocents and turned on their own people. My own father would have been one of their victims, if not for his luck in being saved by Sister Hon and her Communist husband. Uncle Ho did not give importance to the middle class that was the main force in this war against the French, and in his revolution for a better society.

These thoughts flashed through my mind in seconds while the reporter was waiting for his answer. A name was better than no name. I hadn't heard anything bad about Diem, so I blurted out, "Ngo Dinh Diem."

Some months later, I received a copy of a *Congressional Record* containing a speech of Senator John F. Kennedy and Senator Mansfield mentioning my name as a supporter in promoting the idealist Ngo Dinh Diem as leader of Vietnam—someone I really knew nothing about. I had done it again—followed an impulse that caused me regret the rest of my life! Life was like that with me. I made a lot of mistakes out of ignorance, or from pressure to please. To make matters worse, I wasn't sure of the compatibility between my traditions and my own values and the values I admired in the United States.

Decision making to meet up with an unprecedented situation—and there seemed to be many—often gave me something to regret afterwards. I remember the first night I met Hoanh who gave me all kinds of instructions on how to behave properly as a Vietnamese. That same night, after telling me to rid myself of all my friends, he started in on my private life.

He asked me to show him my wallet. "He does not trust me," I thought. I gave him the wallet. He opened it and saw a picture of my English tutor who had sent it to me along with some Vietnamese magazines on my first New Year's in the States. "Who is this?"

"The Vietnamese friend of my family I told you about."

"He must mean something to you, otherwise why is his picture in your wallet?"

"I had no other place of my own to keep it. Anyway he should be placed among my family's pictures."

"If it's true he means nothing to you, can I tear his picture up?"

I was thoroughly taken aback. He didn't believe me after all that! Does he think I am a liar? "Go ahead," I dared him. All of a sudden, I heard in the dark, "shwitt . . . shwitt."—the crisp sound of tearing paper. I turned to him. The picture was torn to pieces. I was dumbfounded. The nerve! He is not real. He is not of this world. He is not someone I could respect. Someone calm and cool like my father. Someone who trusts and respects other people the way my father trusts my mother ... Hoanh's behavior was outrageous, low class! I said that to myself and slept with that and awoke with that until he called me on the phone to announce that he was coming. And I let him come! I let him take me to the main Chicago library to study for hours. Then to the park to listen to open-air music while having our lunch. Now and then he kissed me and made me kiss him back. All done with certainty and authority. And I was happy to have somebody to take care of me so completely, like I had taken care of my brothers and sisters at home.

I was further impressed when one day after the library he took me to a Chinese restaurant and after we ate gave me a gold cross and said, "We're engaged."

I called the Belgian priest on the telephone to let him know and was surprised to hear him order me to return the gift. But a priest was higher in rank than a friend. That evening when my friend came, I attempted to return it. He was furious and rushed out into the dark snowy night. A few hours later I was called out of my room in the middle of the night to receive him standing in the snow with no coat on. He refused to come in and told me that all he had to say was that I had to keep the cross and that things were settled between him and the priest.

Talk about *coup de foudre* (thunder struck) in love. I wasn't sure which one struck me worse, love or shock. He had fought with the priest and run out without his coat, rushing back here from Blackstone, at the other end of town, to Evanston to give me an order. Fighting with a priest about the cross and engagement when the priest certainly knew ten times more than he did on that subject. In spite of this, I found him to be a charming man with a strong sense of leadership. I had no point of comparison.

Neither my parents' lives nor the *Livres Roses* stories had given me practical insight to a man's behavior, the question of leadership and integrity, or the human aspects of love and sex. The only way for me to sort out the problems that confounded me was to, when the circumstances arose, draw out from the confusing maze of Vietnamism, Buddhism, and Catholicism something suitable to my emotions at the time, then rationalize it to make it applicable to the moment — that spontaneous treatment called "improvisation."

My Brother Hoanh, by Vietnamese tradition, became my fiancé. In the spring term, he transferred from Cornell University to East Lansing, Michigan, for his doctoral studies.

When summer came, Brother Hoanh told me to prepare for the wedding. The priest had come to Nazareth to tell me that Hoanh was a very arrogant boy and that I should not marry him. He said he had already sent a letter to my family to warn them about Hoanh. I had also received a nasty letter from my mother telling me that the family had made sacrifices to send me to My Quoc to be a doctor and not to consort with men. She said I should not smear the family name. Surprisingly, I did not feel confused about my decision to ignore both my mother and the priest's warning. I continued to see Hoanh and accepted his proposal for marriage.

The week before our wedding, Brother Hoanh brought two Vietnamese friends from Lansing to see me. I arranged with two pretty Chinese girlfriends to go out with them. We went to the tennis court, and I was surprised to see that Brother did not encourage my two girlfriends to go with his friends. Instead, he picked out the prettier one to play tennis with us and let the rest take care of themselves.

This pretty girl had played ping-pong with me in the past. While I had thought it was just fun and exercise, she kept getting upset whenever I hit the ball too fast and made her lose. She was very mindful about counting the points and arguing over them.

In any case, we were playing on the tennis court, I on her side. Pretty soon the ball was passed back and forth between the two of them; my fiancé rushing to pick up the ball even on her court and to say he was sorry that he played too strongly. All his attention was directed to her. I found myself left out. I stood there smiling to keep my dignity, but inside I began to analyze my beloved fiancé: So this is the man who said he loved me. I have devoted every minute of two years to him by changing my chemistry major, even though I had barely less than a year to graduate, and keeping my body healthy and in good shape—all that in order to show him I loved him and would be useful to him in all matters of the mind and heart. I wanted to leave the court, but I didn't want them to think that I was jealous, the victim of an inferiority complex. My smile wore thin during my discourse to myself. I backed out towards the gate, waving and saying, "Enjoy," and left. I had made a big mistake. I had chosen the wrong man.

I was on the lane leading to the manor where I lived when the two friends of my fiancé and my other girlfriend caught up with me. We continued to walk together. Then I heard my name called from behind. My fiancé was running, trying to catch up with us!

For the whole week I thought and thought. I had no wedding dress, but I postponed doing something about it. Then came the wedding day.

As usual my fiancé arranged everything. Too late — I couldn't back out. I had to consider the adults' face first. I had to stick to my promise. It was amazing how I still always considered those older than me as "adults."

In the afternoon before the wedding, I had bought a piece of nice white material and started cutting it to the shape of a dress. Then I sewed it with the stitches I had learned from a neighbor in Hanoi. I finished just in time for the ceremony. Brother Hoanh told me later that he had had to sleep in his car that previous night, after partying with his friends, because he had locked his key in his apartment. The owner had had to come to open his door on the day of the wedding so he could get his tuxedo.

His professors had organized a big wedding and reception for us with a large crowd of attendants. After mass, we went into the reception room. They all lined up, and the men demanded a kiss from me, and the women demanded a kiss from the groom. This was really awkward and embarrassing for me — kissing complete strangers. I covered my face and smiled. I don't recall if I kissed more than five people after kissing my godfather.

After we ate wedding cake, they told me to give away the bouquet of flowers in my hand. I did not know the custom and did not know to whom to give it. So I excused myself and went in the back to the little altar I had seen hidden in the hallway. There, I placed the flowers under the feet of the Virgin Mary and said Hail Marys. Then I returned to bid them all farewell with my husband under a shower of rice. I thought they threw the rice because we were Oriental.

In Hanoi, my mother, who had objected to the marriage, chose together with Brother Hoanh's parents their own day for our wedding and celebrated it with a classic ceremony. Pictures were taken and shown to us later.

Brother Hoanh's parents had sent from Central Vietnam representatives to ask for my hand. His mother hired nine men in traditional northern dress to carry nine lacquer boxes of betels, nuts, and gold bracelets and necklaces to our home so that my mother could announce our engagement to her relatives and friends. Because of the war, the wedding party was relatively modest. Nonetheless, the customs were carefully observed to show class status. All this was necessary. Mother had our family name to worry about.

After our "American" wedding, we returned to Nazareth, to our new apartment which I had not seen yet; my husband had arranged it all. We slept that night with only our bodies to keep us warm; Brother had forgotten to buy sheets and blankets. The following day, we went without food for almost the entire day. We had no money. Brother told me he had spent all his savings to buy us a new car. That afternoon he drove us to a forest nearby. We shared two boiled eggs and chatted like the little birds around us. I was happy, though deep inside I was unsure about this new side that I discovered in my brother. I didn't mind being poor, going hungry, or sleeping in the cold — I had been there. It was the disappointment in the man, whom I had thought to be my leader, which made me wonder about his abilities and his concept of responsibilities and their consequences. I wondered if he had a plan for our life. And if he didn't, why then had he not talked to me about it so that I could feel that we were in it together for better or for worse? Too many unknowns! I had thought my husband had the marks of leadership and acted with vision. Perhaps I was expecting too much.

The nuns had given me a job in the hospital, washing patients' clothes down in the basement. This exposed me to another aspect of human complications. I worked with an old American woman whose legs were swollen with large varicose veins which, she said, came from working on her feet for twenty years. This struck me with horror. Working like that here in this beautiful country? I told her just to sit down and relax for a minute, but she refused saying, "They don't like it. You can't sit down and work fast. So much has to be done before the work day ends."

Nevertheless, I pulled up a chair and made her sit down and put her legs up. I felt sure that the sisters would not object if they saw the old lady's condition. Besides, one could do a better job after one rested comfortably. The nuns were probably too involved in spiritual matters and neglected our human condition.

Two days later, I was removed to the sewing room. Again another old lady was working there. She pedaled incessantly on a machine. Now and then I heard her moaning about the pain in her neck and shoulders. Again I had to impose my idea, making her rest and giving her shoulders a massage.

This work situation really bothered me. I wondered about the "democracy" of this beautiful country. The poorest Vietnamese in Vietnam would not have had to work half as hard. Our family's maids (every Vietnamese, rich or poor, had at least one helper in the house) and all the maids in other households I knew, took two or three hours of siesta. Though they played with us day and night, they could go and visit their family in their free siesta time or at night after dinner. Even on the rubber plantation supervised by Frenchmen I had seen some "slaves" sitting down and relaxing in the middle of their very slow-paced work. Another thing that troubled me was the way supervisors addressed their older workers on a first name basis, while contrarily, the employees had to call them by "Mr." or "Mrs." I remember noticing that even in France doormen, secretaries, and maids were addressed with a "Mr." or "Mrs." before their names.

Not long before the fall of 1954, Brother Hoanh received a telegram from Ngo Dinh Diem, for whom he had organized talks in the United States. Diem asked him to return to Vietnam with a group of five other students from the United States and Canada.

The trip to Washington, D.C., showed me yet another side of Brother Hoanh. In his new car, he attempted to drive the long distance from Michigan in one continuous stretch. I was spared, I thought, for I had just barely passed the driving test the day before — after a few lessons in the little dirt path by the forest where we went picnicking.

I was lying with my head on his lap, in my half-dream state feeling like a little lamb tenderly protected by her loving shepherd, when suddenly I heard: "Little sister. Little sister. Wake up." I sat up in a hurry. The sky was pitch dark. In front, our headlights shone on two lines of red cones boxing in our car. Before I could say anything, my brother said, "You take over. I'm too sleepy. I must sleep now."

He opened the door and flopped into the backseat out of sight. I scooted over to the driver's seat, my eyes transfixed on the red cones, trying hard to figure out what kind of street I was in. The car was shaking under the heavy rumbling from the continuous flow of passing trucks some dozen yards to my left. My head became feverish. The car pushed forward uncertainly. The cones narrowed themselves, then merged with other cones. Soon my car crossed the lines and cones and suddenly hit the main stream, sucked between the trucks into the tunnel. My hands clung to the wheel, only to protect myself, for the car seemed to float above the road, pushed by the pressure of surrounding trucks. Finally, clearer skies appeared. Brother had risked our lives with my two-day-old driving experience to go through the Pennsylvania Turnpike — one of the most unexpected and harrowing experiences I had ever run across.

The five graduate students held their important secret meetings for two days and nights. On the third day, I and two other wives accompanied them to the airport to see them off. It was a chance for our husbands to be useful to our country. We all welcomed that opportunity.

That same day, I gave the car away to a Vietnamese couple and took a plane back to Kalamazoo — to return to the uncomplicated and disciplined life of school, and to be near the fair and smart Sister Aquinas, dean of studies, who supervised my study; the just and intelligent Sister

Catherine, our school president, who oversaw my daily activities; and the caring and loving nurse, Sister Leonard, who took care of my health as she saw fit. Their influence filled my very being. I relived the simple life of the countryside in North Vietnam, the carefree little girl in my home town in South Vietnam. I had no wants, no wishes.

This bliss of mind lasted six months. In February 1955, I graduated and boarded a plane to rejoin Brother Hoanh in our proud independent Saigon of the independent South Vietnam — freed now "forever" from the eighty-five years of French yoke.

I travelled with a passport allowing me to return to the Vietnam of Emperor Bao Dai. With the intervention of the United States, he had appointed Ngo Dinh Diem as his prime minister. For some reason, the passport in my hand evoked certain dark feelings in me. I remembered my return to Hanoi with my family after the calm and serene life in the countryside — the traffic heavy with jeeps and tanks, the crowd of Foreign Legions, the Redemptorist procession of the eucharist next to the play-girls' living quarters. Would I be returning to the same environment with the same Bao Dai as emperor and the same set-up of a prime minister, only this time propped by another foreign power than the French? My uncertainty, no longer stemming from inexperience, formed a dark cloud in my mind. This time I faced my return to Vietnam with melancholy and passed judgment with the certain bitterness of one who had seen it all before.

My passport read, "Mme. Le Van Hoanh, née Nguyen Thi Tuyet Mai." Traditionally, the family name came first, then a "Van" or "Thi" between the surname and given name to show gender: "Van" indicating a man, "Thi" a woman. In this way, naming a child with a favorite name was made easy: "Nguyen Van Mai" for a boy, "Nguyen Thi Mai" for a girl.

Over half of the Vietnamese population either carried the "Nguyen" name handed down from their ancestors, or adopted it to fit in with the last royal family in power before the French overtook Vietnam. My husband's family name, "Le," represented the longest and last real dynasty in the history of Vietnam.

I contemplated the passport and said to myself: "From now on, forget you are Mai. Forget your past life; forget you existed." A sad feeling embraced me. I missed the "Mai" in me. Our marriage had made my friend Hoanh my superior, my main concern, therefore my life. I had to look after Brother Hoanh's name in spirit and in social functions and be subordinate to him as a wife, attached to him like an appendage. Whatever I did, he had to know. Whatever he did, I didn't have to know because I carried his name, not he mine. Well, nobody had put a gun to my head and forced me to love and marry Brother Hoanh. The priest and my family had objected to the marriage. I had gone on my own, thinking I had picked out a leader for myself—someone knowledgeable, therefore ideal for me and my country. So far my expectations of Brother Hoanh with regard to duty to country had not proven wrong.

In spite of myself, this thought brought to mind a little humorous verse from Ho Xuan Huong (Spring Perfume), a witty and daring poetess: "If I could change my body into a man, becoming a hero would be a simple game." (ca. 1775) A girl of ordinary family, she was twice "second wife," twice widowed. She described her situation: "That one has quilted blankets; this one [herself: second wife] is left in the cold." Her poems and social status did not fit well in the culture of Vietnam, but they reflected the independent spirit of women under the leadership of King Quang Trung, born Nguyen Hue (in the same period as Napoleon Bonaparte). King Quang Trung was the initiator of blitzkrieg warfare, a reformist who advocated equality between men and women, giving back lands to cultivators, and reading and writing in "Nom." (Then, Vietnamese called themselves "Dai Viet" or Great Viets and wrote in Nom, although they still used Chinese characters.) He defeated lords Trinh and Nguyen, who had fought one another, weakening the rare long reign of the Le dynasty (1428–1788) and allowing Chinese troops to reinforce on our border, threatening our independence.

Freedom under the reign of King Quang Trung had also helped to bring to blossom a timeless and powerful masterpiece by the poet Nguyen Du—"The Tale of Kieu"—from which verses older Vietnamese quoted by heart to express the political and psychological traumas they encountered in their lives and in the history of Vietnam. Unlike Nguyen Du whose "Tale of Kieu" was known by many adults, Xuan Huong and her works were banned from the literary classics. The same applied for King Quang Trung, who was quoted in our history books as being a rebel because he had opposed the founder of the Nguyen dynasty who later invited French troops into Vietnam and consequently lost his power to them. The Nguyen dynasty reigned over Vietnam side by side with the French until our revolution in 1945.

It was quite a contrast to come from the cold, harsh winter of Michigan to the warm, humid air of Saigon. Brother Hoanh picked me up at the Tan Son Nhut Airport in a jeep and took me home to a villa he shared with his four new friends: one from the States like him, another from Canada, and the other two, Cuong and Tuan, from France; all bachelors.

Gazing out on the balcony one day, I saw Cuong and Tuan, the French engineers, hopping off a government jeep—one of those left by the French in their abandoned villas or offices. The French returnees looked more easygoing than the other returnees and talked more about everything. From their casual conversation, I learned that they belonged to the Third International Socialist party. They made no secrets about it. It seemed everybody in France belonged to a political party or sympathized with one party or another. I suppose to them it was like a club, some place to chat with somebody.

"Hello, Sister Hoanh. Hope they have something good to eat and plenty of it. I'm starving," said Tuan with his authentic northern accent.

"Oh, I'm sure the food will be good and plenty. I love those big broiled shrimps like they cooked yesterday. I had at least a dozen. I haven't eaten them in years," said the southerner in broken Vietnamese with a French accent.

Just looking at them, jovial and sharp, I felt carried away with love and hope for my people.

Our house was like a market place. Strangers sometimes dropped in from the street and walked through the rooms without anybody paying any attention. One afternoon, a lady I had never met came to see me. She looked fortyish, about my mother's age. We made friends quickly over a cup of tea in our community living room full of laughter, shuffling feet, and noisy typewriters at work. She invited me to her house. I assumed she was one of my neighbors. It turned out we had to take a taxi which took us to the other end of town. There I met the lady's younger sister who said, "Excuse us for the mess. We just returned from Sadec. We haven't had time to unpack yet."

"Sadec! That's the region I'd love to see someday. I've heard so much about the pretty girls there who wash their faces and feet with coconut milk and the farmers who own fields so vast that storks could fly across with their wings stretched out."

"Not any more. The war spread all over. We came here because our houses were burnt down by the the Hoa Hao" (a religious sect influencing the richest land in the Southwest). The lady sighed and continued, "During the war we had to move to Saigon and come back only after the seasons changed to collect dues from the farmers who rented land from us. We had not gotten any money from them for awhile because they claimed that they had abandoned the plots or that their children, their helpers, had left them to join the Hoa Hao army to fight the French and the Viet Minh. This time we came and saw our houses burnt down." My new acquaintances huffed with resentment.

153

Somehow, I did not feel her resentment justified. If she had abandoned her land to find safety and a good life somewhere else, those who stayed behind and were willing to sacrifice deserved to earn what they produced. But I kept my thoughts to myself. Before I left the house, she invited me to attend a meeting at city hall the following day. I agreed to have her pick me up; I thought maybe by then I would know her reason for seeing me.

The city hall was crowded with men, most armed with guns hanging loosely at their sides. The lady said something to a guard who showed her the direction to a room. In the room, men in military and police uniforms sat casually behind small rectangular tables. Civilians bunched together in groups of two and three in the back of the room. I followed the lady to a corner where some civilians were sitting. I thought I recognized the face of a guerrilla I knew among the civilians. Our eyes met, and immediately he averted his to a different direction. I did the same to comply.

Three men walked in and stood behind the podium. The man in the middle, with a gun hanging at his side, spoke up loudly and silenced the crowd.

"Your attention, please. We have here today the majority of representatives of patriotic parties and dignitaries of Saigon. Our discussion is being sent by wire to the palace where Ngo Dinh Diem, a stranger from Central Vietnam, will be listening to our requests. I have here minutes which we have carefully drafted. Most of the representatives here have helped in the drafting of the contents. I suggest we vote on them now. For those who did not join in the previous discussion, the main idea is to tell the stranger in the palace that we did not vote for him to be in there. We never even heard of him. Where was he when all of us here and our families fought in the war for our independence? The minutes are here." He waved the few pages. "If you have any questions, please raise your hand."

With a relaxed gesture, he removed his gun from its holster and set it on the table. Then he looked around impatiently at the audience. Nobody had any questions. "I move that we vote 'Yea' on the minutes," he continued.

Out of impulse, I shot up from my seat and raised my hand.

"Yes, Miss?"

"Sir, I think we ought to take more time to read the minutes before we vote. I don't know what is contained in those pages."

"I told you the representatives agreed on them previously."

"I think some of us here know nothing about your propositions. Can we take a few minutes to read them?"

"No. We don't have the time. I told you the people in the palace are waiting to hear from us through the wire."

"Sorry, Sir. This is a matter of country. We cannot decide blindly. If you don't show me the minutes I won't vote for them." A heavy silence fell.

"May I take leave?" I grabbed my purse and headed for the exit. I heard a gun cocking not far from me.

"You may not leave," ordered the speaker angrily. I pretended not to hear and walked up the aisle toward the door, my eyes fixed on some imaginary object beyond the room. When I reached the door, a man in uniform drew his gun and pointed it at me. I walked on, as if not seeing it. Behind me the lady followed close by. We separated at the end of the street, mentioning nothing about the incident.

On the cyclo I had a chance to think further. I didn't really object to their opposition of Diem. I just disagreed with them on their procedures. I didn't know what else they had written in those papers. As for supporting Diem, I was far from it. He was but a mandarin (an administrator working for the royal family) from the court of Hue, known for its French puppets in the last decades.

I wondered what Diem could have said for himself had he been in the meeting. All the people in the room had most likely risked their lives one way or another during the past ten years of fighting: some for or against the French, others for the Japanese or the Viet Minh or Cao Dai or Hoa Hao sects. Not Diem. He had never had to fight, just resigned and went abroad, and with French permission at that.

In the middle of my brooding, I remembered a conversation with Cuong and Tuan, my new Parisian friends. Cuong had said, "Don't you think it's really haphazard how they settled our independence? Just cut Vietnam in half, gave one-half to Ho Chi Minh and the other half to Ngo Dinh Diem?"

It was interesting to listen to them: open and frank. They had lived in Paris, so they had been able to follow every move of the Geneva Conference from many different sources, often opposing ones. Information we got from the United States was more or less uniform and very brief.

Cuong continued, "I liked it when Mendes France, at wit's end, I'm sure, called the four powers to stop bargaining about who gets what and just find a way to quickly stop the 'Sale Guerre' [Dirty War]."

"It was about time. Thousands of young officers died every few minutes to defend a ridiculous valley! And the Americans! They've wasted enough money supporting the French and British in wars to regain their colonies, all the while claiming to be world defender of freedom and democracy!"

This talk was brand new to me. America involved in blocking our independence? The big powers: the United States, Russia, China, Britain — what had they to do with the French and Vietnamese war? Unable to hold my curiosity, I blurted out, "What valley?"

"Dien Dien Phu," Cuong said, lowering his eyelids a notch, affecting a natural answer to hide his surprise at my ignorance. "That's where the French, under their famous General Navarre, pulled all their forces to make a showdown in a small valley surrounded with mountains. After having dismantled and transported their heavy weapons across the mountains, H.C. Minh troops led by Vo Nguyen Giap mounted their surprise attacks from the hidden trenches they had dug around the camp. The French had to paratroop down their remaining young officers to join forces. These died with the rest of the camp. Meanwhile, in Paris, the big powers were moving in to sponsor negotiations with the Viet Minh. That's how come our country is divided in half: the North to please Russia and China, the South to please the United States and Britain." He paused and said gently, "Don't look so sad, Sister Hoanh. It won't be eternal, the division. In 1956, as stipulated between the French and the Viet Minh, we'll have a national election, and we'll all be one country again."

That had sounded like a sure guarantee to me then. It was the adults who had taught us never to break our promises. (Strange how I kept thinking in terms of "adults." After all, I was one myself.) But now something told me different. I was surprised to find myself so skeptical about the meeting in the city hall and of Ngo Dinh Diem, and of Ho Chi Minh and the whole thing. What worried me most though was that I had involuntarily supported Ngo Dinh Diem again, just because he had been absent from the meeting.

As children, we had settled our differences face to face. Only cowards would gang up and hide themselves behind a leader and induce him or her to fight the battle for them. The leaders would always fight because of them, and get bruises all over which left them sore for days. Were the big powers supporting Vietnam, or were they in it for themselves, I wondered.

Again the lady who had invited me to city hall came, this time to ask me to join the meeting of the Croix Rouge (Red Cross) staff. "Why?" I asked. After the City Hall experience, I felt I could be more blunt.

She replied, "They are selecting a new man for president of the Croix Rouge. We don't want the same old corrupt man who served under the French to have control again."

Since I didn't know anything about the Croix Rouge and couldn't have really judged who was the better candidate, I told her I couldn't attend.

Some time later, I saw the lady's picture in the newspaper. She had been killed accidentally on a trip to her home town, the paper said.

Not too long after this, a dignified looking American lady came to see me. She also invited me to join the Croix Rouge. I put two and two together and figured she must have known the other Vietnamese lady. I didn't join the organization, but we kept in touch. Years later, I was introduced to her husband through the American parties my husband often attended and learned that the husband was officially with the FBI or the CIA or both.

Shortly after the city hall incident, an American from USAID, a friend of my husband, dropped in for a visit. His eyes glittered with sincerity and excitement. "It's incredible," he said. "Just a few days ago, I asked my Vietnamese employees who they would vote for: Ho Chi Minh or Emperor Bao Dai. They had all said Ho Chi Minh. After the city hall meeting, I asked who they would vote for: Ho Chi Minh or Ngo Dinh Diem. They all smiled and said: 'Mr. Diem.'" He lowered his voice and almost shyly said, "We are doing the right thing."

Deep down, we—the young returnees, university students, previous guerrillas like me, and southern elites—who were better informed, had doubts. But we all thought we should give it our utmost and hope for the best.

Brother Hoanh and his returnee friends became absorbed in their projects involving the president and his policies. I became involved in an organization of students to help the homeless displaced by the war and the refugees who came south after the Geneva Conference that divided North and South. My father, who like many of the older intellectuals felt sure that their patriotism had finally found its real foundation on which to build noble dreams, returned to work with a branch of the Department of Public Works in My Tho, a province about forty miles southwest of Saigon. My mother was at the height of her inspiration. She composed a poem a day. All of them were about the blessed bright future Vietnam was going to have—about thanking our Virgin Mary and calling "her children" (the guerrillas) to abandon their arms and return home to reconstruct our new independent country. Some of her works were published in the newspapers.

One weekend, we went to My Tho with Brother Hoanh's parents to visit my parents. From there, the six of us proceeded to the beach at Go Cong, crammed like sardines in Brother's jeep. At a road blockade,

Brother Hoanh swerved to pass and almost ran into an army jeep coming from the opposite direction. He passed the jeep and drove on towards the beach.

While Brother and I were in the water, Brother swimming far out, my attention was drawn to the army jeep that had just pulled up. Two uniformed men jumped out and approached our mothers. Then I saw my mother-in-law's hands clasped together politely in front of her as if begging for something. I got out of the water and while walking toward them heard one of the men say: "No. I want him to apologize. I want him to kneel down and apologize, or I will shoot him."

My husband's mother implored, "Please don't mind him. He is young. He didn't know what he was doing. Make me do whatever, but spare him."

The soldier drew out his gun. My mother-in-law's Hue accent, the same as that of Prime Minister Diem, seemed to irritate him further. "Enough of that. Call him over here."

Then my father walked toward the soldiers. "What seems to be the problem, Commanders?"

The men stood in check. They were not used to seeing unarmed people stand up to their guns. They told him what they wanted. My father said, "Oh, that road. I used to work on that road. I am engineer Phuc. In fact I helped build that road. It looks very shabby now. It could cause a lot of accidents." He offered his hand, "Nice to meet you, Commanders. What army are you with?"

The commanders shook hands and began talking in a civilized manner. "Thought it was somebody else. But if it's your family, Mr. Engineer, no problem then. Enjoy your stay." Before turning to go, one of the commanders said, "Please tell that young fellow to watch where he's driving next time."

The picture of my father slapping the Frenchman flashed back. In the old colonial times, the "oppressed," educated at least, had a chance to defend themselves with dignity. Nowadays, offenders and competitors were to be humiliated and eliminated. I wondered if that was what "independence" was all about: being mistreated and bullied by your own people instead of by foreign Colonialists.

14

HALF OF OUR country was now promised independence from the Communists, from the French, and from the worries of money.

With the powerful support of the United States, the zeal of patriotic intellectuals, and over a million refugees from the North, Prime Minister Diem could now move to "protect" peace by eliminating his potential non–Communist enemies on the local scene.

Colonel Lansdale, who had helped President Magsaysay of the Philippines, was summoned to Vietnam. The Binh Xuyens were the first target. Since Diem had no armed followers, Colonel Lansdale had to recruit from the army of the Cao-Dai religion (One Eye religion), its most anti–French and anti–Communist group led by General The.

Trinh Minh The, their leader, through the solicitation of Colonel Lansdale, agreed to cooperate with Diem to defeat the Binh Xuyens. On the same day of the battle that destroyed the Binh Xuyens, the press reported that Trinh Minh The had "been killed in combat, apparently shot in the back by a pro–French soldier."

Diem gave Trinh Minh The the funeral of a national hero, but the Cao Dais were not satisfied. They withdrew their support, and their Cao-Dai "pope" went into exile with his staff to Cambodia. A rumor circulated that Diem's family had murdered The, but it was never proven.

On the political front, Diem's family prepared a referendum to dethrone Emperor Bao Dai and name Diem chief of state. For the first time in the history of Vietnam, the Vietnamese were introduced to universal suffrage. Diem gave two names on the slates: Diem and Bao Dai. The majority of the populace did not vote because the system was new to them, and because neither candidate had much to offer.

Nevertheless, Bao Dai was defeated, and the Binh Xuyens fled to France. Diem declared "the Republic of Vietnam," making himself its first president.

Brother Hoanh worked for a while in the palace as press officer and had dealings with Mr. Ngo Dinh Nhu, one of Diem's brothers, who had moved into the palace with Diem. He was to pay salaries of employees in the press office with bundles of cash given to him by Mr. Nhu. After a few times, Mr. Nhu, tiring of Brother's insistence on keeping records of expenditures for correct and proper administrative procedure, gave up using him as his trusted aide.

Brother Hoanh was all too glad to be released. Together with an American couple and a group of United States educated returnees, he began publishing an English newspaper, *The Times of Vietnam*, hoping to give Vietnamese information and opinions to the English-speaking foreigners who had swarmed into South Vietnam to report on our "independence." This turned out to be quite a task as the articles had to be set on linotype, and the workers, knowing only French and not understanding a word of English, kept creating new mistakes while correcting the old ones.

Along with this project, Brother Hoanh also had to be available to interpret for President Diem in his meetings with important foreign dignitaries when confidential matters were discussed. Diem preferred to have him instead of the interpreters from the Foreign Ministry.

The day before the president left on his first important diplomatic trip to the United States in 1957, he called Brother Hoanh in and told him to take charge of the national news agency, Vietnam Press. Brother Hoanh tried to explain that he was doing fine with his *Times of Vietnam* and that a private and independent newspaper reflected a better government image, but to no avail. An order by a mandarin head of state was not to be disobeyed, especially in the South Vietnam of 1957.

The same day of Diem's departure, Brother Hoanh had to leave the *Times* to become director general of Vietnam Press. For a Vietnamese to be director of any important organization at the age of twenty-seven was to be in for trouble (his predecessor was a clever M.D. in his late fifties). On the very first day, while re-reading a news release — news coming from world agencies, domestic news, and news from the president's family was to be selected, screened for damaging information, then sent to four different sections of Vietnam Press for translation into Vietnamese, English, French, and Chinese — Brother Hoanh found in the Vietnamese version Mr. Nhu's name misspelled as "Mr. Ngu." The "h" had been replaced by a "g," changing the name from "Mr. Modest or Smart" to "Mr.

Stupid." Brother Hoanh had to recall the copies which stood ready to be distributed all over the country, to local newspapers, to the National Radio, to the Diplomatic Corps, and to the international news agencies. It was impossible to singlehandedly check all the news bulletins before the translation and after the printing. Such was the subtle way the old seasoned Vietnam Press employees, known for their heroin smoking, sought to "break" the new director whom they considered much too young to be their boss.

Realizing how dangerous and conniving these men were, Brother Hoanh had to act fast. He had a time clock installed. Everyone, no exceptions, was to punch in. He knew that several of the intriguing heroin smokers in the French and Vietnamese sections had been putting in false overtime reports claiming to have come to work at four in the morning and left late in the night.

They were furious. To get revenge, they sent him an anonymous note threatening his life and had some local papers criticize the new director for installing a machine to smash out the new ideology, "Personalism" (respect for the person) that Mr. Nhu had claimed for his Can Lao party. Brother Hoanh had to inform the minister of information who was chairman of the board of the Vietnam Press Agency that he was going to fire that very day several employees who felt they could not be fired because they had "connections." Not wanting to take the blame for the men who had been initially recruited into Vietnam Press at his wife's insistence because they were her relatives, the minister did not object.

After the successful handling of this crisis, Brother Hoanh was left alone to manage the Vietnam Press for five years until his resignation. This marked a unique case of stability for the director's post at the Vietnam Press—before his arrival and after his departure, directors were changed every six months.

President Diem's trip to the United States was a big publicity success. He was paraded in the streets of New York. *Reader's Digest* wrote of him as the "Greatest Little Man in Asia." President Eisenhower met with him, and Diem addressed a joint session of the Congress.

He came home triumphant. Those who had doubts about his power saw with their own eyes the full support of the powerful United States. Dollars poured in for the development of Diem's projects. Vietnam became the first showcase of American involvement in freeing an underdeveloped country from colonialism and helping it to realize democracy. If the U.S. Marshall Plan had been successful in countries like Germany and France after the destruction of World War II, there would be no reason for generous Uncle Sam not to succeed in bringing democracy and wealth to Vietnam: such a tiny and remote backward country of 25 million inhabitants who had proven their willingness to pursue happiness and freedom at any cost.

Our returnee friends from the United States played key roles in Diem's government. One became director of the Exchange Office. Another was assigned treasurer to Mr. Nhu's party. Others were sent abroad, at their own request, to do underground intelligence work. About this time, Mr. Nhu created an organization which later became the powerful, secret Social Research Bureau in the presidential palace, supervised by a northerner, a former seminarist.

Brother Hoanh and I joined none of the political activities. At the beginning, together with some returnees from abroad, we organized a night school called Bach Khoa Binh Dan (Popular Polytechnic Education) where practical skills were taught, such as writing English, typing, sewing, and nursing. Later the organization was dissolved for lack of volunteers.

The year that was supposed to reunite the South and the North was 1956. But the previous year, fearing that he would loose his power, Diem had forbidden communication and humanitarian aid to the starving victims of floods in the North and outlawed the Viet Minh and their sympathizers. This move appeared to have had the underlying approval of the United States—President Eisenhower was heard to have said that if the elections were to take place, Ho Chi Minh would probably win. The fire had been removed from the simmering patriotism for one united nation.

South Vietnam appeared to have gotten what it wanted: independence from France. It was rid of Emperor Bao Dai. Excerpts from the American constitution were read with every government move, accompanied by dollars that poured in like rain. But prosperity and corruption came hand in hand. Nobody dared to criticize the military, the merchants, the prostitutes, the crooks or those manners we had traditionally held vulgar.

Nowhere was there mentioned the universal suffrage to reunify the South with the North. For eighty years our country had been divided into three different regions by the French. Before that, by a power struggle between two warlords. "One Vietnam" seemed but an illusive ideal, an abstract, like the words "democracy" and "human rights" that were tossed about in the growing corruption of the last two years. Vietnam's goal and ideal—the unification of a nation—seemed even farther away in our "new democracy" than it had ever been.

162

More bad news kept coming in to poison what little was left of our idealism. Besides the thousands of Vietnamese objecting to Diem's régime who had already left for the North as stipulated in the Geneva Conference, many others also opposing Diem had scattered in the countryside, to be joined later by those who became disgusted with Diem's intrigues. Others, although dissatisfied, did not dare to hope for better. Like my parents, they had seen the other side and what it had to offer. The only unified opposition left was the Hoa Hao religious group who occupied the rich Mekong delta west of Saigon. This group was founded by the popular Huynh Phu So. He had gained the hearts of his countrymen by distributing free medicine and helping them to fight the French and to expel the Communists from their Hoa Hao region. Killed, some said by the Communists, who informed the French of his whereabouts, Huynh Phu So had been succeeded by Ba Cut.

To defeat Ba Cut, Diem sent the vice president, a respectable man and a native of Ba Cut's birthplace, to make contact with him. Persuaded by his compatriot, Ba Cut agreed to meet and negotiate with Diem's representative. On the promised date, Ba Cut came out with a dozen escorts onto the designated road. He and his men were ambushed and brought to trial that same day. The judge who presided over the trial gave false evidence and sentenced Ba Cut to death. Ba Cut was executed on the day of the sentence.

With one stone, Diem had killed two birds. For decades, the Hoa Hao had fought the Communists effectively, maintaining control of the richest region in the South. By killing their leader, Diem had taken away the Hoa Hao's power against the Communists, their control over their rich land. In this way, he deprived these discontented South Vietnamese of a huge, resourceful territory that could be used for underground movement, forcing them to join the Communists if they wanted to fight him. In addition, by using the vice president to trick Ba Cut, Diem had destroyed the credibility of this respectable man and consequently his potential leadership among southern intellectuals.

This incident was reported "directly" to us through the visit of a lady refugee friend of my parents—the wife of the judge who has sentenced Ba Cut. After briefly introducing herself, she burst into tears: "My husband . . . my poor husband. He is losing his mind, ever since the government ordered him to have Ba Cut beheaded. How were we to know who he was. We didn't know. Where we were in the North, we had never heard of the Hoa Hao or the Cao Dai. Knew nothing of the court procedures here," she muttered. "Terrible . . . How my poor husband has been used."

163

We didn't know at first what we could do to help her nor what she wanted from us. But then we realized that all she wanted was for us to publish the news that her husband had resigned, to clear his name from the Ba Cut verdict. Brother Hoanh published the news of his resignation, hinting that there was fraud in the Diem government's trial of the Hoa Hao leader.

By 1957 Diem's government appeared to be well under control. The press, the only means of communication between the populace and between the government and the people, was heavily censured by the Ministry of Information. Newspapers needed permits to circulate. Stories that were unfavorable to Diem resulted in the removal of publishers' permits and worse.

As director general of Vietnam Press, besides handling the endless emergencies of his job, Brother Hoanh had to employ keen politics to delicately balance and compromise between propaganda and truth in order to survive with some dignity.

He had much to occupy himself, and we hardly had the time to talk to each other. Now and then he would casually open and close a topic, while changing clothes for endless cocktail receptions and official dinners. It was always related to politics, or rather the deception of it: "I met an archbishop—at least that's what he said he was—'Archbishop Yupin' and his priest and fighters from the Chiang Kai-shek régime, now Mr. Diem's recruits [Brother continued to call President Diem, 'Mr. Diem,' his old-time epithet] to help fight the Viet Minhs. He was bragging and laughing about using the collaboration of the Nung mountaineers in the High Plateaus—letting them fight and eat live, as they do with their enemies, the livers of the Viet Cong" . . . "Mr. Diem doesn't even trust his own people—he has to rely on Bernard Y. and his Chinese group to check the security of the palace. . . ."

Unlike Brother, somehow I felt strangely immune to the "bad" news created by Diem. Maybe because I had been disappointed a long time ago.

In any case, gradually, Brother and I became increasingly alienated from one another. Perhaps it was because we both felt inwardly ashamed of and disillusioned with our world—after all, we wanted to believe in ourselves and our ideals. We each escaped into our own separate lives.

15

IN SPITE OF my frustrations with my world, I kept myself busy having babies (two babies by 1957). Like most of the Vietnamese women of my time, I saw childbearing as a very natural process and consequently only visited the doctor for the delivery. My new functions as a mother brought new rules and a whole new set of concepts to me. Mother, who had had eight babies of her own, was there to supervise. Every morning she took a cyclo to our apartment from her home settled in the dependents' quarters (consisting of two long rooms) of the villa occupied by a young refugee co-worker of my father. Since political maneuvering had become the main concern of Diem's government, other fields such as my father's were completely neglected. There was no plan nor budget for it.

Mother was adamant in her "advice" which was to be strictly followed by a "good daughter." Mildly I resisted my mother who insisted on various home remedies such as drinking baby boy's urine to clean the system and crawling with arms and legs outstretched, like a cow to get back the stomach muscles. I was given salty, dried meat mixed with ginger for keeping the womb warm; and to keep my skin firm, I was forced to sleep with a charcoal stove below me. I was not to ruin my eyes with reading nor strain my veins with too much walking. And to have milk for my baby, I had to eat boiled pork feet cooked in all kinds of seasonings (medicine herbs). This I did not object to much because it was rather tasty, though I was worried about my belly gathering too much fat. But of course that was already taken care of by the cow-crawling exercise. Every other day, I was to take a steam bath sitting under a blanket, letting the vapor of the citronella grass open and clean my pores, then have the maid rub me yellow with turmeric roots so that a month after the delivery

I would look like a fragile, fair-skinned lady to preside over the traditional party for one-month-old babies.

That was not all—Mother had many of her own "tried" theories to impose too. Since a baby's look and character were influenced from his "egg" (his mother's womb), an expectant mother should only think about nice, good things and carefully choose the *a-ma* (live-in nanny) for her baby, paying close attention to the person's aspect as well as personality. I had seen Mother applying these theories to herself. During her sixth pregnancy, the town used to speak of a soap called Savon Cadum which had a lovely fragrance and a picture of an adorable baby with light brown curly hair and a pinkish complexion for its cover. Mother would use this soap exclusively to wash her face, treating it with tender care. Sure enough, the baby came out with curly hair and a fair complexion, unlike the rest of us who were straight haired and olive skinned. For her seventh baby, she displayed the *Paris Match* magazine with the picture of General Chang Kai-shek heavily decked out with colorful medals by her pillow. This son was born with slit eyes and a face resembling the general.

Having no preference for any particular method or look—Vietnamese, French, or American—I would just experiment in different ways and return to our traditions whenever Mother was around. I felt pretty comfortable as a Vietnamese mother who along with observing the traditions, applied nursing tips prescribed by the French method.

Occupied with our daily activities, we, the little group of five— Mother, my two babies, the maid, and I managed to lead a life oblivious to the problems surrounding us. There was plenty to tend to with two babies, cleaning, shopping, and cooking. (Food had to be bought fresh from the market daily, and in the case of chicken and fish, killed and cleaned.) Though with Brother Hoanh's autonomous budget, he could draw his salary of his own accord, he often liked to express his living standard, which was meager compared to others of his position who had villas and several maids, with his favorite saying, "How many beds can you sleep in? How many cars can you drive at a time?"

At that time, I had no problem with this principle of his. His way of thinking and the way we lived, plus the numerous foreign friends we had, and his easy access to President Diem and Counselor Nhu confused a lot of people. No briberies came near our doors, but no real friends either.

During the first prosperous years of Ngo Dinh Diem's family, between 1957 and 1959, President Diem often asked Brother Hoanh to accompany him on his goodwill trips. One day they went to visit the poor villagers in a flooded area. I was just getting up from my siesta and was preparing for our evening cocktail duty rounds when Brother barged into the bedroom and flung his white silk jacket on the bed.

"I'm tired of these trips." He threw himself flat on the bed. "The president has gone nuts." I stopped powdering to listen. "What a joke. We looked ridiculous in our expensive, sparkling-white silk suits. We zoomed by the poor villagers who had lined up in the hot sun hours ahead just to salute his shiny black Mercedes."

Brother Hoanh's voice faded in the background as I imagined the scene. Diem gave a long speech about "Personalism," Mr. Nhu's new national philosophy. The poor old men, women, and children stood still under the grilling sun. Hot vapor rose from the mud under and around their feet while the president stood on the wooden platform built especially for the occasion, covered with a straw roof. On and on he read his long speech with his foreign accent, foreign idioms, and foreign philosophy. Some men dropped to the ground from excessive heat; others put on their conical hats to cover themselves from the sun. Upon seeing this, Diem stopped in the middle of his speech, called the local province chief and said something to him. The poor fellow, bent in half to show extreme respect, rushed to the microphone: "The president says you may put on your hats." The peasants put their hats on. At this, the president suddenly rushed off the platform and headed for his car. His men followed suit, surprised and frightened, while the peasants shouted: "President Diem Muon Nam [A thousand years to the president]!" Like parrots, they repeated what they were told to say.

Most of Diem's staff didn't know what had happened. Only the men from Hue understood the "mandarin mind" of Diem and his peculiar ways. There were two there, Brother Hoanh and Diem's secretary. They knew that the president was angry, but typical of the Hue people, he was saying "yes" while meaning "no." He wanted the peasants to take off their hats to show respect for his "sacred" presence.

Brother Hoanh suddenly chuckled, "That poor fellow, that province chief. Now he's going to be sacked!"

My head jerked around to look at him, presently lying staring at the ceiling. I knew the bitter sarcasm of his comment came from the disillusionment he was feeling.

"You know what time those peasants had to be there? Four o'clock in the morning. To rehearse ... And we didn't come until eleven!"

I returned to my powdering. I didn't want to add more fuel to the fire. Anyway, we couldn't afford to be late for the cocktail party. Late meant later than those more important in rank than my husband. We couldn't be there too early either — it showed ignorance to be there earlier than those less important than him. Brother had a flair for this protocol—I just tagged along. All of these cultivated mannerisms I couldn't keep up with. At times I became so careless as to call an ambassador a simple "Mister" instead of "Mr. Ambassador" and a general a lowly "colonel." I simply could not remember all the faces that went with the titles. To avoid embarrassment for everybody including Brother, upon arriving at the cocktail parties, I always managed to separate from Brother. It was safer that I wasn't caught making stupid mistakes in front of him.

Cocktail parties were fun in some respects. One had the opportunity to taste the different foods representing the finest of the host's country and also see the latest fashions modeled by the ladies and gentlemen. Unfortunately though, I always felt uncomfortable with this. It was not possible just to eat and watch—it was necessary to make conversation and show one's class and sophistication appropriate to the title one carried.

"Good evening. A nice cool evening, isn't it Mrs. Hoanh?"

"Oh! Mrs. . . . " I returned the greeting gaily, as if I had just found an old friend, but her name slipped my mind.

"Becker . . . I understand it's hard to remember so many names. And it must be difficult for you to try to speak English." She said this with a helpful, kind smile. "I love your dress. What nice embroidery."

"Thank you," I said, embarrassed. What could one say to such nice comments, ever ready on the lips of these nice ladies.

"I've been wondering where one could buy a good piece of embroidered fabric, for a shirt."

"Someday I'll take you to my favorite shop. You can hardly find quality embroidery nowadays. The war has dislocated many good craftsmen."

Mrs. Becker's smiling face suddenly changed to seriousness. "Oh . . . That's too bad." She wanted to show her vast empathy for us Vietnamese and our war, but her smile returned quickly at the approach of another lady who had heard us from a few feet away.

"I wonder if it costs very much, a dress like that."

"Hm . . . about five hundred piasters," I said, surprised at her direct question.

"That much?"

"That much?" I repeated to myself, puzzled. Two hundred piasters equalled only three U.S. dollars. An ordinary American, who taught English conversation to Vietnamese soldiers earned around twenty thousand piasters a month.

"You could buy much cheaper, but it wouldn't be the same quality," I interjected.

Other wives of diplomats drifted over to our circle. I recognized the wife of a USAID man. "We were talking about embroidery," someone said, looking admiringly at her dress — a combined design of Vietnamese and Western fashion. "What lovely embroidery you are wearing!"

"Oh! Thank you. I'm glad you like it. Isn't the dragon interesting?" the USAID wife asked cheerfully, looking down at the dragon curving along one side of her body.

"Embroidery here is rather expensive, don't you think?" commented Mrs. Becker.

"Expensive? This embroidered piece? Why, no. I found it rather reasonable. A piece like this for four dollars?"

Mrs. Becker was delighted with the new information. "Indeed. That is a very good price. You must know a good bargain shop."

"Mrs. Fong, the wife of my husband's secretary, helped me buy this."

Upon hearing the price, everybody became interested in the USAID worker's wife. They exchanged shop addresses excitedly, and some were able to ask her to help them buy their embroidery.

I discovered later the market where Mrs. Fong and other Chinese procured their goods. Actually, there weren't any real bargains, although they were presented that way to the Americans. The Chinese bought what the Americans wanted and charged them prices so that the products, given almost free, would not be construed as bribes.

Gift giving was an art for the Chinese. Only they could perform with such subtlety and discretion. In the years to come when Vietnam and the Vietnamese administrators would seem to be definitely there to stay, some very high ranking Vietnamese would receive similar privileges from the Chinese. For Vietnamese, though, good bargains would be found in much more substantial exchanges — half the price for a five carat diamond, or large deposits into Swiss accounts. In these cases, the gifts were not for obtaining positions in the government (Chinese did not get to work in Vietnamese offices), but for pulling business favors. Where there was an option for an official to do business either with a Vietnamese or a Chinese, the Chinese was always preferred — thanks to their discretion, their worldwide contacts, and above all their disinterest in participating in the coups.

Having destroyed all opposition except the Communists, Diem moved to build himself a dynasty. Diem's four brothers divided their dynasty into four spheres. Bishop Thuc took charge of all the religious organizations. Brother Can governed the Center. Brother Nhu controlled the palace and politics in the South, and Brother Luyen, ambassador to London, was to keep an eye on the diplomats and the Vietnamese abroad.

The sister-in-law, Mrs. Nhu, whose husband was in the palace with Diem, was not to be outdone in importance by the men in her family. From the "cute" young woman that I had first seen in a mountaineer costume at a charity banquet, flirting with young French-educated Vietnamese, she became a powerful "heroine," overseeing all women's activities.

She even created a "women's army" consisting of opportunistic business women and wives of high-ranking officials. To celebrate her "army," she had a statue of herself and her daughter erected on one of the main streets to represent the heroines the Trung sisters. Then, on the holiday itself, she led her army in a parade, herself and her daughter mounted on elephants to recreate the scene of the Trung heroines who had conducted armies of men to fight the Chinese in the years A.D. 40–43. The Vietnamese worshiped these heroines among their ancestors. They guardedly resented the fact that Madame Nhu and her daughter dared to play the role of their saints and patronized the soldiers with their symbolic inspections.

Madame Nhu came up with new ideas all the time. "Enough" never crossed her mind. One day, she met my husband at the presidential palace and told him to write of her as "Madame Ngo, the first lady." My husband said that since Diem was a bachelor, to call his sister-in-law the first lady—a title reserved for the president's wife—would utterly confuse the press and the diplomats. Besides, it was not the Vietnamese way to use family names. He asked her to reconsider.

Later, while my husband was at a wedding of one of his employees, I received a phone call from Mrs. Nhu's secretary at the presidency.

"It's urgent that Madame Advisor speak to Mr. General Director."

When I replied that Brother was at the wedding of one of his employees, she tried to extort the address. I resisted, reasoning that it would be improper for me to help her interrupt the ceremony which Brother Hoanh presided over as guest of honor, unless it was a dire emergency, which I knew it was not.

"Just give me the address, and I won't bother you any more. Would you p-l-e-a-s-e?" she hissed angrily.

When she met with the second "No," she dropped the matter. But not for long. The next day she attempted to reach my husband again at home. This time he was taking a shower, but I told her that he wasn't home. "Why don't you try to call him at his office during work hours. I am sure you'll find him there to deal with official news."

She got the hint and never called him at home again. But of course, she still had to do her bit. A few days later, Brother came home and said

170

that President Diem had criticized him in front of his tennis friends, saying: "Hoanh is influenced too much by his wife. He's even picked up her accent."

Changes took place continuously and rapidly in the streets and businesses of Saigon, while the Diem family strove to establish themselves. "Royal rituals" were exerted everywhere, even among the ministers.

By 1959, it was virtually impossible for Saigon residents to get away from it all. The countryside, with its shady orchards and beautiful rivers, was no longer safe for visiting. The little shacks along the seashore had shut down or become too dangerous for nature lovers to spend the night in. The Viet Congs (Communist South Vietnamese) were known to visit houses in remote areas after dark. The only places left to go were restaurants, concubine houses, or theaters.

Whenever Brother decided to take me out to the movies, we always ran into conflict. Thanks to his trips abroad, he had seen practically all the movies that were shown in town, which consisted mostly of cheap, old films or those that promised huge profits. Brother would drive from one movie house to another. He either didn't feel like seeing the film, or had already seen it and didn't want to see it again. Usually, we would end up going to a restaurant to eat, or I would get out of the car, fed up with our bickering and take a cyclo back home, leaving him free to do whatever he wished.

Today was exceptional. Finally we managed to find a movie that we both felt like seeing. We entered the crowded theater, worried that we had missed a large portion of the beginning of the movie which was scheduled to have started twenty minutes earlier. Nothing was on the screen. In the dim light people whispered nervously. A few minutes had passed when from the back of the screen someone announced: "Order, ladies and gentlemen. The honorable minister of interior and Mrs. Minister have arrived. Let's all rise to salute." Immediately a picture of President Ngo's face appeared on the huge screen and the anthem was played. (Diem had decreed that he be called by his last name, "Ngo," instead of his first name, "Diem." This was unprecedented to the Vietnamese, who reserved that privilege to refer only to kings' dynasties.)

The music played: "Ngo Tong Thong Muon Nam" (Ten thousand years for President Ngo). The audience rose to their feet while next to me my husband swore under his breath.

We were tempted to leave, but their "salute" plan was well thought out. Who would dare to walk out in the middle of our national anthem with a big picture of President Ngo watching from the screen? The obligatory salute to the minister of interior upon his entrance was well orchestrated to synchronize with the obligatory salute of the picture of President Ngo. Even people like us, who were taken aback, were forced to keep our reactions in check unless we wanted to be branded as "Viet Cong." Immediately after the salute, the film began, leaving no time for protest or exit. At the end of the movie, as we were leaving, Brother Hoanh said in a loud voice: "And to think that the honorable minister of interior went to Vinh Long to visit Bishop Ngo Dinh Thuc just last weekend in his beat-up Citroën, dressed in his old clothes. He even lost his voice in the presence of the Bishop!"

The Vietnamese had never been given a place in the world up to this time. Even our Emperor Bao Dai was mocked by the French press as a playboy, and of course the revolutionary Ho Chi Minh who had defeated the French was considered only a Communist rebel. The United States, the most powerful country on earth, was the first to bring Vietnam to world recognition by giving a hearty reception to Ngo Dinh Diem and acclaiming him as a hero—"The greatest little man in Asia." This was a matter of great pride to the Ngos and their followers. Each one fought to get into the spotlight.

16

As DAILY happenings grew intense and barbarous on the political front, Brother Hoanh, now buried under the load of work and deception at his office, grew more and more distant from his family. I suspected he was out fooling around, but I was busy having babies, not thinking about how to prevent having them because of my Catholic background. In any case, Brother was only performing the expected social duty of a normal Vietnamese man of South Vietnam in the fifties. Since my friends also included only those frequented by Brother, I became more aware of the state of my loneliness. I selected incidents which I chose to feed my mind and stewed in them. My innocent outlook of the world, my respect for all those older than myself, the beauty I used to see in love, friendship, and patriotism had all changed into disappointment. I now regarded all I saw with ugly suspicion.

In this spirit of mind I met one of our returnee friends from the United States, now director of the Office of Exchange as well as budget manager to Mr. Nhu's party. He had called me to his office saying that he had important things to tell me. Since he hadn't left word with his receptionist about my coming, I had to state my name and the person whom I wished to see on a form. Upon receiving me, he said (of course with a smile), "You wrote me down as director."

"Yes." I was surprised at his remark.

"It's supposed to be 'director general.'"

"Really. Is that important?" I didn't see the difference.

"You know that your husband's title is 'director general.' He would be vexed if he were called director."

"Oh. That's new. I wonder if he would care. Anyway, did you call me in here for that?"

173

"No. Of course not. I thought I would just let you know. Now to business. You know that the election for the National Assembly is coming up. Are you planning to run?"

"No. What for?"

"They need a few women in there."

"Mrs. Nhu has quite a few women of her own, including herself. She doesn't need anybody else."

"You sound like you are against Madame Nhu. People talk bad about Madame Nhu, but actually she is quite a charming lady. She is very intelligent and social minded. She needs collaborators like you to help represent the Vietnamese women."

"You men are seduced by her charm. Aren't you?"

"No. No. I mean it. I think you two will work well together."

"She doesn't like competition. And I don't like to be ordered around. Neither would I want to be sucked into a situation where I would have to fight with another woman in front of men."

"You are prejudiced. Those are only rumors."

This infuriated me. This friend who had received his education abroad—the friend that we played cards with almost every weekend—how could he be so blind? But then if he could fuss about a "director general" title and be working as budget manager for the Nhu's Can Lao party, he could be a lot of things that I didn't know. He could be a messenger boy for Madame Nhu, and under her instruction, using her husband's party money to buy her fancies.

Looking presently at the director general sitting in front of me, I was suddenly tempted to find out more about his business with his bosses. As treasurer for Mr. Nhu, he could not avoid taking orders form Madame Nhu, who also had a title as leading député in the National Assembly. In 1957, she had used the National Assembly to pass a family law forbidding divorce so that she could revenge her brother-in-law, Chau, and confiscate his property and imprison him. Chau had escaped to France, however. A lawyer and a son of a very rich South Vietnamese landlord, he had filed in court a divorce request against his wife, Madame Nhu's sister, whom he claimed had committed adultery with a French mechanic.

Until this time, family matters had always been kept private, never brought to court. Madame Nhu managed to pass for her own personal gains, the first family law in Vietnam's history.

The National Assembly consisted of members who had been hand-picked by the Ngos at the time Mr. Diem had changed his title from prime minister to president four years before. A set-up arranged to give a picture of democracy at work, it was represented by those serving the Ngos and rich people who paid for their posts.

"Running for office is against my principles," I said. "I consider it my duty to work for my country, but representing it could only come when the people see my worth and want me to serve them. Spending my money to buy my way in is ridiculous."

"I know. But your duty is also to find out if Madame Nhu really is bad for our country. Your friends will benefit from your discovery, too."

"That's a thought."

"Seriously, I myself would also like to know."

"Well, if you put it that way—if I am to run for my friends to find out the truth, then I'll go along."

"Everything costs money. Since it isn't your idea to run, I volunteer to take care of your expenditures. I can't give you the same enormous amount that others put into their candidacy, but I'll pay a modicum cost."

"You know, in my opinion, this game that you are asking me to play is a dangerous one, unlike the poker games we play at your house. You are in it for a minimum cost, but if I am in it, the cost will extend to my life and my family's. You may not believe it; that's why you are still with them. But soon we will all know. I am not afraid. If it is for a good cause, my family would be glad to be in it with me."

"I asked you because I knew that you'd weigh all that and knowing you, you would go for a good fight."

"I will have to be careful, though. I hate to fight only for the sake of fighting. You fight to win. And if you see you can't win you have to know when to quit. Right?"

"That a girl. So you are in?"

"Yes."

"I am glad. Here is, as I told you, my little contribution, sixty thousand piasters. You'll need at least this to pay miscellaneous costs."

Sixty thousand piasters. Around two hundred dollars. Four months of salary for a live-in maid working for an American in Vietnam. Nowhere near the million Madame Nhu had attempted to give me three years ago—and the exchange rate then was one-third that of the present. This money could not have come from Madame Nhu's order.

I thought of when Madame Nhu had tried to bribe me. She had once sent a man to give me one million piasters (the price of a large villa) for me to organize the Girl Scouts, which I had refused. A million piasters without a receipt? I was sure if I had agreed, the messenger would have asked for a cut for his commission, and she would have blown the sum up to a few million in public to smear my name whenever she felt like it. After my refusal, Mrs. Nhu selected another woman, another returnee from the United States, and turned the Scouts into another one of her political support organizations. Till then it had been a nonpolitical organization run by a doctor—together with Powder and myself, this doctor had been one of the first students in the math class opened as an extension to college at Trung Vuong, the only high school for girls in Hanoi.

I had reason to suspect the man who had brought me the one million piasters. He had been with me on an official mission to represent the Vietnamese at an Asian Convention in Korea in 1957.

During the convention, the representatives, coming from the various countries, had elected me to be president of a women's organization for Southeast Asia that they had just created to serve as an example for them to follow in their own countries. I felt honored at this, thinking they had chosen me because Vietnam was then the leading country in Southeast Asia in the fight against Communists and Colonialists. My "partner," however—a spineless fellow—was not of the same mind. He told me I had to refuse because he had not received the order from higher-up for me to accept.

I was infuriated. What were we representing if we could not make up our minds on such simple matters? I decided I was not going to shame my country. In front of the audience at the closing of the convention, I chose to open a crack in the window of our present policies by telling them I could not accept the title because my male partner said he had not checked with the "higher-ups." The audience laughed. I felt I had been able to give them a true image of the government I wished to transcend. I knew I was being mean. I had thought about it the night before and had wanted to forget the matter and accept it as part of life, but the scrupulous teaching of my mother on ethics and my father's stubbornness had left strong impressions on me and inspired me to act.

When the meeting closed, President Sygman Rhee and his wife visited the group. Mrs. Rhee gestured for me to stand at her side for a photo. Again my partner resisted, pulling me back saying, "No," while Mrs. Rhee kept smiling and nodding to me. I jerked myself away, saying, "Ridiculous," to him, and went ahead to have my picture taken with the Korean president and his wife. I did not care very much about being president of an organization or having my picture taken with presidents, but I did care that foreigners take the Vietnamese people seriously.

That evening after my meeting with the director, I told my husband about our friend's proposal for me to run in the election, and he had no objection to it. We both welcomed the opportunity to witness with our own eyes the magnitude of Madame Nhu's influence and scheming on Diem's government.

We decided I should run for the election in Bien Hoa, my childhood home town, a one-hour drive from Saigon.

When I entered the city hall in Bien Hoa at opening time and expressed my desire, I got the runaround until finally a man came out and said that the candidates' list was officially closed as of that day.

I prepared myself for trouble. "So you mean this evening at five, the office's closing time," I reminded him.

He shrugged, caught by surprise. "If you insist." He then asked me to show my I.D. When I did, then he asked me for my birth certificate.

"What do you need it for? They must have my birth certificate where they issued my I.D. My birth date is right on this I.D. and so is my picture."

"The rule says we must have your birth certificate. The original one, certified by the current official at the place where you were born."

That did it. I knew that he was set on giving me a hard time. "All right, why don't you write down for me everything you need?"

After stalling for a moment, unable to come up with anything else, he then said, "That's all. Where were you born?"

"In Nha Trang."

His face lit up with the discovery of another potential problem for me. A birth certificate was the last thing one would carry around, especially an original as requested by him. I would have to go back to Saigon to find it among my papers, or I would have to drive 170 miles to my birth place in Nha Trang to ask the authorities there to reissue me one. I knew I didn't have it with me in Saigon, so there was only one choice. But I was not going to let him see my problem.

"I'll get what you need, and I'll be back." I got into the car and told the chauffeur to drive me to Nha Trang.

"Nha Trang? Madame, do you know that it takes a bus one whole day to get there? Nha Trang is across many mountains, many cities. It'll take at least ten hours round trip if we run like a jet."

"We'll run like a jet. We need to get back here before five tonight."

"Impossible."

"Nothing is impossible. You'll make it."

"Oh, no. Nobody can." Our driver was a solid, quiet man. His attitude was more dignified than that of many of the official ministers in Diem's government.

He shifted the Citroën into gear and drove out in good will, but unconvinced.

We arrived in Nha Trang around one. It was siesta time, especially for government officials. At the city hall, I persuaded the "planton" (building guard and messenger boy) to give me the address of the director's home. The director was having his tea before siesta when I came knocking at his door. After hearing my explanation, he said: "I think I remember your father. I don't think there would be any problem digging out your records. I am glad to help a native here run for a National Assembly seat. Please come with me. I am surprised you made it in such good time. Now you have to rush to get back in time."

We got in my car while he kept on smiling, nodding his head with satisfaction, like a little boy involved in a mischievous plot. At the city hall, the planton opened the door for him, and we entered the building at a quick pace. The director then proceeded to look for the records, fill out the forms, and sign and seal them. Very busy, very efficient. Normally it would have taken ten people to do that job. I looked at this respectful old man and almost cried out of gratitude. Such resilience, such stubbornness in hanging on to hope! He spurred me on more convinced.

The driver looked as if he had already used up all his energy in the mountain crossing. I told him to let me drive and for him to get in the backseat so that he could take a nap. He hesitated, then agreed upon my insistence.

I drove as fast as I could. We arrived in front of the Bien Hoa City Hall at a quarter to five, and I submitted my papers to the surprise of everybody around. The man from the morning regretfully accepted my name. When I walked out, a lady approached me and said, "I am glad you got in. Everybody has been talking about you since this morning. Did you plan to get in this late so that they couldn't have time to dream up any schemes to reject you? I know who you are. My father used to be post office director and my mother used to visit your mother. You know who you are running against? Mr. Lua. You must certainly remember Mr. Lua, the richest man in town before and the most powerful one now. He is not only rich and powerful with all his sons working for his régime, but he himself is the Can Lao party's representative here."

I was dumbfounded at the mention of the name—"God. I'm running against my parents' friend!"

The woman went on, "But don't worry. Nobody will vote for him. He is very rich but very stingy. Our family has been living in his apartment building since the time your parents were here, thirty years ago. Not only does he not give us any discount, he keeps raising the rent. When we told him that we hardly made any income nowadays, with my father retired and me working as secretary, he told us that we were

178

welcome to get out if we didn't like the price. I am glad that you are running against him."

The chauffeur stopped shining the car and opened the back door for me. He seemed to take his time to adjust himself in his seat. When the motor started, he said, "I hope, Madam, you were not late."

"No. Thanks to you."

"I didn't dare to tell you, but you drove so fast around the curves on the mountains, my head kept bumping the car roof. I am really glad we made it. I had some doubts about your driving at first, having seen you looking so fragile in your long dress and high heels."

I just smiled. He had not seen me out every morning at five, at the Club Nautique, rowing my *perissoire* way out to the middle of the river around the big commercial ship and back again, all before he came to pick up my husband at home to go to work.

That night I told Brother Hoanh about the day's events. We agreed that I should return to Bien Hoa the next day and talk with Mr. Lua to get an idea of what was going on. Each province only needed one representative, and there was no use fighting a lost battle.

The longer I lived with my husband, the more I realized that we got along best in matters of country, job, and social standing. We both seemed to enjoy a good, hearty fight for a good cause. As for the rest, we were terribly incompatible — daily matters that I considered important, such as being together and showing that you care — he always seemed to brush off as trivial "women's concerns."

I went to see Mr. Lua the next day. He and his wife both greeted me very joyfully. In three minutes I found out who my adversary was — not him. He had submitted his name, sure that he was the most qualified, especially since he was the province's leader and budget consultant to Mr. Nhu's Can Lao party, but he had been told by his party to withdraw. There was a new runner, Mrs. Nu ("Nu" meaning female), reportedly the concubine of the head of the Labor Union and a protégée of Mrs. Ngo Dinh Nhu.

Mr. Lua urged me to go see another candidate. "You better go check with him. He might be able to tell you more about this election. He is a teacher. Here is his address, and good luck to you. We are glad to see you."

The teacher lived in an apartment in a long complex. When I had explained through his window what I was there for, he opened his door wide to receive me. I was puzzled at the warm welcome of my competitor. Then I found out that he, too, had been dismissed because he was supported by Catholic refugees in Ho Nai.

The Ho Nai refugees, thirty thousand in number, were a homogeneous

179

group of Catholics who in 1954 had followed their priests to the south. Diem had given them an area in the wilderness for settlement. Money and tools were provided by USAID for each family to build a hut and to cultivate their small lots of land in front of their homes to grow vegetables and raise chickens — a self-sustaining program. In four years, the refugees had cleared the whole forest with a few hand tools, built at least twenty churches, made themselves large wooden houses, and created a firewood industry — selling to the residents of Saigon and Cap St. Jacques who were within ninety kilometers of their village.

The Ho Nai people were not only hardworking and anti–Communist, but also extremely obedient to their Catholic priests and their religious leaders.

A few days after the teacher had submitted his name, he was asked to withdraw. He refused and began receiving anonymous notes threatening his life unless he withdrew immediately. Still he refused. One day, two men came, forced their way into his home, and gave him an injection of something which made him dizzy and weak. The last thing he remembered was their holding his arm to sign his name and their saying, "You hereby resign."

When I told him that Mr. Lua had also resigned, he looked confused.

"Ah! So the news must have been reported to Madame Advisor [Mrs. Nhu's title], and she is afraid I'll have the backing of the powerful Ho Nai refugees. And Mr. Lua has the backing of his money and his son, a representative in the National Assembly. Also, his son-in-law is the mayor of Saigon. Madame Advisor obviously doesn't want either of us. So who is it that she wants?"

Brother Hoanh and I both agreed that we were in for a fight. If Mrs. Nu was Madame Nhu's protégée, we were running up against Madame Nhu herself. We had to devise a strategy.

That night, we went to a refugee church in Gia Dinh on the outskirts of town to look for a priest that my mother had known when we were in North Vietnam. He promised us he would talk to the priests in Ho Nai about us and make arrangements for us to see them. That done, we opened the map of Bien Hoa to identify the villages I should visit to make contact with the people. We left out two or three big suburbs of Bien Hoa where we knew Mrs. Nu's husband would certainly send his men to influence residents. The villages I chose were very far away from town and had no access to roads.

Often I had to leave the car on the road and walk alone on dirt lanes separating rice fields. I enjoyed it. It reminded me of my adolescence and refugee days. The villagers were surprised that I came to talk to them "man to man." I was used to it with my army training.

I only had to see the priest in Ho Nai once. The old priest who oversaw the refugees told me just to leave everything in his hands. I should not come down any more so that Mrs. Nu and her people would not know I was getting cooperation from the Ho Nai people.

When the day came for the two candidates to meet to agree on the locations for speeches and the amount of money they should spend on posters, Mrs. Nu was not present. Instead, two big, muscular men from the Labor Union came to represent her. They thought their size and vulgar attitude would intimidate me.

They insisted that only a small number of posters be printed, that there would be no pictures of the candidates on the posters, and that my "platform" should be given to them to inspect so that they could check on government regulations. When I asked them about their platform, they said not to worry because Mr. Buu, their leader, represented the government itself. Having somewhat anticipated this kind of trouble, I tried to ignore them, relying mostly on the good judgment of the people for the election day.

Finally the days of public speaking arrived. "Could you tell me, Mrs. Mai [married women used their maiden name for their own business], why your picture isn't on the posters?" asked a worker at one of the debates where Mrs. Nu showed up for the first time — in the largest suburban village of Bien Hoa. "The 'Mrs.' and the 'thi' were not on the posters either so we thought you were a man."

They all laughed, and I laughed with them. "Now you know," I said. I felt it was no use to embarrass another woman in front of men, so I didn't tell them that my opponents had stipulated that no pictures be printed out and that they designed all the posters themselves.

"You were talking about promoting national businesses, Mrs. Nu?" another man then asked. "Why are you wearing a dress made of imported fabric while Mrs. Mai wears Vietnamese materials?"

"Sorry," replied Mrs. Nu, "I didn't notice."

The peasants, very shrewd in their observations, could be as tricky and subtle as the most sophisticated elites.

Meanwhile, Brother Hoanh had a stack of hand-rolled copies of the election laws ready to give to the young refugees who were selected by the priests to monitor the voting boxes. The leaflets instructed them on their duties: to watch the voting boxes at their posts, follow those boxes until they arrived at the city hall, and see to it that the votes were counted correctly. Brother Hoanh sent the priests the money to cover all transportation, food, and labor costs. They told us that they had already assigned one Lambretta minibus and four young men to each post.

The night before the election, we went to visit with the priests and refugees to verify and coordinate our program. Again we were met with great excitement and enthusiasm.

Brother Hoanh had also contacted the press world, inviting them to come and witness the election with us. The AP, UPI, Agence France Press, and Reuters correspondents among others were in Bien Hoa on the election day. Many of our friends also joined us there.

We spread out in town to observe. Everything seemed to be running along smoothly until about four o'clock. We were gathering to have soft drinks and snacks when suddenly two young men ran in from their Lambretta "bus" and told us that "they" were trying to take the boxes away in the village they were supervising. "They" would not let anybody come in the yard to drop their votes.

I told them I would follow them back to their post. I knew Brother Hoanh should not go with me. He was supposed to be working for Diem. We did not want to risk having Diem consider him a traitor, although at this point we were still in the dark about who exactly wanted to block us. There were five brothers in the Ngo family. Each exerted his own power through his own men. Each had equally powerful influence. But Madame Nhu, their sister-in-law, installed with her husband permanently in the right wing of the Presidential Palace, had the most power. And I was running against her protégée and close aide.

A friend of ours, a returnee from Canada, proposed that he accompany me in case of trouble. We followed the young men in their Lambretta for over half an hour before we reached the remote village. I recalled my long walk with the heads of this village. They had discussed what they would need to make their farming easier—a few more hoes, a few more spades, some better grain, a better well, better dirt roads so that they could commute to other villages in a Lambretta and so forth. I had thought what they asked was reasonable and had told them so.

We entered a courtyard full of soldiers lined up around the fence and standing by the doorway. The villagers seemed to be minding their own business, walking on the dirt path in front of the thatch where the soldiers stood on guard. I saw the two other young monitors sitting by the window, holding on tightly to their boxes. I asked the boys who had brought us where our opponent's representatives were, and they said, pointing to the old man who sat with a box at the other window, "Just that man. He sat there all day, not a single vote for Mrs. Nu. Nobody came to him. That's why they want to take our boxes away."

182

"Who wants your boxes?"

"The captain out there."

I looked to where they pointed and saw an army man standing in the middle of the yard. When I asked him why he wanted to take the boxes away when it was not time yet, he said, "Lenh cua Tong Thong" (Order of the president). Then I asked, "If you take the boxes away, will you let my representatives go with you?"

"No. We will take them in the army truck, and nobody except the soldiers can sit in the army truck."

"That's very unreasonable. You're breaking the voting laws." I spoke loudly for all the soldiers to hear, "The law states that the representatives of the candidates are responsible for the safety of the boxes and should stay with them until they reach the right officials in the city hall."

"I know nothing about that law. I do what the president tells me to do."

"And what did the president tell you to do?"

"To take the boxes away."

"Do you mean to tell me that I and the soldiers should believe you if you said the president sent an order for you to burn this house — that we should believe the messenger's words without checking?"

I turned to the soldiers, "Fellow men, we are here to uphold the truth, our rights..."

Suddenly I heard a gun cocking at my side, and the captain shouted, "Soldiers, this woman said that our president ordered us to burn this house. Shoot her. She is a Viet Cong."

Some of the soldiers automatically raised their guns.

"I think you know I am here to represent your rights," I said, unflinching. Bluff! I thought. Cowards have no guts to take on responsibilities which bring them blame.

My friend came up to me and said, "Sister Hoanh. Let's go. We'll consult with your husband."

I cooled down. He's right, I thought. They would dare to shoot me and my friend and blame our deaths on the Viet Congs. They must have received the order from either Diem or Madame Nhu to gather their troops in this backward area and to say that they had received the president's order. Everybody from high-ranking military to civilians knew who Brother Hoanh was — how close to Diem he was and how important his job was to Diem. No one would dare to hurt him unless he received the order straight from the Ngos. And I wasn't about to give Madame Nhu the chance to claim that she had outdone me personally. She would remain then, in the eyes of the Ngos, an adept, shrewd politician who knew the way to run her people. The Ngos had killed quite a few popular leaders of strong religious sects and imprisoned many others in tiger cages to let them die, burned in lime water after days of exposure to hellish sun. Madame Nhu would certainly not spare me.

"Let's go," I called to my representatives. "We don't need the boxes any more. We already know the truth."

We drove back to Brother Hoanh and the group. Some newsmen were present. I took Brother aside and told him about our venture. We decided that this was not an isolated incident. They had an overall plan to cheat. Brother Hoanh turned to invite everybody to the city hall to witness the arrival of the boxes.

Every time the boxes came in, the foreign press started taking pictures. Whenever the boxes did not arrive with their representatives, the press people would approach the city hall staff in charge to ask them what the reasons were for it. The staff began to get jittery. They moved the boxes to a locked room. Then the refugees from Ho Nai invaded the place with their boxes protected by their own people. A commotion broke out.

Suddenly the whole building blacked out. We waited for the lights to return, but officials said they were having difficulty getting a repairman. The staff apologized for not being able to count the votes at that time. They invited us to go home and not to worry. They assured the press that the votes would be properly counted sometime during the night as soon as the lights returned.

We went out and saw the refugees lingering around their Lambretta buses. All that we could do was to thank them and tell them to go home, we would contact them later.

The next morning, Brother Hoanh went to work earlier than usual. But the minister of interior (the same one who used to force movie houses to hold projection until he arrived) was at his office even earlier. He called Brother Hoanh to report to him the election results from the different provinces. For Bien Hoa he quoted a number of votes for Mrs. Nu, the "winner." My husband quickly checked on the population of Bien Hoa and called the minister back.

"If you need a number, give one that is more realistic. Cheat intelligently. Your 'votes' exceed twice the population. Work on it and let me know soon. The press is waiting for our news."

Several days before, that same minister had called him and told him amicably, "You better cool down. The president complained that you are belligerent." Brother Hoanh had answered, "If Mr. President has something to tell me, he has my phone number."

Two weeks before the election day, while I was on my campaigning tour, my chaffeur had found a note in the car. The note read, "If you do not stop driving for Mrs. Hoanh, you will receive a grenade on one of your trips home." I had had to release him and drive by myself, using my own blue Volkswagen.

Brother Hoanh's position became delicate after the election, but as protection from abrupt disgrace, he relied on the "mandarin" in President Diem—upholding the importance of keeping face in our culture and loyalty to their old relationship which had existed since the days when Diem had been an exile in the Maryknoll Seminary in New Jersey. Then he had insisted on paying for their room with his nickels and dimes whenever he invited Brother Hoanh to come and discuss politics with him. Brother Hoanh had organized many lectures at different universities for him and taken him to conferences for political scientists across the United States—he had even managed somehow to influence me to quote Diem as a potential leader. Mr. Diem also knew Brother Hoanh's family very well. From a highly respected family in Hue, Brother Hoanh's grandfather and father had been high-ranking mandarins who had been sent in 1889 and 1922 respectively on special missions to France. His mother's father had been governor of Quang Tri Province, and his aunt was a good friend of Diem's oldest brother, Ngo Dinh Khoi.

Counting too on his own background and popularity with the press and the Americans, Brother Hoanh was sure that Diem would be cautious about harming him with moves too obvious.

As for me, the "game" was over. I was rather disappointed that it had ended the way it did, quietly fading away. The elections finished, people moved on with their daily business. Friends kept a poker face so as not to betray their feelings. Vietnamese newspapers brushed over the election results, making them sound unimportant. Foreign papers kept quiet so that they could stay on in Vietnam to further witness the show.

Several days after the election, as we were in the middle of our siesta, our maid came knocking at our door and said that two ladies wished to see us urgently. I went to the balcony and saw their car which I thought I had seen following me a few times during my campaigning trips. They walked up the stairs to our apartment, one holding feebly to the other. As soon as they entered our living room, the weak girl dropped flat on the sofa. The other began to fan her and cried out loudly, "Forgive us. My sister and I were very upset at the election results, and she already had a weak heart. I think she's going to faint."

Then she pounded her chest, "I am so angry at the way they cheated you. We promised ourselves if we could find a way to be useful to you to revenge them, we would."

My husband had come down to join me. I told the maid to bring some lemonade and urged them to cool off with it. The fainting girl slowly got up. I saw a pretty young face painted with heavy make-up, the same as with her sister.

"Who are you?" Brother Hoanh asked.

"You probably know Lawyer Loc. We are related to him," the fainting girl said softly. Then she clutched her chest fainting again. As usual, the name did not mean anything to me, so I turned to ask Brother Hoanh who the man was.

"He is in the lumber business. A very rich and well known man."

"Yes, that's him, known for doing lumber business with the refugees. And that was how we got to know the refugee priests. They entrusted us to bring you this message and we rushed here, skipping lunch and siesta, so that you could receive it on time."

"Please, what's the message?" I asked.

"They want you to know that they are preparing to rally in Saigon. Thirty thousand refugees will march in front of the palace to protest for you. They want to know what message you want to give them, what slogans you want them to use. You can write them down, and we will take them back right away. We don't mind going back and forth. We, too, want to help you."

"I thank you for your offer, but don't be so distressed. We'll think of something. Right now, please just take care of your sister. Give us some time."

Their anger was so exaggerated, their devotion so unreal, I felt as if I were watching two actresses performing poorly a part in an act of intrigue. I tried to remember whether their car was the one that I had seen. They were both southerners. The refugees had been very efficient in their communications and very secretive. Why would they use these girls to bring us their message? I stalled for time. It would not be proper for me to excuse myself to talk privately with Brother Hoanh. Besides, that would show that we suspected them.

Luckily, in a moment, the connection between Lawyer Loc and Bishop Ngo Dinh Thuc, Diem's older brother, came to me. Loc was the financial adviser for Bishop Thuc—supposedly to collect funds to help a Catholic university in Dalat. As such, he had the monopoly to exploit a very lucrative region for lumber. These girls were most likely working for them. They wanted to get some commitment from us so that they could incriminate us, using "My Nhan ke" (the pretty girls scheme) to lure Brother Hoanh.

186

I looked at them, sitting timidly, the little sister casting her eyes down shyly, and said, "Please do not tax yourself with this matter. Just go home and take care of your sister. Your health first. Thank you again for your offer." I called the maid to help the younger sister downstairs.

Soon after their departure, Brother Hoanh and I decided to send my youngest brother to the refugee church to tell them that we would be in Ho Nai that night. When it came to confidential matters, I always relied on him. Now that our friends and co-workers knew that the Ngo family was no longer on our side, they would have to watch their step so as not to be associated with us. They had good reason to fear. Sporadic murders, allegedly by the "Viet Congs," of several party members of different cliques who had fallen out of favor with the Ngos were reported on the news.

We ate dinner and waited until it was dark. Then Brother Hoanh drove us to Ho Nai. He parked the car in the street to keep watch while I went across the fields, following the little oil lamps in the distance. Soon I arrived at the front of the church. Standing on the cement court were at least one hundred young men representing the youth group in their village; among them were the priests. They took me to a lower building where the old priest was having a discussion with other priests who represented the Phat Diem district. They were all taking turns smoking a long bamboo pipe connected to a special jar of water which brought bubbles to humidify the burning tobacco. The smoke was strong and filtered with warm fragrance. They told me about the plan—the same one the girls had described—and showed me the banners that they had written. All against Mrs. Nu, nothing about Madame Nhu or the Ngo family. They just wanted the votes to be returned to the person they had voted for. They thought this subtlety would prevent any incrimination. They asked if I wanted to march with them, lead them. I told them that my husband and I had thought very carefully about it upon hearing the news from the two girls.

"What girls?" They were shocked. I knew this would deter them. When I told them that the girls had come to us as their messengers, the old priest swore, "The snake!" I knew he meant Madame Nhu but would not dwell on the subject any further because he did not want to admit that she had beaten them to the game. I told them that the Ngos were very devious. They could shoot down any one of us, then declare it was the Viet Congs disguised among us that did it. I was thinking of what had happened to General Trinh-Minh-The (a mysterious shot in the back!). Then what would we do? The time might be right, but we were not prepared. We would have to plan for the next step at another meeting.

187

They agreed with me and asked me to go out to explain to the young men why it was not yet time to march.

Seeing the disappointment in the youthful faces, I couldn't help but tell them, "It does not mean that we are finished yet. I'll go back and check about this and will let you know. Maybe we can still do it, with more time to prepare."

The next day I made an appointment with my election "financier," the man who had originally proposed for me to run and advanced funds for it. I explained to him what was going on and asked what he thought.

"Well, if you want to be a Joan of Arc, then all glory to you!"

I took his hint. If nobody else knew, he would as a high-ranking official close to the Nhus. He probably was having lots of troubles with them about me. I never knew for sure who had been behind the money for me to run. Madame Nhu may have wanted me in at first to publicly show my incompetence but then changed her mind when she saw the Ho Nai's backing. At any rate, she was not content with merely winning. "Madame Nhu is very furious at you and your wife," reported one of Brother's well-connected tennis friends. "She insisted that Mr. Nhu and Mr. Diem send somebody to investigate your Vietnam Press autonomous budget. She is sure that you took the money from there to help your wife run in the elections. She told them to put you in prison, to teach you a lesson. But Mr. Nhu said you were doing fine at Vietnam Press and to leave you alone."

Some days after the friend's tip, the director general of Budget and Foreign Aid sent his inspector to Brother's office to check on the financial records there. Brother Hoanh let the man work with his accountant for several days, but they could find nothing incriminating.

17

LIFE QUIETLY moved along its course, leaving me alone to ponder on the course of my own fate. The Ho Nai refugees returned to their daily business of going to church and being industrious. Like my parents, brothers, and sisters, they also avoided the election subject, pretending that nothing had happened. Our friends still met with us, but I could sense their reserved feelings towards us. Everyone seemed to be either afraid of us or of hurting us. I waited for Brother to make a move, but in vain. We were only together to solve a crisis; beyond that, we kept our thoughts to ourselves.

The leadership qualities he had demonstrated had been an inspiration to me. What I had thought purely "intellectual" in him had proven to be practical and brave. He had the shrewdness and charisma of a leader and conducted himself with integrity and composure. Through these qualities, we had been able to divert our enemy's attack and discover their weak points. The defense stage had passed. Now came the most crucial point, the preparation for a show of force on our part.

But in this he was not with me. A "man of integrity" nowadays was a mixture of new and old cultures which made him impossible to comprehend. I could not read his mind. Perhaps he was being too much the "noble mandarin" not wanting to fight over "petty" issues. I had thought our retreat was only a strategy. Now it looked like we had retreated for good. The exhilarating excitement of our concentrated effort to meet the challenge seemed to have ended in quiet resignation. Though I had thought about our children and our responsibilities for their welfare, I did not anticipate a major problem about this—my family had survived through the worst of the revolution which had daily exposed us to disaster and death. Life proved to be beyond us humans to take or reject.

189

"Troi sinh voi, Troi sinh co" (God creates elephants, so He creates the grass for them to feed on) my mother often said. I was feeling fatalistic.

Left alone to ruminate, I went through a depression without knowing it.

Then it occurred to me that maybe I should take some time off to clear my mind. I set out to enroll in the Saigon Law University. They rejected me, saying that my B.A. had no place in the French system and that they could not find my Hanoi school records. I went to register in an art course. They told me I had no background in art and no recommendations. I tried to take piano or violin lessons, but the few teachers in Saigon were too busy with other more "productive" projects than teaching music. Professional artists were not highly regarded in our Vietnamese culture which considered them dilettantes: "Dan ca, xuong hat vo cong doi nghe." (Art, music, dancing, and singing are for idle people who are good for nothing.)

Feeling reduced to nothing, I wondered if the past few months had not been merely a figment of my imagination. Was life only what was running through my head? Was the morning exercise, the routine eating and talking and playing with my children something invented for me to survive from day to day? My life seemed purposeless. Tomorrow seemed only a dreary prolongation of today, worthless and senseless in the dark, deep pit of Saigon. And when the day ended and nightfall began, when struggling birds came back seeking warmth and protection in their nests, what did I, a human, get for consolation? Lying in bed waiting for Brother Hoanh to come home or not to come home? And when he did come another problem presented itself. Our two children slept in the living room. When one of them cried the other would start in, too. Their cry would mount to our room, making Brother nervous so that the maid would end up carrying the older child out into the street to calm him down with the fresh air. Whenever this happened, my head would scream at the injustice. I could do better; we could do better. Why did we choose to stay trapped in this?

With his position, Brother Hoanh could have easily obtained a better house or more money. But no, his position as a close aide of Diem put him in a delicate situation. He would have to decide on his own salary and fight for his own housing. He wouldn't do that, as the "mandarin" in him considered that somewhat too materialistic and below him. The regular salary of a director general would be too little for his needs. Other directors before Brother Hoanh had been more established in the sense that they already owned a government house. For cash, they would resort to discretionary funds in which they could exaggerate their spendings.

But to Brother it was a disgrace for a director to charge the government with expenses that were not clear. Well, I saw all that, but where did that leave me?

Brother Hoanh did not seem to care where we lived, what we ate, how we survived the day. Most days he wasn't even home. I struggled to live decently within my class, but I could never reconcile the feeling of hypocrisy that kept nagging at me. What was the purpose of working for a government that we did not believe in and meet with "friends" who were only interested in exploiting the day's work and not a bit concerned about the future? What was the use of keeping up a façade that we were good, honest, and disciplined and didn't care for money—the picture of a mandarin of integrity—in this deceptive world of pragmatic politics?

Again I heard my baby crying in the street, but my husband didn't seem to care. I knew there were many problems and dangers for him at work—but maybe, I told myself, maybe he did not realize what was going on at home, because his mind was so much on other pressures. If I could explain to him and share with him my feelings then he could understand.

The following day during lunch I talked to him, trying to be as calm and thoughtful as possible. Suddenly he blew up. "Where is all your money?! If you don't have it, go to work for it!"

I was struck by his mean words. Hadn't I proved myself enough?! Wildy I jumped up, climbed the three flights of stairs, four steps at a time, and took my jewelry box out. I threw it bouncing down the stairs with the jewelry given to me by my mother and his flying all over.

"Here's all the money you made!" I screamed at the top of my voice, which echoed back and surprised me with its vulgar sharpness. It was the first time in my life I had fought in the open and so violently—and not for something idealistic, but for such a base thing as money.

I ran back to my bed and wept loudly, like a mad person. So low, so low had I sunk. I remained in that depressed state of mind until evening. Then suddenly I remembered I had some pain killers given to me before my delivery. I swallowed the whole contents of the bottle.

I was traveling over a green meadow spotted with colorful flowers; ever so lightly I passed over them. The view in front of me was soft, the air around me calm and sweet . . .

All of a sudden I saw the ceiling. Its white and confining corners pressed down on me. Heaviness sunk me back to life. My eyes lowered to pick up a form in a European suit, lying at my side. Brother Hoan's voice sounded faintly, "Little sister, you are back. You've been sleeping for a day and a half. Are you all right now? . . . I didn't know whether you wanted me to call a doctor."

Tears flooded my eyes. Tears flooded my soul. I dreaded returning to this place. Why hadn't he been concerned that I could have left him for good? Why hadn't he called the doctor? Was it because he was afraid of a scandal? Or was it because he respected my will? I would never know, and perhaps it was just as well.

He left for work. I lay there with my eyes closed until the bright morning sun pried them open. I went to my dresser and looked into the mirror. The same face of yesterday reflected back. I had relied too much on him as my leader. He had abandoned me. Worse, he had shown me that I was stupid to rely on him. Or did he really think I wasn't doing my duty? He had told me to go to work. I had thought my place was at home — to keep myself healthy, to dress well, and to act well and think well; to take good care of my children so that he could be proud of his family in public and happy to have good company at home. I had thought my job was to give him support and constructive criticism and to stand by him in his troubles.

I did not want to think any more. In an effort to shake off my state of misery, I put on my new European-style dress which had flowers the color of eggplant, my favorite color. I had had it tailored before my pregnancy and had not been able to use it since — having had to get back into shape to wear Vietnamese clothes during the elections. No wonder I was lost. One day Western, the next day Asian; one day with an American partner, the next day with a mandarin husband!

Chi Ba had taken the kids to visit the neighbors. I drove my Volkswagen to a classy café on Catinat Street (the Vietnamese Champs Elysées). In the past I had always been with my husband when I went out in public, but today I was determined to shake loose of my old idea of wifely behavior and to test my own independence.

Sitting at a small round table for two, I noticed a man from the bar smiling at me. Since I met so many of Brother Hoanh's friends and hardly ever remembered their names or faces, I thought this man must have been one of them. I smiled back. He came to me and asked my permission to sit at the table next to me. I told him the table was not occupied and that he was free to sit anywhere he wanted. He was a young Frenchman with a romantic look and a handsome face. I sat and sipped my tea, and he his drink.

As I was getting into my car, this same fellow peered through the opposite window to ask me if I could give him a ride to his car, which he said was in the shop. When I asked him where the garage was, he said, as if he knew, in the same direction I was going. Along the way he asked to be dropped off at a large garage, and asked if he could see me again.

I replied that it was no secret where I lived and that I had a husband and two children and left it at that.

At home I thought about the encounter, and somehow it made me feel good about myself. For years I had lived in Brother Hoanh's shadow — always behind him, always seeing only what he saw. He called me stupid, so I thought I was stupid. He criticized my looks, so I thought he had good taste and I bad taste. He went out with other girls, so I thought I must be distasteful in some way. What had happened today, however, had reminded me of my own identity. The world looked to me the same as when I was a young girl. Life still ran its happy course in the midst of problems and intrigues. I was determined to change my "wifely" concept.

It seemed that maybe Brother Hoanh did care after all and had his own plan for getting out. He became absent from the house more often on Saturdays and Sundays, and at the same time he saw Diem more often. Whether because of my complaints or because President Diem told him to pay himself better now that they were spending more time together, we were able to move into a nice villa and had more money to buy better furniture, hire a good cook, and give parties for our diplomatic friends at home.

During this period, the Ngo family seemed to have settled down. Each knew his rights and boundaries. Madame Nhu was pleased with the harem of women at her disposal. It now included women pharmacists, lawyers, and teachers who joined the International Women's Club and the Phu Nu Lien Doi (Women's Solidarity movement). They held social gatherings with other women in the diplomatic corps.

I did not join either of the groups, neither did I frequent diplomatic cocktail parties any more. But one day, my husband told me there was going to be a cocktail party given at the Presidential Palace in honor of two relatives of President Kennedy. Out of curiosity, I went and was invited to Madame Nhu's reception the following day.

After hors d'oeuvres served on the lawn, we were all asked to go inside to listen to Madame Nhu, presenting the work of her Phu Nu Lien Doi organization.

I happened to be standing next to the sister of President Kennedy (or so I was told), when an American uniformed man, dressed in white, came to invite her in. She turned to ask me to join her. I declined. She asked why. I told her that Vietnamese women had been doing social work and attending to our civic duties for hundreds of years and that was how we kept our country strong and helped our men to fight for Vietnam's freedom. Madame Nhu's women's organization was a collection of wives of high-ranking government officials and business women who did no social work except for appearing in public gatherings next to Madame Nhu. They either were obligated to join because of their husband's jobs, or hoped to get business contacts by being near to the "Sun power."

President Kennedy's sister then turned to the uniformed man and told him that we both would stay outside; we could witness the meeting from the window. The uniformed man returned with two chairs for us.

Madame Nhu spent half an hour speaking in English to over a hundred Vietnamese attendants and two Americans. She told them that her organization was the first of its kind to draw women out of their homes and get them interested in attending to the country's needs. She closed the meeting by asking some "important members" to stand in line with her to greet the guests. She and the Vietnamese shook hands with one another in their *ao dai*, Vietnamese dress. When my turn came, I clasped my hands together and placed them in front of me at waist level. Madame Nhu had offered her hand to shake, but seeing me, she pulled her hand back and imitated me, except that instead of placing her hands at waist level, she placed them in front of her chest. Again she proved she knew nothing about our Vietnamese culture. One only raised one's hands to the chest to show respect to people of higher status; between persons of equal status, the hands would be at navel level only.

For a girl who used to sit quietly in the crowd, among friends, I was surprised to find myself seeking so eagerly the understanding of foreigners as if my own life depended on it. Somehow, by instinct, I guessed that Vietnam's fate depended on the way Americans understood Vietnam and its people.

On October 11, 1961, when my third child was eleven months old, my husband came home and said, "Let's pack up. We are going to leave for America tomorrow. Tell nobody, not even your parents."

I was happily surprised, although I wished Brother trusted me more, at least on things that concerned us both. I packed our clothes into four suitcases and the next day sent our chauffeur to my parents to ask them to come and see us. All that I could tell them was "good-bye" and for them to take what furniture they wanted and to get rid of the rest.

We arrived at the airport just before the plane took off. An American friend of Brother Hoanh, who was the Saigon manager for TWA, handed us the tickets with the seats already assigned.

My dear Brother Hoanh! Whatever surprises he made, whether pleasant or painful, they always took my senses away. He had left us in the dark for three whole years. During that time I had been crying inside—

wanting to escape, yearning to see signs of my husband's resolution to leave Diem's corrupt regime to preserve his dignity! Now, with an order of a few words, he wrenched the five of us, wife and children, away from our homeland, friends, parents, roots. Was I to be considered his possession? What a dictator! Yet how glad I was to be getting out of this hell. I was happy Brother was taking us out, although it would seem that he did think I was stupid and untrustworthy after all. Only when we were thousands of miles away from home did Brother Hoanh feel safe enough to tell me, his own wife, what had happened.

Several months before, seeing that Diem was happy with the reports of his reelection, Brother Hoanh had taken the opportunity to tell Diem that he had an Associate Nieman Fellowship offered by Harvard and wished to ask for permission to return to his studies (it was a good pretext and a lucky coincidence). Diem, shocked at the sudden request, did not respond. Months had passed. Meanwhile, Mr. Nhu's office had been drafting an order to appoint Brother director general of information, besides being director general of the Vietnam Press. Finally, after eight months of maneuvering among the Ngo family members, Brother had been granted permission to leave, supposedly only without his family, as stated by the minister at the presidency who said that it was Diem's order.

Confident that Diem was only bluffing, in an attempt to either discourage him from leaving without his family, or to keep the family as collateral for his return, Brother went ahead and sent the permit to leave to police headquarters, requesting passports for the entire family.

Thus Brother Hoanh had left one of the best jobs in Diem's government for an uncertain future in the United States.

18

A BORROWED place, a borrowed time, a borrowed life. We were the poorest among the Nieman Fellows who were a select group of journalists (mostly Americans) invited to Harvard for one year of unstructured research and study. In Cambridge, we slept in army surplus sleeping bags and used a fold-up square table for dining. Brother Hoanh had brought along his typewriter, so I bought him a huge used vibrating lounge chair to massage his tired muscles after long hours of typing. He first wrote an article, on my behalf, "Electioneering South Vietnamese Style," which was published by *U.C. Berkeley Review Asian Survey*, then a book, *Is South Vietnam Viable?* which was published in the Philippines in November 1962 (twelve months before the 1963 coup against Diem). He could not afford to wait for the decision of the American publishers who had told him of their year-long process of evaluating the book for the American market. The people in Vietnam were dying by the thousands every day. The Diem régime was becoming more and more unpopular as a despotic family dictatorship. Non-Communist groups were shifting to the Communist side. We thought the American public should be aware of this.

Before Brother Hoanh had the book published, he sent a confidential copy of his manuscript to General Lansdale, hoping that he would, in one of his trips to Saigon, give it to Diem to read, and from there Diem could see his mistakes and correct them. Then there would be no need for publication. Instead, Brother Hoanh received a letter from his father saying that Diem had visited him at his house in Dalat and mentioned that he was disappointed in Brother Hoanh whom he had treated like his own son. If Brother Hoanh needed money, Diem would buy his land in Thu Duc and send him money. My father-in-law, who was quite a character, outspoken and frank, had replied that "if money was so important to Hoanh, he would have stayed back in Saigon."

My father-in-law's letter convinced Brother Hoanh that Diem had known all along what was going on but chose to close his eyes and take sides with his family. Brother Hoanh gave up hoping to "reform" Diem and had his book published.

While Brother was busy with his book, I handled our expenditures. I regained my self-confidence during this period. All things considered, my mental and emotional health improved tremendously. Education for my children became a priority in America. However, unlike in Saigon, for my children to enter a good school I no longer had to ask my "contacts" to get them on the list of students allowed to take the entrance exams! As for myself, I was able to put aside some money to take singing lessons at the Boston Conservatory of Music—I who had not had one singing lesson in my life!

At the end of the year, when our visas expired, we had to stay on in the United States as we could not return to Vietnam nor travel abroad. Tran Van Dinh, then counselor at the Vietnam Embassy, signed a form to deny us our six-month visa extension. Dinh, who had always come to my husband as his close friend to have good Vietnam Press reports on his diplomatic missions! He now had secretly conspired with our friends Vo Van Hai, Diem's private secretary, and paratrooper Colonel Thi in the 1960 coup against Diem. It was sad to find out that he was an unscrupulous opportunist! We had not believed it when we had been told that he had reported on Hai and Thi's conspiracy to Mr. Nhu immediately after the coup aborted. Such a well-spoken, educated fellow; yet how treacherous underneath the façade.

Brother decided he wanted to be alone so that he could actively become involved in politics. He took us to live with one of my sisters, Golden Cloud, who had settled in Arizona after her graduation from Nazareth College. Brother went away to teach journalism at the University of Missouri, awaiting changes in South Vietnam.

In Phoenix, Arizona, my children and I shared a house with Golden Cloud and her family—an American husband and one child. We spent our days, my three children in school, and I working part-time as a salesperson at a recently opened May Company.

Together with Golden Cloud, I hired a Mexican nurse to help us cook and care for the children. I also rented an old, manual typewriter and started learning to type on the heavy keys. In this way, I hoped to be able to work on my own time when I became proficient enough. My simple daily chores left me free of anxieties, and I felt my life there was just a transition period.

Meanwhile, the political situation in Vietnam was deteriorating rapidly. Many left the régime to join the Viet Congs whom they thought of as their South Vietnamese compatriots. Two rebellious attempts to overthrow Diem had been aborted.

In 1963, Madame Nhu was in the states for eye surgery. She wore big sunglasses to face the press. They asked her about the monk who had burned himself in public protest against the Ngos—to shock the world into realizing the desperate state of the people under the Diem régime.

"All they [Buddhist leaders] have done is barbecue a bonze," she mocked.

Her inhumane remark made the U.S. and the international public realize that she was indeed a "Dragon Lady." Mr. and Mrs. Chuong, her parents, who were ambassadors to the United States and the United Nations were embarrassed and resigned from the Diem government in protest. Brother Hoanh saw the opportunity, and together with Richard Dudman, the *St. Louis Post Dispatch* Washington bureau chief (who later wrote *Forty-five Days with the Enemy* after he was released by the Viet Congs) invited Mr. Chuong to give talks about his critical views on the Diem government and Mrs. Nhu's pernicious role in the Ngo family régime.

Mrs. Nhu was more than just a spoiled sister-in-law of the president; she was a recklessly ambitious and unprincipled woman. As it turned out, during the Buddhist crisis, Mrs. Nhu had conspired with her psychotic younger brother, Tran Van Khiem (in the eighties, Khiem killed his parents, allegedly because of an argument about family inheritance), to assassinate Diem's and Nhu's closest aides (Tran Kim Tuyen and Nguyen Dinh Thuan) and to sabotage their attempts at reconciliation with Buddhists.

In my seclusion, I followed the events in Vietnam almost with indifference. Until suddenly one day I found myself shocked by the televised scenes of the aftermath of the coup d'état in Saigon. It was November 2, 1963, the day after the coup. The TV also showed an APC (armored personnel carrier) parked with its lid open. The commentator was announcing that President Diem and Mr. Nhu were in the tank, stabbed and shot several times. A single man, identified as Colonel Nguyen van Thieu (the same who later became president of Vietnam), was descending the huge vacant steps to survey the APC. His blank and waxy face had the cold look of a coroner checking to make sure that the bodies were in fact dead.

Brother Hoanh and I talked long distance. We were both shocked by Diem's murder — such a demonstration of unnecessary violence from the Vietnamese who normally gave the appearance of being meek and submissive. For the following weeks, we watched, uncertain about the future developments in Vietnam.

Right after Diem's death, his brother Can, known as the "Terror" in Hue, was killed in prison after his fortune was extorted. The two other brothers, Ngo Dinh Luyen and Bishop Thuc who were outside Vietnam at the time, settled in France and Italy respectively. Madame Nhu was reported to have left the United States for France, leaving behind enormous unpaid bills. She told the press she did it intentionally "to make the American people pay for the murder of the Ngo family." Then came the assassination of President Kennedy ten days later. While the world was in mourning — even my baby-sitter, an illiterate Mexican woman who had entered illegally into the States, threw herself on the floor of my house and grieved at the televised scene — Mrs. Nhu found her chance to lash out her morbid venom to the press, saying that "she was pleased that her family was revenged."

In November 1963, immediately after the coup, Brother Hoanh, whose book had been taken secretly into Vietnam through the Philippines and was widely known by the elite and the coup makers, was invited back home to work for General Minh, the leader of the coup that overthrew Diem. General Minh was quiet and an unusually large-boned man for a Vietnamese. He had frequently played tennis with Americans in Diem's time. He was so quiet and "simpatico" that the American VIPs thought of him as a knowledgeable and wise man. However, after three months of leadership, General Minh was removed, and Nguyen Khanh succeeded him. Khanh's "reign" proved even more confused than Minh's. In those days, Saigon was ripe with rumors about coups, counter coups, and daily demonstrations by Buddhists and Catholics against each other.

Upon our return from the States, Brother Hoanh was given a big villa and appointed deputy of information minister, the existing minister being a general. He refused the job because he did not see any sense in doing propaganda work for the Saigon generals who did not seem to know what they were doing.

From 1963 to 1965, the country was left without a government. The military leaders reportedly dealt in cocaine and heroin. Together with some Americans, they used American planes to transport and exchange dollars for drugs from Hong Kong and then shipped the drugs back to sell to U.S. soldiers in Vietnam and to Vietnamese.

The security of Vietnam was left to whomever wanted to take over. Saigon was guarded by a group of Cao Thang students who used as weapons tools they made in their machine shops.

Their eighteen-year-old leader, A (Asian), came to us one day and said that General Khanh's aide had handed him a package of cash which he had brought along to show Brother Hoanh and to seek his advice. He said they wanted him to lead his group to demonstrate in favor of the Buddhists when called for. The son of a "blue collar" worker and a Catholic, A confessed he knew it was a bribe and wanted to return the money, but he was afraid of antagonizing General Khanh and the Buddhist monks he supported. We praised A for his work and honesty and told him that his intuition was the most valid thing he could rely on in moments of doubt, and we advised him to return the money. Meanwhile, Brother Hoanh obtained from his American friends a number of transmitters that he distributed to Catholics and Buddhists so that they could communicate among themselves and avoid the clashes provoked by vicious rumors spread by politicians.

While the Vietnamese generals were fighting among themselves, Americans were trying to make sense out of the political confusion in Saigon and to design some kind of Vietnam policy. They concentrated their efforts on fighting Communists in the field as if Vietnam were their own country and the South Vietnamese their guests. Americans in South Vietnam became so involved, each with their own "counterpart" or favorite Vietnamese politician, that they lost track of the basic goal of the U.S. presence in South Vietnam — to help the people of South Vietnam stay free and independent.

One evening when he was very depressed, Brother took me to see Colonel Pham Ngoc Thao, whom Brother thought to be better informed and more dignified than most Saigon military officers. Bishop Thuc and President Diem had used him to report on suspected corruption among chiefs of provinces. His contribution to the success of General D.V. Minh's coup to overthrow Diem had been a major one. He and his men had made a suicidal attack to gain control of the National Radio Station in Saigon which was a key target for coup planners. We visited him on the day he was preparing to be sent to serve as Military Attaché to the Vietnamese Embassy in Washington, D.C., in spite of his insistence that he would be more useful at home. The visit over, he slipped off the holster and gun at his side and gave it to Brother Hoanh, saying, "Be careful! You, too, are being very closely watched by Khanh's secret police. Keep this, my personal pistol; it may be useful some time." Brother Hoanh was pleasantly surprised to receive a "personal" pistol from a man he had only met a few times at official meetings during Diem's régime. He gave the gun to me to keep.

During this period, when there were many rumors of coups, Brother Hoanh was out every night to find out the news. My younger brother came to stay with me during this time. One night, while I was sleeping alone in my room with Colonel Thao's gun under my pillow, I heard my brother scream in the next room. I went to wake him, and he told me that a ghost had come, shoved him out of his bed, and told him to get out of the house. After a while, we returned to bed. Then I dreamed I saw a ghost with long hair trying to pull my blanket down—I fought to pull the blanket back up so I wouldn't have to see its face. My brother was awakened by my scream; he came and woke me up. For some reason, I immediately associated the ghost with the gun. I removed the gun and locked it away in my trunk, thinking that this would lock the ghost away. A few days later, I heard of Thao's death. Colonel Thao had come home from his mission in the United States, and he was involved in a coup to overthrow General Khanh. Immediately after the coup had failed, he went into hiding because generals Ky and Thi were after him. He was caught hiding in the Ho Nai Catholic community near Bien Hoa. Some American general had tried to ask Ky to guarantee Thao's security, but while negotiations were taking place, the lieutenant colonel guarding Thao received orders to eliminate him quietly—Thao's private parts were crushed while he was flown on a helicopter from Bien Hoa back to Saigon. Thao's unusually cruel murder was kept a secret, but rumors quickly spread that General Thieu was masterminding Thao's murder, because Thao knew too much about Thieu's intrigues with the Catholic and the Can Lao groups to solicit their support in his favor against generals Ky and Thi. If Thao were left alive, under interrogation, he would have revealed compromising secrets about Thieu.

19

IMPROVISATION was called for in all aspects of life, especially for those Vietnamese who tried to remain dignified, intellectual, fashionable, and carefree in spite of their strict culture and the hopelessness of the war situation. Catinat Street, our showcase, renamed Tu Do (Freedom), was like a mirror of the Vietnamese people. Formerly the Champs Elysées of the Orient under the French, it no longer brought back the flavor of the elegance of the past. Dark soot stuck to the proud curbs where in the time of the French a cleaning truck had sprayed water early every morning for the prisoners to sweep clean. The street had become a marketplace in lieu of the former calm and chic ambiance. Many bars were squeezed in between the once elegant shops, and in the shop windows, cheap handicrafts were piled one on top of another to attract American GI's, Australian Rangers, and Korean and Thai soldiers. In colonial times, this street had been the only place where the French and a few Vietnamese with money and connections appeared together besides the big cathedral under whose roof "masters and servants" came to worship their common Catholic God.

No matter how I tried to divert myself, walking down Freedom Street never failed to take me back to the past, to the "good times"—a sharp comparison that left me hopelessly nostalgic.

Today, while waiting for the light to change at a street corner, I caught myself standing in front of a large window exhibiting Japanese toys. In the past, Vietnamese had shown a dislike for Japanese toys, known to be very *gia tao* (artificial)—falling apart quickly. Then it was commonly agreed that the Japanese were tricky, keeping the quality products at home and selling us the cheap stuff.

As I was contemplating this, I heard someone say "hello" behind me.

I looked in the glass and caught a glimpse of a GI grinning at me. I smiled back into the glass hesitantly. Old-timers would not have approved of conversation between a Vietnamese "lady" and a stranger who was a foreigner, especially a Caucasian. But in the old times no stranger would have approached a "lady" like that either.

"Do you speak English?"

For a second, the virile look of this Caucasian, his bronze tan and his clear blue eyes stirred a pleasant feeling in me. Then his practical question promptly brought me back to reality. I thought, I wish he would say something different, something the Frenchmen would use, an old trick, but it worked every time: "Are you Lotus, or Moon, or Rose? Haven't I seen you somewhere before with your friend Autumn? Or Spring?" The question would trigger an answer, affable or scornful, depending on the mood of the girl or the look of the boy, leading to a conversation.

Bah, that's the way they are, I thought. Maybe clumsy, shy. Maybe they just didn't want to waste time.

I must have looked very cold because the GI moved away, perhaps figuring he had mistaken me for a playgirl. I moved to cross the street.

A pleasant river breeze flitted by, sending a delicate Shalimar perfume into the cool air. I held on to the flaps of my dress while my eyes caught sight of a girl in a miniskirt farther on, raising her hand to call a cyclo on one of the side streets. When she leaned her well-proportioned five-foot body forward, the surrounding activities seemed to pause as the hem of her miniskirt hoisted up, showing all her thighs and part of her underwear, then teasingly dangled back to its normal position. Lately, such "porno" scenes had become a part of our daily surroundings.

Ironically, since Diem's time, Freedom Street had been reserved only to cars and limousines. Taxis and cyclos had to use the side streets. The same with Cong Ly (Justice) Street—kept "one way" to yield a clear road for visitors and dignitaries who came to town from the airport. The underprivileged called these streets "Limousine Freedom" and "One Way Justice."

As I walked past the little park which used to be the pride of Freedom Street in front of the theater, now a parking lot for bicycles, I turned left, trying to find a cyclo on the side street.

Suddenly I was halted by a sharp shrilling sound. I looked up from my daydreaming and saw an American GI jerking his gun at me, a few feet behind the barbed wire and sand bags. I stood bewildered for a second. Behind me I heard running and alarmed confusion. I swung around and heard the police shouting.

203

"Get off the curb!"

Caught by surprise, I stepped off quickly. Then, regaining myself, I chided, "What's going on? What did I do wrong, Mr. Policeman?"

"You are not supposed to walk near the curb, Miss."

"Oh, sorry, I thought I was supposed to walk only on the curb and leave the streets for automobiles and tanks. Is this an exceptional rule for our exceptional American friends?" Then I turned toward the GI who still pointed his gun at me, his jaws set tight, and said, "If you don't want anybody to bother you, why don't you move somewhere quieter?" The Americans had turned the whole building in the middle of our "showcase" street into some kind of secret headquarters.

Shaking my head, I started to cross the street.

Just then a cycloman pedaled toward me and asked, "Where to, Miss? You are right, Miss. Those Americans are sons of God. They have barbed wire, sandbags, trucks, jeeps right on the corner of Tu Do where the authority forbids us tiny quiet cyclos to pass." I had a hard time convincing him to let me pay afterwards. He insisted that I had done him a favor by speaking up. The good man pleased me, yet right away I wondered if he weren't Viet Cong. Only they would be concerned about matters like these, and only they would do anything for free, I thought to myself. I did not make further conversation for fear that he was a real Viet Cong trying to recruit me or that the authorities might think I had contacts with the enemy. But at the same time, I regretted having to deprive myself of the company of a good, honest person. But that was how we managed to survive in Vietnam.

Despite my desire to remain detached from my world, I found myself doing quite a bit of social work related to children. Since I had sent my own four children with their maids and a cook to live in a rented villa in Thu Duc (half an hour's drive from Saigon) for better air and a country life, the unfortunate plight of other children without parents or shelter had become even more troubling to me.

Today as I passed before the office window of the orphanage that I had been frequenting for some time, I caught a glimpse of Jim drooping in an armchair, his sunburnt face sad. My social work had led me to become fond of Jim by the end of 1965. We had much in common since he, too, was interested in the welfare of children. He was an American I thought would make an ideal husband, ideal father, and ideal soldier for my country. I held a secret romantic love and respect for this man of integrity.

As I entered the office, he did not stand up but rather looked at me like a wounded bear. I sat down in a chair near him.

204

"Hi, Captain."

Without returning the greeting, he just said, "Try to catch this." His hand was holding a rubber frog, the other hand held loosely to the rubber control. I obediently reached out my hand, palm open, and the frog landed in the middle of it. He smiled wanly. I was late, so the children had already been called inside. Jim looked so troubled I suggested we step out to the garden to have some fresh air. We walked into the yard scented with the perfume of the "princess" flowers perched high on the tall tree. The ivory-colored flowers were scattered sparsely among the dark green leaves, yet their delicate fragrance helped to distinguish them. The small, finger-shaped buds opened like bright stars when in full bloom. One single flower could scent a large room with its mild fragrance which was not as strong and sweet as the jasmine's. My head barely reached Jim's shoulder. I, who was five foot two, considered myself fairly tall by my countrymen's standards. But I loved the feeling of being protected by his tall muscular body.

"How was the battlefield?" I asked, smiling up at him.

He looked down at me tenderly. Our eyes met. A sweet thrill ran through my body. He sighed and vaguely gazed into the distance.

"I've never seen such horror. They were all old women and children. When I saw them I couldn't control myself any more. I jumped into a jeep and went looking for Charlie. I wish I had found them—I'd have shot them all."

I yearned to comfort him. Perhaps it was his childlike sincerity that attracted me so much.

"I love you, Jim," I murmured within myself. A moment passed. This is the time for me to share with him my feelings, I thought. It may help him to see clearer the true Vietnamese politics and maybe not blame himself for his failure in comforting those poor people. Very seldom did we have a chance to touch on a political subject. Looking straight ahead, I ventured, "You know, if you had, you could have killed one of my cousins. Many of my relatives and friends still are with the Communists. Some were forced to stay, and some of them like the Communist government better than these corrupt régimes. They may have killed those poor innocents in trying to 'liberate' them, to force them to reject the help of the enemy."

A complete silence fell, and I felt Jim's eyes on me. I looked up to see him staring at me disbelieving, as if he had just discovered that I was a Viet Cong. My God, I vexed him, I thought. How could he understand— if he did he wouldn't be here.

"Oh, Jim. I know this is not the time to talk about things like this.

Some of your friends, too, have been hurt, killed. Forgive me, okay?" I said, reaching for a jasmine flower across a cactus bush.

"Watch out!" Jim pulled back my arm. The front of my dress was caught in the cactus thorns. I turned to see his smiling face, and knew his doubts had been brushed away.

Luckily I didn't get around to finish expressing my thoughts. He would have certainly thought I was a Viet Cong if he had heard me compare that horror inflicted by the Viet Cong to that inflicted by the South Vietnamese and American soldiers. These tried to "free" villagers under the control of the Viet Congs by throwing napalm bombs, hoping to burn the Viet Congs inside the villages, then moved in and tried to heal the wounds of the survivors with medicines, to provide loving care with nurses, and to brighten the hearts of the orphans with chewing gum. The strange U.S. policy in Vietnam: Burn and destroy Vietnamese villages in order to "free" them!

Our villa used to be occupied by the Binh Xuyen who used to cooperate with the French police in Saigon. Perhaps because of its terrifying reputation, this villa had remained vacant since 1955. It was a large two-story house with a dependents' quarters and a dirt-packed garden. The garden looked quite nice and roomy, so I thought I would use all of our money to fill it with white and blue marble gravel (as some French yards were) and hire a gardener from the director of the zoo and botanical garden to plant some flowers along the walls. I missed them, and I thought I could afford to treat myself some.

Then to complete my dream of living American style, I went to the Chinese section of town to buy a water heater. Since Diem had granted citizenship to the Chinese who wished to become Vietnamese citizens, the Chinese had spread out into what used to be the Vietnamese section of town. They did not have to comply with our draft laws because they had good connections and their Chinatown (Cholon) to hide in. However, like the Vietnamese, they could apply for business and import licenses. Vietnamese who resented the way the Chinese exploited their newly acquired Vietnamese citizenship under Diem suspected a special connection between Diem and the Chinese. These suspicions grew stronger after the 1963 coup, when Diem and his brother escaped through a secret tunnel in the Presidential Palace, to seek refuge in the home of a rich Chinese in Cholon.

Buying a water heater in Vietnam was as difficult as buying a car. When we were under the French, we had exported many agricultural products, from rice, coffee, sugar, and tea, to rubber. Since our independence, we had had to import practically everything, even rice, which came from the United States, and kitchenware, using American aid dollars to import goods, mostly from the Japanese.

Finally, I had everything as I wanted it. My children even had membership cards to the Cercle Sportif and the Riding Club about three blocks from our house. We went there every day after school for them to take judo, ballet, swimming, and riding lessons, and to dine there with Brother Hoanh whenever he came to play tennis. It was a good life for once, I thought, and Mother would love to try our hot shower sometime.

I had used it fewer than five times myself when one afternoon Brother Hoanh announced before going out with friends, "We are leaving this government house. I quit my government job as of this afternoon."

All I could think of was: Not again! Was it Fate or was Brother trying to play God with his sudden decisions with such important consequences? Frankly, we could have stayed in that government house if we had wanted to, even though he had resigned his government job: everybody in Saigon used to do it. But it was a question of principle for Brother, and we had to move out, because he had already so decided.

We not only had to move but move quickly. He told me that he had agreed to let a "friend" of his, a Colonel Pham Van Lieu, use the house as a meeting place for youth groups. As it turned out, that "friend" of Brother merely took the house for his own personal use, forgetting about youth group meetings of any kind. (This same colonel later as a refugee in the United States formed one of those émigré anti–Communist organizations [rackets] claiming to "liberate" Vietnam. In fact he was only interested in taking advantage of poor unsuspecting soldier refugees who were all too eager to believe in and contribute to any organization which promised to bring them back to Vietnam as "heroes.")

Finding a house in Saigon at this time posed a very big problem, more difficult than finding a job. Even six years ago, before the influx of refugees to the city, I had had a hard time finding an apartment. But I had to scramble.

Mother had many friends, so I went to talk to her. Upon hearing my problem, she immediately sent word to a business lady, the potential mother-in-law of my younger sister. The next day my brother-in-law-to-be came with the news that they had found an apartment, "only, it is haunted," he revealed. The apartment had been left with an Indian "watchman" for several years until for some unknown reason, he had hung himself. No renters since had lasted more than a few months. They either became very sick, lost their fortune, or got so scared that they had moved out. If we didn't mind the ghost, we could move in. I didn't mind. We left the government house and moved in the next day.

Brother Hoanh was now jobless.

In the midst of my concerns about money, a friend dropped in and asked if I could help him with his business at the PX (Post Exchange). He wanted me to ask Americans not to return his defective Sony radios any more but instead give him a chance to send his Japanese technicians over to open a repair shop in the PX. A strange proposition, but I ventured, "That's a reasonable request. Why don't you go ask them yourself?"

"Well . . . They don't want to see us any more because they said our representatives made promises and didn't carry them out."

"I know nothing about business. Especially yours. I don't see how I can help you. I don't even know what the PX is."

"I think it would be easier for somebody who's been to their country, and charming, to talk with them."

I brushed aside his flattery, but surprised to know that the PX also did business with non–Americans, I was tempted to find out more. He added, "If we get the repair contract and are able to sell more products, we will reserve a commission for you on all our future shipments."

"No. If I do this, it's out of curiosity. I don't think they'll listen to me, anyway."

"It's normal to take a commission. That's business. That's how you make money. I make my living through my commissions, too. The PX as a company also charges a fee on items sold through its concessionaires. So I will keep you a commission."

I took a quick siesta, then set out on my business venture. The PX was huge, and there were all kinds of security measures. I was screened, sent to wait, then finally shown in to see the colonel who managed the PX. He sat at a desk surrounded by other desks and soldiers walking busily to and fro. Very unlike our government departments, the atmosphere seemed very democratic and relaxed. I took a liking to the manager right away. He in turn told me that I sounded trustworthy and that he would give the Sony business another chance.

When I returned home and told the friend to go in and sign the contract the next day, he was very excited. The business transaction completed, however, I never heard another word about a commission from him. This was my first disappointing experience in business. Though I felt I had not really done anything to deserve a commission, I resented the fact that he had broken his promise. My only consolation was that the experience was an eye-opening one for me and that I found out something about the PX.

Once again, it looked like Brother Hoanh did have a plan after all. He told me about his intention of importing Honda motorcycles. He had visited a factory on a previous official trip. He thought that without public transportation in South Vietnam and with the scarcity of the Lambretta and Vespa mopeds, being sold at blackmarket prices by a French firm, Honda motorcycles would be useful to the common people.

We were lucky that the government was still in a state of confusion and that there were people who were eager to associate with Brother Hoanh in business although they would not risk collaborating with him in politics. We embarked on the enterprise with four associates, including Brother Hoanh: one respected elderly engineer who was nonpolitical; the second, a priest representing the archdiocese of Saigon which owned the famous Caravelle Hotel and agreed to let us use its annex street floor as a showroom; and the third, a Japanese who knew about Vietnam business. At first, nobody needed to contribute any money, just their name, and Brother Hoanh would do all the work.

Brother didn't realize what he was in for until he flew to Japan and found out that Nomura Trading had had the exclusive agency of Honda in Vietnam for over ten years and was not able to penetrate the market but still refused to get out. After one week of negotiating, Brother and his elderly engineer associate were able to have Honda sign over to them the exclusive agency. They returned home to obtain import licenses, only to be met with the minister of economy who tossed away the idea, saying there was no foreign currency to buy (though we were told by his assistant that the file about Honda was kept locked away in his drawer). In vain, we pointed out to him that the price of a Honda would be one-third of the price of an imported Lambretta. Later, we found out that the entire Ministry of Economy secretly worked for the French. That explained why even the powerful Nomura Trading Company, which was very shrewd in their business dealings (trading with North Vietnam from a section of their building in Japan while working with South Vietnam and the United States in Saigon) had not been able to pierce through the "French network."

Brother Hoanh decided to change tactics and introduce Hondas to the GIs through the PX. This was where my experience with the PX came in handy. Recently a grenade had been thrown into a crowd killing an American who was waiting for his military bus. Brother told me to quote this to the PX people and convince them that individual transportation would save time and lives. I arrived at the premises a little before lunch hoping to see their manager, the colonel, but found out that he had been replaced by a group of civilians. I waited and after a while saw three civilians come in. They were approached by the soldier who had received me, and he told them that I was waiting for them. One man in the group looked at his watch and said that it was already lunch time. As I followed the soldier to be introduced, I overheard their discussion and suddenly came up with an idea: "Gentlemen, may I suggest that you come to our restaurant to have lunch. You have to eat anyway, and I want to tell you about our project which would be of great use to you. A transportation project, to save the lives of many GIs."

"Hey. She's a real business woman, isn't she?" They laughed among themselves.

"I don't know about that," I said embarrassed. Then seeing their encouraging smiles, I added, "Our Honda motorcycle business has an office at the Caravelle Hotel and the restaurant on top of the Caravelle has the best view in town. Please accept my invitation, and let me use your phone to call ahead."

"She's dynamic, too. Go ahead." They all looked at me with big smiles. I felt like an actress performing the part of a hostess in her social hour.

We arrived at the restaurant to be greeted by my husband and his associates. Then we were led to a long table covered with an impeccably starched white tablecloth and decorated with a beautiful bouquet of flowers in the middle of shining silverware.

Surrounding us were Caucasians speaking many foreign languages. The fantastic view overlooked the cathedral, the famous Catinat Street, the Majestic Hotel, and the Saigon River.

Many "garçons" were in attendance, and the French chef even came out to invite our guests to his entrées after beautifully prepared hors d'oeuvres. With the best wine and soft classical music in the background, the atmosphere made one feel lavishly rich and elegant. The scene completed my public relations work.

Who would have ever believed that just a month ago, Brother Hoanh had been unexpectedly asked by his associates to pay five thousand piasters for his shares. He didn't have the money then and had to ask me to try to get a loan. I had gone from our rich relatives to our rich associates. All in vain. Nobody would lend us the money. I had returned home from that miserable morning of rejection feeling totally consumed by the discovery of the baseness of people. I couldn't eat, couldn't sleep.

That afternoon, before returning to the scheduled meeting, Brother had told me if any good news turned up to come and see him at the Caravelle. It was hard to imagine what might have "turned up" though. I had thought of the charity organizations to which I had given double or triple that amount, but I couldn't very well ask them to lend me back some. Finally, I had decided to go to the Cercle Sportif and forget about the whole matter. As I went out of the house, I met my younger sister, Blue Water, and her American friend playing with my children. As I bade them farewell, the friend said that he was about to leave too and that we could share a taxi.

In the taxi, I had kept putting my face out the window to hide my tears. He asked, "Are you mad at me? Why don't you want to look at me?"

"Sorry," I had said, trying to hold back my tears, but they kept flowing.

"What's wrong, Mai. Tell me."

"No."

"What happened? Tell me. Am I not your friend?"

"It's awful. I don't think you should know . . . I hate to tell you my secrets, but I can't lie to you either."

"Yes. Please tell me. That's what friends are for."

So I had told him how I felt about those mean people, and how I hated to find that out.

"Did you ask them for a lot?"

"That's the thing. Just five thousand piasters, a few hundred U.S. dollars."

"I have eight hundred dollars hidden away on top of my closet. Now and then I have to check to see if it's been stolen. Please let me help you."

"No. You put the money away for emergency use. I don't know when I can pay you back."

"Please. It's only part of one month's salary. We are three minutes from my place. It won't take me two minutes to run up to my room. If you don't let me loan you the money, I'll sit in the taxi and follow you wherever you are going."

"You are funny. Thank you." Whatever happened to our Vietnamese "friends"? I thought with bitterness.

We were saved. My husband was allowed to remain an associate. In just a short month and a half, I had learned all the ruses and intrigues of business dealings, I felt.

After the meeting with the PX people, Brother Hoanh asked me again to raise some capital for the business operation. Their first capital of $3,200 had been used on their trip to Japan to negotiate the contract. He told me I might want to approach the old friend who had put out the money for my election campaign.

After the coup killing Diem, this old friend had been imprisoned for a time because he had served the old régime as treasurer for Mr. Nhu's party. As his friends, we had tried every possible way to ask for his release, vouching for him and arguing that the old régime had had good and bad people, and he was not bad.

I was on my way to see him when I met him in the street. I told him about the Honda project and asked if he would be interested in joining the venture. He said he would and asked me how much he needed to invest. Without having given much thought to how the meeting would come out, I was not prepared for his question. But no sooner had he asked than, to my astonishment, I found myself telling him "one million piasters." Since he had handled millions before, I guessed I would need to make the figure big to interest him.

"What's my share in it?" he asked.

"You come and work with Brother Hoanh in the firm. Whatever profit we make will be divided half and half between you and us." He agreed, and tearing a piece of paper from his little notebook, he scribbled a message to his mother-in-law and told me to take it to her at her diamond shop—a very chic diamond shop in town. She opened her huge safe in front of me and handed me a bundle of cash saying, "This is one million piasters. I shall wrap it in a bag for you." I walked two blocks from there to the Caravelle and gave the bundle to Brother Hoanh and told him the story.

It was strange the way things happened. I didn't know how I had come up with the amount for the deal so quickly and was not even surprised that our old friend went along. From the five thousand that nobody wanted to loan to the million—and half of the shares in profit—I thought it must have been the Indian ghost, former owner of our apartment, who contrived the whole deal and prompted me to act as I did.

Tet, our New Year, was approaching. On the last day of the old year, a chauffeur from Brother Hoanh's rich aunt delivered an antique flower pot containing a bulb of fragrant narcissus called Thuy Tien (Water Fairy). A note from our aunt said that the bulb had been specially brought from China and expertly trimmed in such a manner as to bloom for Tet. When I had lived with my family in Hanoi, I used to see my mother try to do that herself, but always unsuccessfully—either no flowers would appear, or some would blossom long after New Year's Day. I returned the antique bowl, thinking it was too expensive for our aunt to have intended to give it to us (the difficulty with borrowing five thousand still fresh in my mind; an antique bowl was then worth about twenty thousand piasters), and kept the bulb with its few leaves in a soup bowl on our living room table.

At the stroke of midnight, firecrackers commenced to blast gaily from every house in the city, including ours. Brother Hoanh and I were sitting on the sofa in front of the bowl of Water Fairy. I thought out loud, "What if the Viet Congs attack us? Nobody would hear their guns." As I was saying this, my eyes strayed to the bulb and caught sight of it miraculously spreading its fragile, white petals out of the water, sending forth a delicate scent which immersed even the heavy burnt smell of the firecrackers. There was indeed no other more appropriate name for these flowers than "Water Fairies," for right then and there I felt as if little white fairies had come and lifted me up into the air and told me that my luck had turned around. "I shall be the luckiest person in this world!" I exclaimed.

20

ONE BRIGHT morning not long after Tet, I awoke with the idea of opening a laundry shop to wash the uniforms of American GIs. Thinking I just needed to arrange for some washing facilities to be in business, I set out in my Western dress to look for the laundry shop I had once passed near Catinat Street. I took a cyclo to Catinat, then started heading down the side streets. I remembered seeing a sign, "Tiem Giat Van Cam" (Laundry Van Cam), somewhere in the area. "Van Cam" was the name of a famous theater in the past that everybody knew about.

In one of the shop windows there was a "Laundry" sign. I went in to inquire, but to my disappointment it wasn't the shop I was looking for. The "Van Cam" shop had moved to somewhere on Nguyen Hue Street. I returned to the cyclo and patiently the driver and I searched both sides of Nguyen Hue. After some time, I spotted under a glass counter a neatly folded shirt, with next to it, two jars of coffee beans. The sign was covered by an awning. It was about twelve o'clock when I entered the shop and found out that it was in fact owned by Mr. Van Cam. I was introduced to his third wife, called "Ba Ba" (Mrs. Third), a portly lady with a baby complexion and two gold teeth, who told me that Mr. Van Cam was not in but would be back for lunch, "unless he was detained by Ba Hai" (Mrs. Second).

The coffee looked fresh in the jars, so I asked her to sell me some. As she scooped out the fragrant toasted beans, she told me the whole history of her coffee. It was a retail business of Mr. Van Cam who had given it to her for her living income. "These are very good coffee beans from Bara. Lots of customers and restaurants like them." After listening to her for a while I decided to leave a message, saying that I would call

214

Mr. Van Cam to talk about a laundry business. As I crossed the street and was about to get on a cyclo, I heard a boy calling from Mr. Van Cam's shop, "Miss, Miss. Mister Van Cam is back." Turning around I saw a man in black Western trousers and a white shirt walking with a large black umbrella in the middle of the hot sunny day, his gold teeth flashing brighter than the bright sunlight. I came back and was invited into a small room behind the counter. I introduced myself by telling him that I wanted to know about his laundry facilities and that I might be interested in giving him some customers, maybe a large number of customers.

"My laundry is the biggest in town and the oldest. I wash and iron sheets for hospitals and big hotels. I also do laundry for very prominent people around here. In fact, if you have time I can take you to my facilities right now so you can see I am not bragging."

"Can you take in more?" I inquired.

"Sure. Half of my machines have not been in operation since the French soldiers left."

So his facilities are really big, and he's had experience with military uniforms, I thought. I asked, "Would you want to sign a contract to rent that unused portion to me?"

"Yes. What do you have in mind?"

"How much rent would you charge for a month?"

"Depends. I could even cooperate with you."

"No. I just want to pay you a straight fee. Tell me your price."

He gave a figure. I said too high. He lowered it. I agreed and told him that I would pay him the higher figure if business was good.

"I think I'll like working with you. You are smart and generous."

"If I make money, I don't mind seeing you make money too. It would be for your own benefit to introduce me to good workers and maintain your machines properly."

We signed a contract—a few words on paper—stating our terms. I went with him right after that to his plant where laundry was being washed in huge metal bowls containing agitators and hung on long clotheslines stretching out over the rooftop. In another building across the dirt pathway, other men were doing the ironing. There were empty shelves all along the walls. I made a brief assessment of the place, then told Mr. Van Cam that my men would return that afternoon to arrange things.

I returned home and told Brother Hoanh about my intention of hiring one or two secretaries who knew English. Brother Hoanh told his chauffeur, who had returned after the siesta to drive Brother back to work, to go call on two secretaries who had worked for him in the past.

215

They arrived on their bikes promptly, and I employed them on the spot. I took them to the plant so they could clean up the shed that Mr. Van Cam had been using as an office and now rented to us. Then one of the secretaries, the male one, accompanied me to the ironing section to arrange the shelves, number them with chalk, and alphabetize them. I guess I got this idea from working in the library when I was a student in the States.

From there I proceeded to the PX to make my offer. Sure enough, they needed a laundry contractor who could take care of the whole camp. Till then they had been using families who picked up only twenty, thirty pieces at a time — there was no control over the return laundry items nor the sanitary requirements.

They sent a man to see the facility, and I explained to him how I was going to handle the washing, drying, and sorting of their uniforms. On that same day, I got the contract with the PX, which from then on brought me hundreds of thousands of piasters a day. All I had to do was to supervise closely during the first few weeks!

I was more than ever convinced that I was blessed by the Indian ghost and that noon time, as was believed, was the most sensitive hour during which powerful spirits returned to earth.

Our Honda business was also doing well with the GIs, but we needed to break into the Vietnamese market which was difficult, because the French detected our "invasion" and guarded their interests tightly. Luckily, Brother Hoanh came up with a novel idea. He sent Honda brochures advertising the motorcycles with sharp images and low prices (one-third that of the Lambrettas) to the four corps commanding generals. They were asked to post Honda catalogs for their Vietnamese soldiers to see and sign a list if they were interested in buying Honda motorcycles. The marketing idea was new, the price was good, and the new buyers would not need to beg their sellers to sell at black market prices as was customary. In no time the lists were returned and over twenty thousand signatures of new Honda customers. Brother felt it was important to use this "grass-roots" approach to introduce Honda motorcycles into the Vietnamese market, despite the opposition of the French company, which insisted on maintaining its lucrative monopoly. Brother was confident that the weight of some twenty thousand families of ARVN (Army of the Republic of Vietnam) soldiers who had signed up as the first Honda customers, would convince both the Vietnamese and the American authorities to abolish the monopoly situation and to open the market for other makes of motorcycles.

This opening up of the motorcycle market to provide cheap transportation for the population also suited the wish of General Ky who had been making endless speeches on the need to help the South Vietnamese people, especially ARVN soldiers.

Anyway, to make sure our first shipment of Hondas would go through smoothly, Brother Hoanh asked me to find Nguyen Cao Ky's men and show them the brochures—at that time, Ky had just replaced Khanh who had had to leave Vietnam as a "roving ambassador." By then I had a laundry concession in the Tan Son Nhut Airport, so I went there to see the man in charge. I met Col. Luu Kim Cuong, Ky's right-hand man and Tan Son Nhut base commander. I showed him the brochures and told him that it would make General Ky very popular if he let his men buy the 50cc Hondas. In addition to its low price, this Honda used very little gas and had good resale value.

I became so carried away with enthusiasm that I forgot I was there to make money. Having heard Brother Hoanh say that the Hondas had been flown over for the GIs, I promised to fly in eight "Police Honda, 450cc" and eight helmets in time for the forthcoming ceremony when General Ky would preside over the symbolic distribution of Hondas to ARVN buyers. I was a bit concerned when I told Brother Hoanh the outcome of our conversation—having given away the cost of bikes that size and the flight transportation—but to my surprise, he didn't protest.

We flew the 450cc Hondas and the helmets. The distribution ceremony took place, and the French monopoly over motorcycle imports ended.

Meanwhile, we needed to firm up prices with Honda in Tokyo. At the time the Saigon government made it difficult for men of draft age to obtain exit visas to go abroad. Since Brother Hoanh could not get an exit visa, I went to Japan in his place.

At the airport in Tokyo, I had to call up the Hilton Hotel to have their limousine transport me to the hotel—I only had a few dollars on me lent by a friend who had just returned from Hong Kong. The hotel people had only to guess who was going to pay! Credit cards were not yet available, and as Vietnamese we were not allowed to own foreign currency. The government allowed the exchange of a small amount of foreign currency, but I did not go through the exchange because I knew that what was allowed would not have been enough for me to cover my Tokyo expenses anyway.

For two days I tried in vain to contact the Honda people. On the third day, with still no answer from them, I had to threaten to sue them. On the fourth day, three Honda men were sent over. We sat in the lobby and talked for over three hours, or rather, they did the talking in Japanese

217

with now and then their translator turning to ask me a question. Each answer would be translated into and discussed in Japanese for half an hour before another question was asked. At the end of the session, they said they would send a car the next day to take me to their office.

The following day I was greeted by a Japanese chauffeur who welcomed me to a huge, black Cadillac decorated with two Honda flags. The limousine blocked the entire stairway to the entrance of the hotel. The uniformed chauffeur opened the door for me and saluted me in Japanese with his head bowing low, almost to his knees. We went through the narrow hilly streets, staying on the left-hand side. I was near having heart attacks with the fast speed on the narrow roads, in the huge car, and with the left-hand drive. Upon arriving, a male secretary ushered me through several halls and offices crowded with small desks and male employees diligently minding their jobs. Finally, we came to a small guest room where I was left alone. Then another male employee came to serve me tea and left. I waited, and fifteen minutes later two men entered the room. We greeted each other, and then they exchanged papers among themselves and seemed to wait for something. Some time later three more men joined us and the meeting commenced. The translator was a different one, and they were all new faces. I guessed the men of the previous day were messengers who had come to report on me and my English.

The same process of "investigation" went on from nine thirty to one thirty, with only green tea to feed my poor empty stomach. I imagined they wanted to know how long I could last. Fortunately, I was familiar with this type of questioning from the Communist sessions I had been exposed to. Talk leading to nowhere. They all knew from the start what they wanted. They just wanted to know who they were dealing with, and based on this they would conclude who would be getting what.

At one thirty I was about to pass out. My head was keen and clear with ideas thanks to the caffeine from the tea, but my body could no longer sustain me. I decided I was not going to play along with their rules or traditions any more. Acting like an ignorant woman, I stopped them in the middle of their discussion in Japanese and said, "I'm starving to death. Can we eat first and resume this meeting after?" Two of them laughed spontaneously. The others needed a translation; then they all laughed. Now I knew that two among them knew English. Again it took them fifteen minutes to discuss among themselves, then the translator said, "Yes. We'll stop to eat now."

Two of them excused themselves and left. The others sat and waited for the translation back and forth. I decided to eat French food. They

218

were all delighted with the idea. Since the Japanese had built their own larger duplicate of the Eiffel Tower, anything French was in.

We resumed the meeting after lunch, and I continued to sit and listen to their discussion and translation until five. At the end of the meeting, the translator announced that I was invited to dinner that night, to which the entire group nodded approvingly and laughed in unison.

We went to a bar full of businessmen and "hostesses" to attend to them. I was introduced to two of the hostesses. Each stood smiling sweetly at my side, and one brought me a glass of whiskey and soda, urging me to have a sip while the rest of my group downed their drinks one after another, with the coquettish solicitation of two pretty hostesses at their sides. I was later to learn that Japanese companies paid for their public relations expenses — the more prestigious the name of the company, the more hostesses and drinks — the larger the bill, the more powerful the company.

After the drinks, the hostesses led us towards a sliding door into a corridor where they were replaced by an older lady with the air of an overseer, sweet yet efficient. She ushered us into a large room carpeted with straw mats, empty of furniture except for a long low table surrounded with colorful lounging pillows and set near a huge painting on the wall. The decoration was basically calm, devoid of any sense of lust or grandeur. She ushered us to the pillows, whereupon another set of hostesses rushed in like little birds with their small steps and greeted us in high chirpy voices.

I was seated between two of the men, one of them reminded me of a samurai. In the middle of the "Hai . . . Hai," "Dozo," and giggles of the girls, the samurai-looking one turned to me, raised his sake cup, and toasted in English. He explained to me that a geisha would come out to sing for us near the end of the dinner and the girls were asking a lot of questions about me. He apologized for his company not contacting me the first two days. They had never dealt with women and had been shocked at the idea. After much debating, they had decided to treat me like another *man*. That was why the hostesses were serving me tonight and trying to please me as if I were of the opposite sex, though they couldn't help asking questions to satisfy their curiosity. He spoke fluent English and had very good manners. When the men had enough drinks to relax them, the room echoed with laughter.

"Welcome to Japan," toasted the man sitting opposite me. "Do you know that sitting next to you is our respectable prince?"

The samurai laughed with embarrassment.

"True. He is with our firm, but first he is a real prince, descendant of the royal family." No wonder then that he behaved with such poise and sureness.

The next day it was back to work again, with the same seriousness and intensity of the day before. We concluded business at four, and I told them I didn't need their car to return to the hotel, but to please find me a taxi. I had planned to meet an acquaintance of Brother Hoanh at the Vietnamese Embassy. By the time I arrived at the embassy, it was officially closed. While we sat and talked in the office, I noticed a car with a Honda flag drive up. Surprised, I asked what they were doing there and found out that they had come at the request of the Vietnamese ambassador.

"The ambassador! What business does he have with Honda? I was legally issued a visa to come here to talk business with that firm. I did nothing illegal."

"No. They came for different reasons. Here," he reached in a drawer and took out a cable. "We received this from the minister of economy, unofficially telling the ambassador to make Honda reserve for them 3 percent on any sales you make."

The crooks! That was more than what they had agreed to pay us as their exclusive agent. And I had tried to keep the price and our commission down to help our people buy cheap! Nomura Company already wanted 7 percent, and on top of that reserved the shipping rights so that they had full control over us. Honda would have to jack up their prices to cover for all the commissions. They must have thought I was naïve to ask for so little profit. Even so, when I had finally agreed to 3 percent to cover only our costs, they had tried to squeeze me down to 2. I learned one thing: it was hard to do well and still be good and decent.

The embassy friend showed me Brother Hoanh's cable to him asking him to warn me that a newspaper in Saigon had written about my trip saying that it was illegal to negotiate for commissions. We both contemplated the conniving policy of the ambassador and the minister of economy. There was an appropriate Vietnamese saying for it: "Vua danh trong, vua an coup." (Sounding the drum to warn the coming of danger while robbing in the midst of confusion.)

The next two years were an uphill battle for us in the Honda business. The French made their last attempt to destroy us before pulling out. They maneuvered secretly to have our house searched, and it was published that we would be court-martialed for keeping foreign currency in the house (a few dollars). Once we discovered who was causing all the trouble for us, we solved our problems without too much difficulty.

By 1967, after a year and a half of our existence as Honda's exclusive agent, nearly half a million Honda motorcycles were sold to the South Vietnam market. This drew wild attempts to block our success. The old minister of economy was replaced with a new one who was even greedier for a share in the business and managed to pass many new import regulations — hints that Honda business should be paying bribes. Honda and its shipping agent, Nomura, connived to take over the business. As soon as we passed them the GI orders from the PX and told them to prepare for a big order of over twenty-two thousand motorcycles from South Vietnamese soldiers — barely six months after the signing of the exclusive contract — Honda illegally allowed Nomura to issue proforma invoices and take orders directly from potential customers. Honda finally achieved their goal by taking away our exclusivity, arbitrarily and for no valid reason, at the very time when our sales made phenomenal increases in 1967. Not only did they breach their contract with us, but they did not pay the millions of dollars of commission they owed us.

Successful as we were, there was not a single day that we did not have problems with Honda, Nomura, the Ministry of Economy, the police, customs, and local competitors. Somehow we managed to keep our heads above water and move forward in spite of adverse conditions. People wondered who was behind us; some even thought we had the support of the CIA!

Brother, who pioneered the Honda business more as a new "political exercise" than as a money-making proposition, was disgusted by Japanese business practices. But his mind was already preoccupied with the bigger problem: what good was the Honda business if South Vietnam itself went down the drain?

After Brother Hoanh lost interest in the Honda business, I had time to concentrate more on my own business. The laundry was bringing me so much money I decided to try other ventures. I decided on exporting shrimp, which would be a new business. It would take time for others to catch up with me, and it would bring in the first money abroad made by Vietnamese. I had once observed a village of refugees on a shrimping expedition from a shore near Cap St. Jacques. They went out at three or four in the morning and returned around three or four in the afternoon — a line of thirty or forty wooden boats, each about thirty feet long, speeding towards shore as if in a race. Shrimp poured out from the hulls of the boats in large volume, to be hauled to the market in huge bamboo baskets lined with layers of ice. Many spots along the coasts of South Vietnam had access to shrimp in quantities.

I went to USAID to inquire about exporting shrimp and asked them for their technical help and approval for funds to purchase fishing supplies for fishermen. They said they could teach villagers to freeze shrimp on the spot if I could provide freezers and boats to transport shrimp to Saigon before shipping it out of Vietnam. With their involvement, I knew I could get help with licenses to import freezers and other fishing materials.

While I was working on the new project, the PX contacted me and told me they could help me buy laundry machines through their post if I would open up a laundry outfit in one of their isolated camps. I was willing.

They sent me by helicopter to a spot in the middle of nowhere near Sadec. We landed in the camp which was full of helicopters. I was in my *ao dai* (Vietnamese dress). Many young men came out from their bungalows to watch—they said they had never seen a Vietnamese dress before because they had never been in town: they spent their rest and recreation time in Japan or Southeast Asian countries. In Vietnam their time was spent training, looking for Viet Congs, and rescuing their own people. At the end of their term they would be flown back to the States.

I met with the commander of the camp, and the contract was signed to be executed immediately. The commander said that he was happy I could start the business there to take care of his men's uniforms on the spot. He also said to involve the villagers, if I could, for he had had no business dealing with them previously.

I returned home ready to start all kinds of new projects. But just as I stepped inside the house, my telephone rang. My husband's cousin was on the line, telling me to come to the Grall hospital right away. My husband had been shot, and he needed me. He had been calling my name on the flight from Hue back to Saigon. It was Monday, May 29, 1967.

The news was such a shock it numbed me. Like a robot, I called long distance to the commander to void the contract and cancel the helicopter trip scheduled for the next day when I was supposed to go to organize the business. I had thought I would go to the village first to see whether or not I should hire the villagers and set up my plant there, or on the military base.

Strange! I didn't feel pain or sorrow. My cousin's words echoed in my mind.

"Calling my name, hm?" She had repeated that more than three times, as though that were the only important event in the whole accident. She must have been impressed that he loved me so much. So much that even in his unconscious state he remembered my maiden name—

222

the one he had stopped using since our marriage, to identify me only as his wife, Mrs. Hoanh, Sister Hoanh . . . Mr. Hoanh's property to be used or discarded at his own pleasure.

Was her excitement the result of a long yearning, an imagination long nurtured with tender, bitter love for her own husband? Flashing to mind was an image of my cousin helping her husband to build up their pharmaceutical business from scatch — the business that had made them the envy of town — while he had supposedly been doing his "intellectual" work. He acknowledged her worth by getting a few concubines and having more children. Meanwhile, she, still striving to make him recognize her intelligence and importance in *their* business, occupied herself with the "dirty" task of manipulating and intriguing with the Saigon authorities.

The cyclo screeched to a halt in front of the steps of the hospital ward. I stepped off thinking, I wish I could believe in this again — this idea of love and be loved. After all, it's just plain logical and natural — if you love a dog and treat him well, he will love you back and be faithful to you. How come it doesn't work that way with humans though? We who claim ourselves to be the superior race, the image of God!

21

MY COUSIN waved to me from an open door of the surgery ward. Her husband came out of the room to join us. She said Brother Hoanh had passed out again due to the strong dose of pain killer so there was no use in seeing him right away. She described how her husband had had to run on foot to different laboratories to find blood for my husband when Hoanh had had an amputation in the Hue hospital. Then he had had to arrange for the flight back to Saigon this morning. The city of Hue was still in a horrible mess after the Viet Cong terrorist attack. The hospital was full of patients moaning and groaning. There were not enough doctors to operate on the wounded. Many were left to die.

The V.C. had attacked in the night and targeted the Huong Giang Hotel on the River of Perfume in Hue. My husband was wounded by a bazooka round the V.C. had shot through each hotel room at the level where the air conditioner was installed, so the room occupants would be killed even if they lay down on the floor.

Brother Hoanh moaned. We all went in. He looked at me, pale but alert.

"Hi."

"They cut off my leg," he said, lifting the stump up under the white sheet. "I lost my leg."

The stump didn't look too terrible under the sheet. The way he put it was very dramatic. Suddenly a picture of him running on the tennis court, always the last player to quit, flashed to mind giving me a pang. I tried to ease his pain: "I'm glad you're still alive, and looking good, too. Your mind is still very fast."

That didn't make him feel any better. He turned away and dropped into silence. That night I slept in a bed placed next to his. His regular, faint breathing in the silent darkness made a strange impression on me. At first I felt exhausted, then sorry, just sorry, for whom or what I didn't know. Then tears slowly ran down my cheeks when the sound of the breathing brought on the image of Brother Hoanh with a stump. I tried hard to imagine him standing up with one leg. Would he be like those one-legged soldiers I saw in hospitals, sitting miserably on the bed, or jumping awkwardly, drawing either pity or careful avoidance from people? No. He couldn't look like them. But how else? I had never seen a cripple doing any work except for crawling on the curb, begging for money. But that, too, was rare. We Vietnamese were so conscious of "looks" that we would avoid even looking at an "abnormal looking" person for fear of being contaminated. Now that I was with one, I was surprised to realize that, in a country wrought with war such as Vietnam, there weren't more with Brother's misfortune among the elites, or even the Saigon people.

My mind kept switching from the present to the future, then back to the past. There was nothing in any of these images that could help to give me a concrete idea of what my life was going to be like. One thing for sure was that my life was going to be with him and for him again!— just when I was getting used to being happily independent again, dedicating my energies to my own life and interests.

On the third day, Brother felt better and the doctor told him to walk around with his crutches. We thought it would be a good idea to go out and see a bit of the town. We had a pleasant ride on the cyclo through busy streets until we reached Catinat. Suddenly, I didn't know what I had said that made him so upset, but he jumped off the cyclo and started hopping toward the curb, yelling, "Enough. Let me out. I'm a cripple. No cripples here!"

I had to apologize and beg him to return to the cyclo so that we could go back to the hospital. The abrupt incident served to shock me out of my muddled state. I sat at his bedside in the dark, and we talked about our future. We decided that he should go to America for treatment and that the kids and I would join him there when we could get our passports.

The following day, when I returned from my brief trip to the house to check on the children, I saw him sitting up in his hospital bed, his face red with anger. He had just met with the Honda people and the vice president of our company. "The bastards! They want me to transfer my power to them! They think I am dead because I have an amputated leg. I'll show them." In the life I had had with him before, he had never talked with me so much about himself, and so openly. It took a tragedy to bring us together and make my Brother aware of the force of unison.

While Brother Hoanh was home waiting for permission to go abroad, General Lansdale came to visit us several times. It was probably his presence in our house and the traditional Vietnamese beliefs that cripples were worthless which resulted in Brother Hoanh promptly receiving an exit visa.

Then came my turn to obtain permission. Under normal circumstances the Ministry of Defense, the Ministry of Interior, and the police worked hand in hand to speed up the process for a visa, which was given only to those in government favor. I was sure that we had not done anything to give cause for denial. While conducting our business, we had neither received nor sought favors. Furthermore, some of our Saigon business competitors would be happy to see us disappear from the competition. Thus, I thought it would be a usual procedure to be permitted to accompany a husband abroad for medical care and rehabilitation not available in Vietnam.

I was wrong. The first two weeks I concentrated on the minister of interior, who was known to have received bribes. In Saigon, bribes were a fact of life. The trouble with us was that even if we were willing to pay, nobody was willing to take from us directly because we were too well-known there.

After having my friends bribe the Ministry of Interior people, I went in and asked to see the minister. For the next two weeks during office hours, I sat posted at the long bench outside his office, like a prisoner waiting to be called for my sentence. I was called two or three times to be told that I had to wait and that the paperwork was being processed, but there were some problems with the children—"Why do they have to go? Couldn't they stay with their grandparents?" This kind of problem seemed to indicate that either the man wanted more money or had no power to decide. I suspected he had no power to decide my case. I then went to the police headquarters where my papers had been submitted at the same time as to the Ministry of Interior. My driver had a friend, a secretary there. With my money he had bought some gifts for her to distribute among the staff, so my papers should have already reached the head clerk in the visa section.

I went to the police headquarters and sat two days in a row, once again on a long wooden bench, waiting. Nobody paid any attention to me. My name wasn't called for an interview. Finally, when I thought the head clerk had seen my face long enough to think that I had been humiliated enough, I asked to see him. I told myself that in dealing with people less fortunate than me I had to be very careful not to hurt their pride, but also not to give them the impression that I was totally helpless. It was a fine line, for if I looked like them, why should I be treated any different from them? What rights did I have to think my family should get out of the country and enjoy peace and comfort while their families had to suffer and their kids fight in the war for me? For pure psychological effect, I had "armed" myself with my two-carat diamond and a nice silk dress, expensive but not flashy, to show that I had money. I hated doing this. I hated to be so manipulative, but again, this was another fact of life I had to face. And there was no room for mistakes.

The head clerk called me to his desk and told a clerk to get my file. A chill ran down my backbone while I followed the clerk with my eyes. He went though the shelves full of files, stopping now and then to take down a pile of old greenish folders, searching and putting them back on the shelves. Finally, he found my file. He brought it to the head clerk who was already busy working on another file. Fifteen minutes passed. Then, slowly, he reached for my folder, opened it, and flipped through the file. With the attention of a conscientious head clerk, he scrutinized the birth certificate of each child. Finally, he looked up: "You and the girls can go. The boys must be kept on the reserve list for our military service."

"At the ages of eleven and eight months!" I exclaimed, having lost my patience.

"Well. Maybe your first boy can go. The law says the first son can ac-company his ill father to take care of him and to receive his will in case...."

"But Sir. My younger son is only eight months old."

"He will grow up before you know it."

"Eighteen years from now? Isn't that a bit too early to worry about another war?"

"Don't worry. There'll always be another war." He gave me a kind smile, "If you believe the war will soon end, why are you trying to run away?"

I politely thanked the head clerk before I withdrew, all the while tell-ing myself that I had to find another person, the right person, and give the right amount of bribe.

On my cyclo ride home, I tried to draw out my little plan for bribery, but my aching head kept being distracted by the remarks of the head clerk. "He's just a clerk," I told myself. "He's jealous that I might be able to go out with my family while he, his children, and his wife might be stuck here forever. An understandable jealousy!"

But why do I want to leave the country? Why am I going through so much trouble? All my family's here. My business is here. I'm considered wealthy here. I've maids to take care of my children and cook my meals, a driver to drive my car, and money to buy any luxuries I want, even another fortune to make if I so wish. Why do I want to run away? My husband is no longer here to trouble my mind. The corruption, bribes. I hate it. It dehumanizes people. Ah! The bribes, but that's the daily business of living. After all, wasn't it thanks to bribes that one was able to stay in business in Saigon? Friends called our Honda business "the bottomless treasure." Everybody knows nothing lasts forever in this life! So grab it while it lasts. Look at Mr. T. and Mr. N. who had bought themselves and their families, sisters, in-laws, high posts in the government. They used their influence and money to monopolize all import businesses. The commissions gained from buying products in foreign countries they kept abroad. The profits in local currency they used to build up more prestige and power. And look at Mrs. Thieu, our president's wife, with her military bank, collecting dues from the millions of ARVN soldiers (real ones and fake names on the padded military payrolls) and using billions of piasters for their shady transactions. If the Communists were to arrive, they'd be the first to know. They'd just pick up and leave, fly abroad, make a call to their Swiss bank, order some of their money to be transferred to their new accounts. Fat accounts make good contacts. With money, they'll start their life anew, good, brilliant, "hard-working" like any other "respectable" people of the world. See? What's wrong with that? Use or be used. That's the name of the game. Democracy, freedom, anti-communism, these are only words or at best slogans.

The cyclo rode on in the midst of noisy engines and smog. I raised my handkerchief to cover my nose. I was brought back to reality: "Is this what you want to live in? Raise your children in this hell?" I resumed my bribery plan.

It took me several trips to be able to finally intercept Major Tu Duong (Charitable Sea), the young police official. My driver said he had had a hard time getting himself introduced to the guards and Mr. Tu Duong's secretary and could only manage to give them small gifts: an imported shirt or two to each. He had heard that the major was a difficult man.

"Sir, may I see you a minute? It's about my passport."

He turned to me, an embarrassed look on his face. "Uh, I have some important paperwork I need to rush out."

"Sir, it won't take but a few minutes. They said you are the only one who has the authority to help me." Uneasily I insisted, not being used to having to beg for favors.

He then looked at the guards around him. They were busy looking elsewhere or turning away. They all knew me by then. He entered the anteroom of his office. I followed him. A male clerk stood behind his desk, occupied with the files he was sorting: "Good morning, lieutenant colonel." He pretended not to see me.

At the door to his office, I stopped following the lieutenant colonel. He entered and left the door open. I stood outside waiting.

"Captain Cay. Would you ask the lady in?"

The secretary in uniform gave me a big smile. "Madame, please come in."

"Thank you." I crossed the long tiled floor to the chair in front of the lieutenant colonel's desk. He remained standing the entire time.

"Please take a seat," he said kindly.

"Excuse me." I adjusted the back flap of my Vietnamese dress and slid onto the seat.

I explained my situation to him. He looked straight at me while listening attentively. He rang for my file. In just a few minutes it was brought over. He read it carefully. Then suddenly I heard, "Nonsense! Your eight-month-old son on the reserve list?"

I looked at him. A ray of hope flashed through me.

He rang for Captain Cay. "I approve their exit visa. Do the necessary papers; then bring them in for me to sign."

He picked up his pen and wrote a few lines across the last sheet of the file.

"Insane. Keeping a baby on the reserve? Madame, check with the secretary as to when you can come to get your permit. May your family go in peace."

Totally disbelieving, I stood up, my hands automatically brought up together and placed high on my chest, my head bowed low. Respect and gratitude filled my whole being. "Thank you. My children and I are forever grateful to you. May God bless you." Taking a few steps backward before turning around to leave, I felt like a little girl again. How wonderful it was to be in the presence of a respectable person.

I returned the next day to get the passports myself.

During the entire night before I had prayed that nothing would happen to Major Tu Duong, the police headquarters, or Saigon itself.

Safe now in the sky with my four children by my side, I looked down at the brown patch of land below, the Mekong River and its many tributaries and canals. I imagined I could see live shrimp and fish jumping in the baskets immersed in water at the bottom of the sampans gliding

229

leisurely along the canals. I visualized little boys my older son's age pedaling their small boats with their legs and letting their dreams skip boundlessly over the cool waves.

I heard my son laughing softly next to me. He was gazing out into the clear blue sky. I wanted to ask him what was so amusing and share his laughter with him, but I refrained, remembering an instance when he was five and laughing by himself, looking at the water while we were crossing a bridge. I had asked him then, and he had slowly turned around, smiling, and said, "If I tell you, Ma, it won't be funny any more." It struck me that he was quite a philosopher, but then again, children seem to be natural philosophers endowed with boundless imagination and ingenuity.

Looking down at the land we flew over with its rice fields, rivers, mountains, and forests, I thought of the rich resources of Vietnam. So much potential buried under such a fertile undeveloped soil! With such an abundance, such a variety, such a richness were we blessed. If only it could be tapped and used to secure the happiness of the millions who were still hungry and homeless, poor and diseased.

The voice of the air hostess announcing that drinks would be served awakened me from my daydreaming. Yes, South Vietnam was at war in 1967, and the war destroyed everything and everybody. No family, rich or poor, smart or dumb, was spared. It was because of the war that I had to leave Vietnam again.

Maybe one of these days peace would return to Vietnam and the vast potential of the country could be fully developed. I could only pray.

Leaving for the third time, I had the impression that I might not be back again — at least not with my entire family. In January 1964, only two months after the coup overthrowing Diem, without hesitation nor calculation for the security of my family, I had left the United States to return to South Vietnam with my husband and children. I remember how we had written to the Immigration and Naturalization Office in Kansas City to thank them and to inform them that we no longer needed permanent U.S. residence papers since we were "going home."

I was looking with nostalgia at the familiar landscape of South Vietnam through the airplane window. As if seeing it for the last time, I was trying to take mental photographs of the rice fields, the bamboo, the coconut trees, and the meandering loops of the Mekong River below. I then realized how much I was attached to this land, my homeland.

I asked myself why my life had to be so divided between Vietnam and the United States. Wouldn't it be simpler just to choose one of the two and stick with it? If that were possible, then I would not have to make these cultural adjustments between life in the United States and life in Vietnam.

But such was my lot it seemed, to bridge two different worlds, for my own personal sake and for a better understanding between Americans and Vietnamese. I have often thought that maybe the Vietnam War could have been avoided if Americans had understood the Vietnamese better and vice versa. But I also remembered the times in 1962 and 1963 when we had tried and failed to voice our views through American newspapers, as they did not want to publish our articles.

We were now preparing to land at the L.A. International Airport. On that mid-summer morning of 1967, the Los Angeles sky was bright blue — much like the sky over Saigon.

Walking through the long aisles of the airport, I was straining my sleepy eyes in search of my husband. I was moving nervously with the rushing crowd of passengers, carrying my eight-month-old baby boy in my arms and trying to hold on to my other three children. My two daughters were clutching tightly to the flaps of my *ao dai*; my eleven-year-old son was acting like an adult, holding his youngest sister's hand protectively. I was walking in a daze, looking ahead of me, trying to locate among the crowd a man with crutches. I imagined him with one leg missing, stabilizing himself on crutches. He would be standing apart, away from the tall, husky Americans waiting at the gate.

Suddenly, out of the crowd, I heard a familiar voice: "Mommy! Mai! Over here!" I turned to look in the direction of that cheerful voice. To my great astonishment, I saw my husband *walking* on his own two legs towards us. He had a smile on his face, and he was wearing a smart grey suit. A miracle! He looked absolutely "normal"! My legs suddenly became so weak that I felt like falling. My mind frantically searched for an answer: "His stump, where is his stump? Am I dreaming, or is this real?"

Then he was in front of me, standing on his own two legs. My body nestled securely in his arms. My face lifted to receive his kiss. No sooner had we finished embracing, when Brother, in his usual brusque manner of old, quickly began hustling us all along to the exit while matter-of-factly recounting to me how his good friend Dr. Omar Fareed had helped him to get his artificial leg so quickly. I was thankful to Dr. Fareed, for it was obvious that through his care Brother was able to begin to think positively and function normally again.

At the car, again like in the "good old days," Brother shoved me and the children in and drove us directly from the Los Angeles Airport to our new home in Newport Beach, as sure of himself in the maze of traffic and freeways as a native Californian.

I hope my children will forgive me and understand us better for the problems we gave them during the sixties and seventies. They only knew we had uprooted them, taken them away from their friends and the luxurious comfort they had in Saigon, to plunge them into a totally new culture, a new environment where the conflict between anti-war and pro-war movements was heartbreakingly tearing adults and children apart. I hope they have forgiven us for abandoning them with their problems, while we used our savings to fly between Washington, Paris, and Saigon, trying to "solve" the bigger-picture problems!

It was a dilemma for me, and for years, until that dilemma was finally resolved by the collapse of South Vietnam in 1975, I was like a psychological somnambulist. I walked around in a daze, with a thousand unanswered questions in my head, unable to sort them out, never fully conscious of what I was doing and never sure of the purpose of my actions.

One thing I was sure of was that the more we probed and searched, the more discouraged we became. Comparing the two sides, we found that the Communists seemed to know what they were doing and where they were going. Our anti–Communist side, the Saigon generals and politicians, were constantly fighting each other, devoting all their energy to power intrigues and corruption schemes, stealing as much as they could without any regard whatsoever for the fate of the "Free Vietnam" that they were supposed to represent. I felt sorry for my children for having to face their friends in school as South Vietnamese. How could I explain to my children why we had to be in America when American soldiers had to go to Vietnam and risk their lives? How could I explain to them about our shameful "leaders" who had defrauded their own countrymen and caused the death of thousands of Americans?

On the doomed day of April 30, 1975, Saigon fell into the hands of the Communists who were themselves somewhat surprised by their sudden victory. Nobody—except maybe President Thieu and the CIA—knew exactly why and how it happened the way it did. According to General Phillip B. Davidson, a very knowledgeable military historian (*Vietnam at War, the History: 1956-1975*), on March 11, 1975, Thieu and his top generals, including the chief of the joint staff of the ARVN, General Cao Van Vien, and the prime minister, General Tran Thien Khiem, had a breakfast meeting where Thieu discussed his intention to abandon the northernmost portion of South Vietnam, considered as indefensible. The generals not only did not object to this idea, but General Cao Van

Vien even supported it, saying that he himself had embraced the idea for a long time.

That fateful decision spelled the beginning of the end for South Vietnam and was the main cause for the final defeat of the Army of the Republic of Vietnam (ARVN).

By mid-March, Ban Me Thuot and the Central Highlands were gone. One million or so soldiers were left to fend for themselves in chaotic retreat, while whatever generals were in with Thieu had already returned (as ordered by their commander in chief) to the safety of Saigon. As General Davidson put it, the rank and file of the ARVN could fight and did fight bravely, when properly led (e.g., ARVN Eighteenth Division at Xuan Loc), but it was the abysmal failure of South Vietnamese leadership that caused the final collapse of South Vietnam.

But surely the generals must have known that such a decision for a massive retreat without careful advance planning would be catastrophic, so why did they choose to go along with Thieu's decision? The only explanation I can see for this is that in their calculations, they saw they had nothing to lose.

At its best — since the United States had invested huge amounts of resources and above all Uncle Sam's prestige as the number one power and defender of the Free World had been committed — this withdrawal plan would serve as a ploy to embarrass Americans and jolt them into reversing their previous decision to abandon South Vietnam. To Thieu and his Saigon generals who had grown totally dependent on the United States for winning the war for them, they speculated that the United States could never let go of Vietnam. Therefore, if Americans at this critical juncture decided to make a comeback and shore up the truncated southernmost part of South Vietnam, there would still be the rich Mekong delta and Saigon for Thieu and his generals to control and continue their corruption rackets.

At its worst, if Americans failed to return and South Vietnam was definitely abandoned, Thieu and his generals would still be on the priority list of "American assets" to be evacuated from Saigon. Traditional U.S. generosity would not allow any other course of action. Thus Thieu and his generals would safely enjoy in their golden exile the fruits of their corruption. Most important, they would not have to worry about prosecution or inquiry by any successor government in South Vietnam. With no country left, who would have the authority to bring Thieu to justice? Besides, the fall of South Vietnam being for all appearances a tragic military defeat, who could pin the blame on Thieu? In this context, Thieu's adamant refusal to allow any viable alternative in South Vietnam after his escape was a good calculation which worked out very well for him and his generals.

Thieu and his generals thought nothing of the Vietnamese people and their poor soldiers. And they thought that as long as they met the three usual requirements for Americans to consider them good men— speak good English, drink good whiskey, play good poker—they could fool their American mentors into accepting whatever politics they found suitable for their schemes. As General Davidson so aptly described, "From Thieu on down, ARVN leadership reaped the whirlwind which eventually befalls the inflexible, the incompetent and the cowardly."

Among those who lost the most to Thieu were the ARVN soldiers, the millions who were drafted and had to risk their lives to bring riches and glory to their commander in chief, the president of South Vietnam.

Not until April 6, 1975, the day Phan Rang fell to the advancing Communists and the shameful distintegration of the one million man ARVN became irreversible did a handful of ARVN soldiers have the chance to take revenge against Thieu. Their battle lost, frustrated, angry, hungry, they turned toward the gravesite of Thieu's ancestors in his hometown of Phan Rang and bulldozed the tombs to the ground to show their contempt for their commander in chief.

Following the events in Vietnam through American television, I saw the horrible scenes of the "Convoy of Tears," with thousands of refugees fleeing abandoned Pleiku in the Central Highlands and the desperate efforts of traumatized soldiers to escape, some clinging to the wings of departing airplanes taking off from abandoned Da Nang. It was a heart-breaking sight.

But why did I feel so strongly? Hadn't I known all the time that this day was going to come? But still it hurt. And the disgraceful circumstances accompanying the loss added insult to injury.

In 1975, Nguyen Van Thieu sat at the head of the massive corruption that was South Vietnam. During his eight years as president, Thieu had knowingly appointed corrupt civilian ministers and corps and division commanders, who with his blessing and protection had sold guns, rice, and radios to the enemy. They had padded their division payrolls with phantom soldiers, sold deferments from military duty, trafficked in narcotics, and smuggled scrap metal.

In his final days in Saigon, Nguyen Van Thieu wanted to make sure that after him, there would be nothing left in South Vietnam. Key to the success of Thieu's scenario for a "golden" escape from Saigon was the timely manipulation of lie and deceit.

Ailing Tran Van Huong (whom Thieu had installed as his vice president especially to protect his escape) and Duong Van Minh (who did not see that succeeding Huong as the last president of South Vietnam he would be surrendering to the Communists in three days), being too busy with their own schemes and blinded by the vision of the lucrative opportunity provided by the post of president, hurried to accommodate Thieu in order to get rid of him.

Ironically, Minh had especially requested Americans to arrange for Thieu's departure from Saigon so that he himself could have room to maneuver. It was for Minh a repetition of the 1963 situation when he was afraid of Diem's presence in Saigon after the coup, so he secretly gave orders to his trusted aide to have Diem killed. Intertwined with these intrigues by Minh, other secret schemes and intrigues by other Saigon generals and by American policy makers converged to further confuse the situation.

Frank Snepp in his book *Decent Interval*—an insider's account of Saigon's indecent end as told by the CIA chief strategy analyst in Vietnam—wrote that Minh took one thousand dollars (only!) from CIA Station Chief Polgar who had CIA General Timmes deliver it to Minh personally. This ridiculously small amount given to Minh was to be used as travel expenses for his emissary going to Paris, supposedly to negotiate a "peace solution." It was also Minh himself who asked CIA's Timmes to see to it that Thieu was sent into exile.

On April 26, 1975, Nguyen Van Thieu, the strong man of South Vietnam, was sneaked out of the country by CIA agents, with several "mammoth suitcases" loaded with gold and money. Besides that loot, Thieu reportedly also received $100,000 given almost "officially" by U.S. Ambassador Martin to "help out."

That evening, driven after curfew to Tan Son Nhut airport by CIA agents, Thieu was ordered by his American escorts to hide his face for fear that angry ARVN soldiers manning the checkpoints might make trouble and prevent his escape.

With Tran Thien Khiem—another Saigon general who had been a candidate for the position of "South Vietnam's strongman"—Thieu fled Saigon on an American air force C118, on his way to Taipeh where he had stashed crates of antiques and boxes of gold and diamonds, sent earlier to his older brother, the ambassador there, for safekeeping. A few days before his escape, Thieu had managed with the help of his wife, Nguyen Thi Mai-Anh, and her Chinese relative Ly Long Than, to steal tons of gold from the National Bank of Vietnam.

The cowardice of Thieu and his generals revealed in several well-documented books published after 1975, thoroughly turned my feelings of shame and doubt into plain anger. In the annals of history, it would be hard to find more undignified escapes by former chiefs of state than that of Thieu. Probably partly in jest to alleviate an otherwise shameful reality, once it was discovered that Thieu had fled, rumors in Saigon had it that he might be the reincarnation of a dead Cham (people from the former "Champa" Empire) from Phan Rang, taking revenge on the South Vietnamese for the killings the Vietnamese had inflicted on the Chams centuries before. The Cham people had in fact built their capital city somewhere near Phan Rang, the hometown of Thieu. The Vietnamese had almost exterminated them, so now the Chams were taking revenge by placing Thieu-the-reincarnated-Cham as president over the South Vietnamese and were heaping disgrace and humiliation on them by letting them see how their chief of state sneaked out of Saigon, like a thief and a scoundrel.

It was a shameful page in Vietnamese history, a most painful waste of lives and resources for the United States. I hope there will never, never be another Vietnam War.

Epilogue

1990. ONCE again, after two and a half decades of restless "roaming" in the States, I found myself looking out the window of an airplane and marvelling at the landscape of my native homeland, Vietnam. This time, however, my husband was by my side. Together we gazed at the mesh of canals weaving amid patches of brown and green rice fields. There was not the bitterness and hopelessness that I had once felt, but rather a sense of wonder — wonder at the healing power of nature and at our own power to discover new meanings to our life.

I didn't really need to return to Vietnam to recall memories of my youth, yet I was urged by the feeling that being there in person would probably cure my feeling of nostalgia.

After much socializing and "catching up" with old friends, I finally had the chance to do what I had long been yearning to do — to lose myself in the peaceful rural life, moving in slow motion with nature. That was the charm of old Vietnam. This picture of serenity had disappeared during the forty years of war to reappear now with the return of peace, giving the people of Vietnam something to hope and live for.

Swinging leisurely in a hammock under the cozy straw roof of a gazebo in a remote country house, I took in the surrounding scenery with relish. Not too far up, across the calm, lazy river was a large tree overhanging the water. Sweetly, gently, the memory of my rubber tree and carefree childhood embraced my soul.

I felt an urge to search for my tree, to see if it still flourished and had withstood all the changes, like the many people whom I had managed to see during my visit in Vietnam — those who had entered into and disappeared out of my life over the years. To my amazement, we were able to reminisce and enjoy our experiences anew as if time and distance had not separated us at all. Their energy and enthusiastic outlook in spite of a lifetime of struggling were an inspiration to me.

Sadly, Minh and Lien, my onetime army buddies and close friends from my hometown were both gone now, but Nhan and other survivors of the group remained for the most part unchanged. "Captain Nhan," my old reckless captain in the guerrilla army, looked in fact the very embodiment of his belief that "life is what you make of it." His belief had kept him unchanged, the same Captain Nhan, young in spirit, outspoken, enthusiastic in outlook, despite a lifetime of hardship, constantly fighting against foreign enemies while trying to survive under the tight restrictions and starvation régime of his Communist comrades-in-arms. It was not an easy task for Nhan who, with his independent southern ways, did not join the party.

Maybe to compensate for his starvation days with the guerrilla, Nhan now proclaimed himself a Capitalist. He and his family lived in a villa in the center of town which was considered luxurious by local standards. It had been "sold" to him, he said, by a friend, a rich doctor with Viet Cong connections, who had decided after 1975 to leave for France. He could have rented his villa to foreigners at high prices, but he decided against it because he wanted to keep it as a meeting place for his old guerrilla friends. He had good connections in town, but he refused to get involved with the shady quick-buck deals which were popular there. Instead, to make an honest living, he opened his front yard as a garage to repair and clean motorcycles. He showed me a recent picture of him and his wife celebrating his sixty-second birthday, "Western style," with cake and flowers. He was dressed in an expensive double-breasted suit that he wore with bright suspenders—a style he had admired on "bigshot French imperialists" in the forties.

Nhan liked to make me laugh, and he was proud of his sense of humor. Yet below his optimistic appearance, I could sense that Nhan had deep-seated frustrations. He felt that many of his surviving guerrilla friends, not as enterprising as him, who had suffered so much during the war, deserved better now that peace had returned.

Daydreaming in the hammock, my mind drifted to my cousin in North Vietnam, Dr. Quang, who had a personality opposite Nhan's, though he also believed that "life is what you make of it." Ten years older than Nhan, at seventy-two he impressed me a great deal because he seemed always undisturbed and always contented with his lot. Calm, reserved, modest, my cousin, I thought, lived like a real ideal Communist.

As the director of an important hospital in Hanoi for many years, his contacts were extensive and his patients ran the social gamut from ministers to peasants. In his younger days, as a practicing professor of surgery, he used to be invited by hospitals in Europe to give demonstrations of the liver surgery techniques that he had developed during the war years—techniques that had been made simple by necessity because of wartime conditions and yet were very effective compared to modern technology.

Dr. Quang always appeared happy with his lot, no matter how bad it might have appeared to others. He received a monthly salary equivalent to about twenty U.S. dollars (like most doctors and other professionals in Vietnam today). He and his family lived in very Spartan quarters, on the second floor of a very old villa within the hospital compound—two rooms and a hallway for a family of five including his wife, his daughter, his son-in-law, and his grandson. He could have lobbied for the return of the bigger villa that he used to occupy with his parents prior to 1945. But he did not bother going through the complicated procedures to evict the ten or twelve families who had settled into that villa.

Yet he was really happy with what he had and with the way he lived, receiving his friends and hospital patients at his leisure, helping his wife with housework, eating very frugally, surviving with the combined small salaries of his and his wife's. He saw no point in trying to obtain more or own more, though this did not please his wife who complained to me. It made me remember my complaints about my husband in the past, under Diem's régime, only at that time my husband was very *un*happy with the régime.

Every day, in the summer, my cousin pedaled his old rusty bike to the club near the Ho Chi Minh Mausoleum (reserved for high-ranking party members) to take a quick swim and chat with his old friends. Then he pedaled back home and walked to his office at the hospital. He rarely used his chauffeur and his official car—only for diplomatic or official functions. He had a couple of Western suits that he only wore on special occasions or on foreign trips; he felt more comfortable with his simple daily attire—a shirt, old pants, and sandals.

During the months that I spent with my cousin Quang in Hanoi, I was very impressed by his simple way of life and his contented attitude toward life. He was living like a monk, contented with little and happy with his lot. I thought that it would be wonderful if everyone in Vietnam were like him. Such simplicity and such patriotism. Then I started wondering about the new trend in Vietnam which considered people like my cousin obsolete. The new-trend people were worried about making more money and getting rich fast. They liked to own modern gadgets and wanted a comfortable life, just like in capitalist countries.

How much longer will cousin Quang's generation be on this earth to preserve this wonderful concept of simplicity, dignity, and happiness? Things are moving so fast, and misguided changes in people can be as destructive as wars. While I wished them to have a better material life, I also wished they would go out of their way, once again, to fight this important "moral" battle for Vietnam. Maybe, at last, they would find a happy middle way for all Vietnamese — including us overseas Vietnamese (Viet Kieu) — combining, in their unique Vietnamese way, the best of both Socialist and Capitalist worlds, for the sake of their generation and their children's.

In front of me, on the calm water of the river and with the peaceful countryside in the background, a large wooden boat quietly slid by, carrying in it an oversized load of colorful ceramic jars, decorative pots, and stands. The boat barely kept afloat — with a mere few inches showing above the surface of the water.

To the boatman, this thin line of wood above water must have been his vision of equilibrium, a reminder of safety. Somehow, I felt a profound anxiety for that critical margin. It reminded me of the thin line in my own existence. Till now I had looked at life as only a hazardous experience, with me as the boat carrying a fragile and heavy load, going nowhere but in the big circle of time.

As I watched the precarious boat float calmly on the river, however, my anxiety for the boat gradually disappeared. In that miraculous moment, I thought that I had learned a new, precious lesson for living: that no matter what my life's boat might have to carry, whether solid gold bars, or colorful fragile ceramics, or common colorless gravel, I should constantly watch for balance. I do hope that somehow Vietnam will find its own balance. With balance, life becomes the lovely current of our dreams.

Selected Bibliography

Since the end of the Vietnam War in 1975, the literature on Vietnam has grown enormously. However, for the purpose of this personal account of my life, I have listed here only a few selected works which I found useful as confirmations of what I have seen and witnessed on my own. Besides these books, references to the articles and books that I and relatives of mine wrote as far back as 1962 on our own Vietnam experiences are also indicated.

Please note that most Vietnamese retrace their family names to the five important dynasties of Vietnamese history: Dinh, Le (Early), Ly, Tran, Le (Later), Nguyen. So to distinguish the millions of Nguyens, Les, or Trans, Vietnamese use their surnames as both first and last names. Thus Gen. Vo Nguyen Giap is *not* referred to as "General Vo," but is famous as "General Giap."

Bao Dai, S. M. *Le Dragon d'Annam*. Paris, Plon, 1980.
Corson, William R. *The Betrayal*. New York, W. Norton & Co., 1968.
Davidson, Lt. Gen. (USA Ret.) Phillip B. *Vietnam at War: The History, 1946–1975*. Novato, CA, Presidio Press, 1988.
Dawson, Alan. *55 Days: The Fall of South Vietnam*. Englewood Cliffs, NJ, Prentice-Hall, 1977.
Dudman, Richard. *Forty Days with the Enemy*. New York, Liveright, 1971.
Fenn, Charles. *Ho Chi Minh*. New York, Charles Scribner's Sons, 1973.
Gibson, James W. *The Perfect War: The War We Couldn't Lose and How We Did*. New York, Vintage Books, 1986.
Halberstam, David. *The Best and the Brightest*. New York, Random House, 1972.
Hatcher, Patrick. *The Suicide of an Elite: American Internationalists in Vietnam*. Palo Alto, CA, Stanford University Press, 1990.
Kahin, George McT. *Intervention: How America Became Involved in Vietnam*. New York, Alfred A. Knopf, 1986.
Karnow, Stanley. *Vietnam: A History*. New York, Viking Press, 1983.
Lansdale, Edward G. *In the Midst of Wars: An American's Mission to Southeast Asia*. New York, Harper & Row, 1972.
Le, Khoi Thanh. *Histoire du Viet-Nam, des Origines à 1858*. Paris, Sudestasie, 1981.
McCoy, Alfred. *The Politics of Heroin in Southeast Asia*. New York, Harper & Row, 1972.
Mai-Oanh (pen name of author's mother). *Chin Nam Loan-Ly, 1945–1954* (Nine

Years of Vicissitude). Selected poems published by Quynh-Giao Poets' Society, Saigon, 1963.

Mus, Paul, and John McAlister. *Les Vietnamiens et Leur Révolution*. Paris, Éditions du Seuil, 1972.

New York Times Staff, *Pentagon Papers. The Secret History of the Vietnam War*. New York, New York Times, 1971.

Nguyen, Mai Thi Tuyet (the author). *Electioneering: Vietnamese Style*. The Asian Survey, University of California Berkeley, Vol. II, No. 9, November 1962.

Nguyen, Son Thanh. *Nhan-Dan Dong Bang Song Cuu-Long Anh Hung (The Heroic People of the Mekong Delta Region)*. An unpublished autobiography (1987) by the author's Viet-Minh commander in 1945, southern Vietnam region.

Nguyen, Thai. *Is South Vietnam Viable?* Manila, Philippines, Carmelo & Bauermann, November 1962.

————. *A Vietnamese Speaks Out*. The New Republic, June 8, 1963.

Nguyen, Vien Khac. *Histoire du Vietnam*. Paris, Éditions Sociales, 1974.

Sheehan, Neil. *A Bright Shining Lie: John Paul Vann and America in Vietnam*. New York, Random House, 1988.

Snepp, Frank. *Decent Interval: An Insider's Account of Saigon's Indecent End Told by the CIA's Chief Strategy Analyst in Vietnam*. New York, Random House, 1977.

Tran, Gen. Tra Van. *Vietnam: History of the Bulwark B2 Theater, Volume Five, Concluding the Thirty-Year War*. Ho Chi Minh City, Van Nghe Publishing House, 1982 (translation by the Joint Publications Research Service, Arlington, Virginia).

Van, Gen. Dung Tien. *Dai-Thang Mua Xuan*, in Vietnamese. Translated into *Our Great Spring Victory: An Account of the Liberation of South Vietnam*. New York, Monthly Review Press, 1977.

Vo, Gen. Giap Nguyen. *Nhung Chang Duong Lich-Su (The Historic Episodes)*. Nha Xuat-Ban Van-Hoc, Thanh Pho Ho Chi Minh, 1976.

Warner, Denis. *Certain Victory: How Hanoi Won the War*. Kansas City, Sheed Andrews and McMeel, 1977.

Westmoreland, Gen. William C. *A Soldier Reports*. Garden City, NY, Doubleday & Co., 1976.

Index

243